D0205926

DICTATORSHIP, WORKERS,
AND THE CITY

DICTATORSHIP, WORKERS, AND THE CITY

Labour in Greater Barcelona since 1939

SEBASTIAN BALFOUR

CLARENDON PRESS · OXFORD

1989

Oxford University Press, Walton Street, Oxford. Oxford OX2 6DP

Oxford New York Toronto
Delhi Bombay Calcutta Madras Karachi
Petaling Jaya Singapore Hong Kong Tokyo
Nairobi Dar es Salaam Cape Town
Melbourne Auckland

and associated companies in
Berlin Ibadan

Oxford is a trademark of Oxford University Press

Published in the United States
by Oxford University Press, New York

British Library Cataloguing in Publication Data
Belfour, Sebastian
Dictatorship, workers and the city: labour in Greater Barcelona since 1939.
1. Spain. Labour movements, 1939–1988
I. Title
335'.00946
ISBN 0–19–822740–X

Library of Congress Cataloging in Publication Data
Balfour, Sebastian
Dictatorship, workers, and the city: labour in Greater Barcelona since
1939/Sebastian Balfour.

Bibliography: p   Includes index.
1. Labor and laboring classes—Spain—Barcelona—Region-
-History—20th century. 2. Trade-unions—Spain—Barcelona Region-
-History—20 century. 3. Spain—Politics and government—1939–1975. 4.
Spain—Politics and government—1975-
I. Title.
HD8590.B342B35   1989   331'.0946'72—dc 19   88–29154 CIP
ISBN 0–19–822740–X

Set by Burns and Smith, Derby
Printed in Great Britain by
Biddles Ltd., Guildford and Kings' Lynn

PREFACE

THIS book began as an attempt to explain one of the most puzzling aspects of contemporary Spanish history. The transformation of Spain from a dictatorship to a democracy can be traced back in great measure to the failure of the regime to keep workers in check in the factories, mines, shipyards, and offices. Yet the working-class movement has been the poor relation of the new democracy. From one of the most militant, it has become one of the least organized in Europe. The interpretations of the so-called 'crisis of unionism' in Spain have centred on the economic recession and the political process of the post-Franco period. In this book, I shall seek for the explanation also in the conditions of the dictatorship itself. Accordingly, the book traces the experience of the Spanish working class, concentrating on the area of Greater Barcelona, from the victory of Franco's armies in 1939 to the devastations of recession in the late eighties.

While it focuses on a specific area and period, the book seeks to cast light on a broader question: the nature of working-class dissent in authoritarian societies and the role of workers' movements in the struggle for political change. The history recounted here has relevance for the experience of workers in other countries and other periods—in particular, Italy, Argentina, Chile, Greece, Portugal, and more recently Poland. Its analysis of the relation between industrialization, urban growth, and militancy has also a significance beyond the concrete case of Barcelona and Spain. During the research leading to this book, also the theme of the city as a formative influence on the development of the labour movement imposed itself. It became clear that in the peculiar circumstances of Francoist society, the workers' movement in each area of the city and its industrial belt developed its own identity according to distinct patterns of urban and industrial growth.

Because there are virtually no other studies of labour history set in the Franco period, this is of necessity a hybrid work, belonging in part to a new tradition of historical investigation that examines the relationship between the ecology of the working class and the labour movement, and in part to the more conventional history of the labour movement as a study of organizations and ideologies. The dearth of serious accounts of the experience of workers under Franco meant that I had to use a wide range of sources, not all of them very reliable. Over a period of five and a half years I interviewed dozens of people who played a key part in the labour movement or on its margins, and their oral testimony plays a major role in this history. I went to considerable efforts also to track down archives that seemed to have vanished into thin air, and to trace other, private archives assembled at great risk during the dictatorship and then put away afterwards in lofts and suitcases because no one seemed to be interested in the history they are part of. By far the most exciting discovery was the archives of Franco's secret police in Catalonia, stored in the vaults of the Civil Governor's mansion in Barcelona, and untouched since the dictator's death. To leaf through the piles of dusty files was like seeing a familiar scene from a completely new angle.

A crucial limitation of any social history of Francoist Spain is the absence of reliable data. The bureaucracy either failed to collect statistics in a systematic way or, if it did, embellished them. Figures relating to demography, strikes, wages, and the like are only approximate and the historian is obliged to an uncomfortable extent to rely on interpretation. But the wide variety of sources used here is also part of an attempt to understand the complex nature of working-class protest by examining cultural factors such as tradition, as well as structural features such as the different configurations of urban and social conditions.

The book is set in a broad chronological framework. I have tried to establish a balance between the narration of the main episodes that marked the history of the labour movement in Barcelona, a description of the conditions and culture of the working class, and an analysis of labour protest against the background of the political, urban, and industrial environment. Chapter 1 begins by examining the destruction of the old institutions of the labour movement after the Civil War and the degradation of working-class life in the forties. The earliest expressions of popular dissent in the first two decades of the dictatorship are analysed, in particular the General Strike of 1951.

The focus of the book is on the period between 1962 and 1976. Chapter 2 describes the social transformation brought about by economic growth in the sixties, together with the changing shape of Barcelona and its satellite towns. These changes are then related to the experience of both the indigenous and immigrant working class. The rise of new forms of labour organization and militancy is analysed in Chapter 3, as well as the vicissitudes of the clandestine organizations of the opposition. Chapter 4 departs somewhat from the chronological sequence by making a comparative study of the labour movement in the four main industrial centres of the province. The different patterns of tradition and leadership and of industrial and urban structures in each area are contrasted.

The sources of growing militancy in the early seventies are then discussed in Chapter 5 with particular reference to the immigrant community. The variation in the kinds of labour agitation in the three main industries of the area is also highlighted. Chapter 6 examines popular and political dissent in the last three years of the dictatorship. Through two case-studies of local mass strikes, the nature of labour protest is contrasted with the perspectives of the opposition. The rise of the new union movement is traced within the broader context of political change in the mid seventies. The book concludes in Chapter 7 with a discussion of the relationship between the crisis of unionism in the eighties and the effects of economic recession, political reform, and the heritage of Francoism on the labour movement. The experience of the Spanish workers' movement, finally, is related to broad questions of militancy and political change in authoritarian societies in general.

During the period of my research leading to this book, it seemed to me that a kind of collective amnesia descended on Spain. It may be that the burial of the immediate past was part of the price of the peaceful transition to democracy. But it does not help us to understand the present. It has also meant that the credit for the political transformation of Spain has gone to those who negotiated its terms in the last year or so of the old regime, rather than to those thousands of individuals who fought and suffered over many years to achieve democratic rights. It has been a privilege for me to meet some of these people and I wish to thank those who generously shared with me their experience of the past. In particular, I want to thank José Luis López Bulla, Manel Ludevid, Jaime Aznar, Fausto Miguélez, Jaume Sobrequés, Jordi Calvet, Pere Ysàs, Carme Molinero, Xavier Marcet, and many others whom space does not permit me to mention. I owe a special debt of gratitude to Professor Paul Preston, who supervised the doctoral thesis on which this book is based and who was an unfailing source of support and stimulating advice. Neither he, nor anyone else mentioned above, bears any responsibility for the judgements that lie in this book nor any errors that may occur in its pages. Finally, I want to thank my daughters Rosa and Marianna and above all my wife Gráinne for the sacrifices that they have had to make for the last six years.

S.B.

February 1988

CONTENTS

LIST OF MAPS

LIST OF TABLES

ABBREVIATIONS

ACD	Asociación Católica de Dirigentes (Catholic Association of Directors)
ASO	Alianza Sindical Obrera (Workers' Syndical Alliance)
CCOO	Comisiones Obreras (Workers' Commissions)
CNS	Central Nacional Sindicalista (National Syndicalist Union)
CNT	Confederación Nacional del Trabajo (National Confederation of Labour)
CONC	Comissió Obrera Nacional de Catalunya
COS	Coordinadora de Organizaciones Sindicales (Co-ordinating Committee of Union Organizations)
CUD	Candidaturas Unitarias y Democráticas (United Democratic Slates)
ELA-STV	Eusko Langille Alkartasuna (Basque Workers' Solidarity)
FAI	Federación Anarquista Ibérica (Iberian Anarchist Federation)
FLP	Frente de Liberación Popular (Popular Liberation Front)
FOC	Front Obrer de Catalunya (Catalan Workers' Front)
HOAC	Hermandad Obrera de Acción Católica (Workers' Brotherhood of Catholic Action)
JOC	Juventud Obrera Católica (Young Catholic Workers)
MSC	Moviment Socialista de Catalunya
OSE (OS)	Organización Sindical Española
OSO	Oposición Sindical Obrera (Workers' Syndical Opposition)
PCC	Partit Comunista de Catalunya
PCE	Partido Comunista de España
PCI	Partido Comunista Internacional
POUM	Partit Obrer d'Unificació Marxista (Workers' Party of Marxist Unification)
PSOE	Partido Socialista Obrero Español (Spanish Socialist Workers' Party)

PSUC	Partit Socialista Unificat de Catalunya (United Socialist Party of Catalonia)
SDEUB	Sindicato Democrático de Estudiantes de la Universidad de Barcelona (Democratic Union of Students of Barcelona University)
TOP	Tribunal de Orden Público (Tribunal of Public Order)
UGT	Unión General de Trabajadores (General Union of Workers)
USO	Unión Sindical Obrera (Workers' Syndical Union)
UTT	Unión de Técnicos y Trabajadores (Union of Technicians and Workers)

1
Defeat and Resistance 1939–1959

All the posters on the walls
All the leaflets in the streets
Are mutilated, destroyed, or run in rain,
Their words blotted out with tears
Skins peeling from their bodies
In the victorious hurricane.

(Extract from 'Fall of a City'
by Stephen Spender)[1]

THE VICTORIOUS HURRICANE

On 26 January 1939 Franco's insurgent army marched into
Barcelona. The capital of Catalonia had fallen with hardly a fight.
The militiaman who had told the English poet John Cornford

But if ever the fascists again rule Barcelona
It will be as a heap of ruins with us workers beneath it[2]

could not have predicted the mood of defeat that hung over the
city in the last year of the Civil War. The euphoria that had
greeted the revolutionary upheaval of the second half of 1936
had given way to demoralization and despair. Between the epic
defence of Madrid in the autumn of that year and the fall of
Barcelona there stretched two years of war, bitter internecine
strife, and betrayal of the Republican cause by the Great Powers.
Barcelona had suffered countless bombing raids, the shops were
empty, and people were hungry and weary of war. The streets of
the city, according to one witness, 'were littered with paper,

[1] Cunningham (ed.), *Spanish Front* (Oxford, 1986), 358
[2] 'A Letter from Aragon', ibid. 259–60.

torn-up party and union membership cards, documents'.[3] Many of the officials and activists of the parties and unions in Catalonia that supported the Republic had fled. Others had been summarily executed as the Nationalists had seized town after town in their advance on the city. The invading army, as it paraded through the urban centre, was greeted by crowds of supporters from the well-heeled sections of society, those who in 1936, in George Orwell's words, had been 'lying low and disguising themselves as proletarians',[4] and many middle-class people, relieved that the war was over even if their feelings about the coming regime were mixed. Behind the troops came the local employers who had fled during the first days of the revolution, intent on reclaiming their expropriated businesses. There began the systematic elimination of all the institutions associated with the Left and with Catalan Republicanism.

The single party of the new regime, the Falange, took over the centres of power — the mass media, local administration, and the forces of law and order. The Church, celebrating the victory of the 'Crusade' over 'atheism' with open-air masses, imposed on the defeated population an archaic and oppressive morality. And the military tribunals set to at their gruesome task of purging Catalan society of so-called enemies of the new regime. Armed with a panoply of repressive laws, the judges had almost unlimited scope to punish. Less than two weeks after the fall of Barcelona, a retroactive Law of Political Responsibilities was issued allowing the courts to try people for acts committed since 1934; among the crimes it listed was that of having betrayed 'serious passivity' towards the Nationalist cause since the uprising in 1936.

The purge laws obliged people to resort to elaborate bureaucratic procedures to try to prove their innocence. It was necessary in order to work to obtain a certificate from the authorities; for many this was merely a credential of provisional liberty until they were required to appear before the judges. Indeed, the number of accused people was so high that they

---

[3] Fraser, *Blood of Spain*. (London, 1979), 482. For the bombing raids, see J. M. Solé i Sabaté and J. Villarroya i Font, *Catalunya sota les bombes* (Barcelona, 1986). For a contemporary description of the atmosphere in Barcelona shortly before the entry of the Francoist army, see Louis MacNeice, 'Today in Barcelona', in Cunningham (ed.), 359–61.

[4] George Orwell, *Homage to Catalonia* (London, 1962 edn), 9.

were tried in batches. In the old town of Sabadell and its region, some 20 miles from Barcelona, the Falangist authorities had opened almost 59,000 files on suspected enemies of the regime, out of a total population of 74,000.[5] Throughout Catalonia thousands of people were imprisoned or sent to work in punitive labour battalions. The least fortunate, some 3,385 people, were executed after appearing before the military tribunals.[6] A disproportionate number of these victims were from the countryside, reflecting not only the bitterness of the agrarian conflict during the Civil War but also the difficulty for the land labourers of escaping arrest.

The employers were given a free hand to sack their staff. A supply of fresh unskilled labour was available out of the throngs of Nationalist veterans who hung about in Barcelona hoping for a job as a reward for being on the winning side. Many of the tram workers, who had formed a powerful union in the thirties, were replaced by ex-soldiers almost all from the Francoist stronghold of Valladolid.[7] The reprisals were particularly harsh on civil servants and municipal staff because of their association with the institutions of the Second Republic. In the factories, however, judging from the few available accounts, the purge was more random. Indeed, there were a few notable cases of clemency.[8] Strong paternalist ties had existed between many employers and their work-force before the Civil War. Class conflict in the industrial centres of Catalonia had been less virulent in the thirties than in the agrarian South or in the capital of Spain. For all the strength of anarcho-syndicalism in Barcelona, considerable support had existed among the working class for the Catalan Republican movement, the petty-bourgeois-led *Esquerra Republicana de Catalunya*, which many of the smaller factory-owners had joined.[9] One out of every ten employers had stayed

[5] A. Castells, *Sabadell: informe de l'oposició* (Sabadell, 1983–7), V1 26. 76.

[6] J. M. Solé i Sabaté, *La repressió franquista a Catalunya 1939–1953* (Barcelona, 1985), *passim*. Solé i Sabaté's figures, based on a painstaking search in each village and town of Catalonia, do not include, however, the summary executions that were held before the military courts were set up.

[7] V. Alba, *La oposición de los supervivientes* (Barcelona, 1978), 99.

[8] For eyewitness accounts see F. Candel, *Ser obrero no es ninguna ganga* (Barcelona, 1968), 89–100; and L'Avenç, 'Les condicions de treball d'ença de la guerra civil', *L'Avenç*, Jan. 1981. pp. 23–31.

[9] For a discussion of the 'populist' Republican tradition in Catalonia see E. Ucelay Da Cal, *La Catalunya populista* (Barcelona, 1982).

on after the Revolution of 1936 in his collectivized firm to work alongside erstwhile employees as a consultant or manager.[10] Others, returning after two and a half years' absence, found their machinery and stocks in a better condition than when they had fled. The spirit of revenge was also tempered by the shortage of skilled labour, allied to the post-war demand for manufactured goods. Moreover, in the new conditions imposed by the military regime, the employers were to be given plenty of scope to exploit their workers.

Indeed, the main objective of the new order was to restore fully the capitalist system in the factories, mines, offices, and landed estates and to ensure that it would no longer be threatened by social unrest. The Nationalist uprising of July 1936 had been motivated less by the programme of reforms of the Popular Front government than by the fear that the social struggle in the city and the countryside would get out of hand. The new system of industrial relations, enshrined in the Labour Charter of 1938, was intended to stamp out the class struggle for ever. Labour legislation under the Franco regime denied workers the right to organize collectively in defence of their interests. Strikes were classified initially as crimes of sedition and were to be tried by military courts. The whole working population was enrolled into a new corporatist structure modelled on the Fascist corporations of Mussolini's Italy, and variously called the *Sindicatos Verticales*, the *Central Nacional Sindicalista* (CNS), and the *Organización Sindical Española* (which will henceforth be referred to as the OSE or the State Union).[11]

The OSE organized the active population into 28 trade unions each representing a different economic activity; in turn these were divided into branches of industry. They were 'vertical' in the sense that both workers and employers were incorporated in the same union. All workers (or 'producers' in the new jargon of the regime) had their union dues deducted automatically from

[10] For collectivization in Barcelona, see J. Brademas, *Anarcosindicalismo y revolución en España 1930–1937* (Barcelona, 1974), 189–96; Fraser, pp. 210–36; M. Seidman, 'Work and Revolution: Workers' Control in Barcelona in the Spanish Civil War', *Journal of Contemporary History*, July 1982; Candel (1968), 27–40.

[11] The early attempt by the radical wing of the Falange to make their union organization, on which the OSE was based, a force independent of the State was easily foiled. For further details see S. Ellwood, *Prietas las filas* (Barcelona, 1984), 113–54.

their pay-packet, while the employers were obliged to make a contribution for each of their employees. The officials of the new organization were Falangists appointed from above. Yet, although the OSE had its own legal identity, it was to all intents and purposes an instrument of the State. An array of laws decreed in the five years following the Labour Charter ensured that the new organization could not act independently of the State. Its role in the management of economic policy became a purely advisory one. The Law of Work Regulations of 1942 gave the Ministry of Labour the sole prerogative to determine wages and conditions of work throughout the country, thereby denying the OSE even a formal role in representing the interests of workers or employers. Indeed, Franco was reluctant to invest the OSE with any political power for fear that the delicate balance between the coalition of interests on which the regime rested would be tilted in favour of the Falangists. The State Union, however, was given control of a vast legal and welfare apparatus that in the coming decades would play an important part in the lives of millions of workers.[12]

The new State, while denying workers the right to organize collectively, purported to defend the right of the individual 'producer' to a secure job. It was as if a tacit social contract was being offered: in exchange for obedience to the employer the worker was given a number of benefits, the most important of which was job protection. The employer, in turn, was responsible to the State for the economic well-being of the firm. Notions of hierarchy and discipline were tempered by the paternalist role that the State assumed. Thus the arm of the regime reached into every aspect of shopfloor life. The Ministry of Labour determined the working conditions and the rates of pay for every category of worker in each of the 28 branches of economic activity established in the new corporative structure. Likewise, the internal rules of each factory and workplace were modelled on these regulations. At the same time workers' grievances were to be dealt with individually through the Labour

---

[12] For further details of the structure and ideology of the OSE see M. Ludevid, *Cuarenta años de sindicato vertical* (Barcelona, 1976); M. A. Aparicio, *El Sindicalismo vertical y la formación del estado franquista* (Barcelona, 1980); and J. Amsden, *Collective Bargaining and Class Conflict in Spain* (London, 1972).

Courts, which depended on the Ministry. The role of the State as dispenser of justice and arbiter of wages and conditions of work was to have enduring consequences on the ideology and habits of Spanish workers.

Yet the conditions imposed on a defeated working class in 1939 could hardly be described as paternalistic. The fear that the Sabadell textile boss, Marcet, detected among workers in his town that a 'new era of slavery' was about to begin was not unfounded.[13] Government decrees forced wages down to 1936 levels though prices had risen over 50 per cent; a 48-hour working week was reimposed where during the Republic the demand for a 40-hour week had been successful in some industries; overtime was made compulsory; and in many cases workers were obliged to give their labour free of charge either as a 'personal contribution to the State' or as 'reparation for damage' to industry during the Civil War.[14]

Low wages and a demoralized working class supplied the conditions for a rapid accumulation of capital. Factory employers were not the only ones to benefit. The autarky of the forties, the result partly of the Allied economic blockade and partly of the ideological choice of the regime, forced the government to take control of the supply, movement, and price of goods. But official food rations were insufficient to keep families above subsistence level. Nor was the quantity of goods available from government stocks enough to keep the textile and engineering factories in Barcelona going. The consequence was a flourishing black market or *estraperlo*, on which many a future magnate made a fortune. Although black-market dealings carried the death penalty, corruption was so widespread that the Civil Governor of Barcelona between 1945 and 1947, Bartolomé Barba Hernández, admitted he could do little about it.[15] The opportunities offered by the new society enabled the rich to get richer and a class of parvenus to rise to wealth on the misfortunes of the poor.[16] While the *Diagonal*, the avenue that cuts diagonally through

[13] J. M. Marcet Coll, *Mi ciudad y yo* (Barcelona, 1963), 25–6.
[14] Candel (1968), 107.
[15] B. Barba Hernández, *Dos años al frente del Gobierno Civil de Barcelona* (Madrid, 1948), 11–37.
[16] For the immediate post-Civil-War economy in Catalonia see J. Clavera, 'Industrialització i canvi de conjuntura en la Catalunya de la postguerra', *Recerques*, no.6 (1976), 205–21.

Barcelona, was filled with cabarets for black-market racketeers, the factories were filled with tuberculosis sufferers.[17]

Disease and malnutrition stalked the slums of Barcelona and those of the surrounding industrial towns. Life for the working class in the forties was dominated by the search for food. The Sabadell Chamber of Commerce, in its report for 1939–41, noted that 'Output of labour tended to decrease in all industries as a result of lack of food, the most marked fall occurring in those industries which require greater physical exertion'.[18] Hunger and the long workday, exacerbated by many hours of overtime, took their toll of the health of working-class families. The local employers' federation of Terrassa was prompted to express concern at the rise of tuberculosis and nervous diseases among the local population.[19]

Yet conditions in the countryside were far worse. From the end of the war, a flow of semi-starved migrants from the interior of Catalonia and from the South reached Barcelona and the towns in its industrial belt. The authorities made sporadic efforts to turn them back. Occasionally the police swooped on immigrants arriving at the station, who had spent their every penny on the train fare, and sent them back south.[20] Official ideology frowned on the city as a source of vice, while the countryside was extolled as the fount of traditional Spanish values. (It was no coincidence that the cities had returned massive majorities for the Popular Front in the 1936 elections.) But the post-war boom in textiles led some employers to take a very different view. According to one report, the eccentric Mayor of Sabadell was supposed to have hired a train to bring immigrant labour from the South, exclaiming 'Let them come, let them come. The spinning-wheels must keep turning.'[21]

Doubly stigmatized by the regime as a centre of labour militancy and of Catalan separatism, Barcelona lost the opportunity of post-war reconstruction. The welfarist rhetoric of the new regime belied the almost total absence of public investment in urban development, housing, schools, and health.

[17] Candel (1968), 108.
[18] Cámara Oficial de Comercio e Industria de Sabadell (COCIS), *Memoria comercial e industrial*, 1939–41.
[19] J. Calvet i Puig, 'El creixement industrial de Sabadell durant 1940–60', *Arrahona*, Autumn 1981, pp. 84–5.   [20] Marcet, p. 291.
[21] Quoted many years later in *Diario de Sabadell*, 20 Oct. 1979.

The fact that housing and urban policy were under the control of the Ministry of the Interior, whose main responsibility was law and order, gives some idea of the regime's priorities. The arrival of immigrants—between 1941 and 1950 over a quarter of a million made their way to Barcelona and its industrial belt—multiplied the deficiencies in housing and services caused by war and urban neglect. The inner-city slums became saturated, and shanty towns sprang up like mushrooms in the suburbs or in the waste lands of the metropolis. In Sabadell, some immigrants set up their homes in prehistoric caves overlooking the river Ripoll. One of them recalls the journey to Catalonia from his family home in Badajoz in south-west Spain:

We lacked many things. There were seven of us children . . . our mother was the one who suffered most from the hunger. The land there was the property of big landowners. In 1950 . . . there was no work and we decided to come here [Sabadell]. We had a small house that my father had inherited . . . and we sold it for 7,000 pesetas [about £98 at the time]. The money was used to pay off debts to the shopkeepers in the village and to buy a cave in Sant Oleguer in Sabadell that cost us 3,000 pesetas, which we did through someone from the village. The rest was for the journey.[22]

LABOUR PROTEST IN THE FORTIES

Absorbed in a life-or-death struggle to survive, the immigrants were hardly in a position to challenge conditions of work in the jobs that they were able to find. It is not surprising therefore that the earliest protests were staged by the traditionally organized workers in the old textile industry and in the long-established engineering factories in Barcelona. During the darkest years of the post-Civil-War period between 1939 and 1945, such actions went largely unrecorded. Some shop-floor petitions were organized, and there were go-slows and short stoppages.[23] But disaffection more commonly took the shape of absenteeism or personal quarrels with foremen and supervisors.[24] By all

[22] Alvaro García Trabanca interview, 17 Nov. 1983, Arxiu Agustí Serra (AAS archives).
[23] Jaume Viladoms interview, Mar. 1967, AAS archives.
[24] Barba Hernández, p. 58.

accounts pilfering on the shop-floor was common practice. Many workers hid wool, tools, wire, or anything of value under their clothes when they left work. In the textile firm La España Industrial, the management had a network of informers to report on thefts.[25] The police had to call off their investigation of petty theft in a Sabadell cotton firm after the management appealed to the Mayor, alleging that if the case continued most of the staff would be charged and the factory would have to close down.[26]

It is only towards the end of 1945 that there was a sudden increase of collective labour protest in Catalonia. The causes were twofold. The defeat of the Axis powers raised hopes that the end of the Franco regime was in sight. As early as the autumn of 1943, disgruntled communiqués of the Sabadell Falange were noting the 'effervescence' and 'great happiness' among people of the town when the news of the capitulation of Italy came through.[27] The second reason for the rise of strike action was the spate of power cuts that took place in the autumn of 1945 and that severely eroded take-home pay. Government statements habitually blamed the shortage of electricity on the 'enduring drought' (*la pertinaz sequía*) from which Spain was suffering, but it was also clear that Catalan industry bore the brunt of the cuts. It was symptomatic of Franco's attitude that he should refer, in the course of a speech in the same year, to 'the huge and dangerous industrial concentrations of Barcelona and Vizcaya'.[28] Workers affected by the cuts were either not paid for the periods of idleness or given inadequate compensation. Textile workers in the town of Manresa were required to report for work upon pain of sanction or dismissal whenever the power supply was due to be switched on again, whether it was day or night.[29]

The first widespread action was held on 8 May 1945 to mark the end of the war in Europe. For a few hours, the factories in Barcelona were silent and only a few trams circulated in the streets as workers celebrated the defeat of the Axis powers by

[25] L'Avenç, p. 26.
[26] Marcet, pp. 200–1. For more evidence of pilfering see Castells, 26. 44.
[27] Castells, 26. 92.
[28] From a speech to the third Congreso Industrial Sindical 1945, quoted in G. García de las Heras, *La huelga general del 12 de marzo de 1951 en Barcelona*, Tesis de Licenciatura (Universidad de Barcelona, 1980), 82.
[29] Ll. Ferri, J. Muixí, and E. Sanjuán, *Las huelgas contra Franco 1939–1956* (Barcelona, 1978), 78.

refusing to turn up for work.[30] However, despite the efforts of the clandestine opposition press to link labour dissent with the politics of the thirties, the strikes of 1945–6 centred around bread-and-butter issues–demands for wage rises, for adequate bonuses, and for company stores where food supplies would be on sale at cost price.[31] From January 1946, a wave of strikes swept across Catalonia and into Madrid and the Basque Country, shaking the regime in the most precarious moment of its history. The most important of these actions was the general strike in Manresa in protest at the docking of one day's pay over a compulsory feast-day on 24 January 1946. The 'holiday' was in celebration of the anniversary of 'liberation' of the town by Franco's troops in 1939. Such was the solidity of the action, the employers and authorities were forced to concede not only the day's pay but a cost-of-living bonus and the installation of company stores throughout the town. The Civil Governor of Barcelona, Bartolomé Barba Hernández himself, held a meeting with workers from factory committees set up to deal with the allocation of points for family allowances.[32] Less than three months later, another widespread strike broke out in the textile town of Mataró on the coast north of Barcelona. It was sparked off by the arrest of some workers during a stoppage in a local firm in protest at the inadequacy of food rations. After three days of street incidents, the town came to a virtual halt on March 26. That day, a march of women workers held back a Civil Guard assault with stones.[33]

A remarkable characteristic of both these strikes was that they were led by women textile workers. In the later struggles of the labour movement women workers would play a much more passive role. No easy explanation can be offered as to the relative decline in their militancy. It can be argued that the actions of 1946 and 1947 were strikes about subsistence and concerned the

---

[30] For an eyewitness account see Angel Cortes, 'Quan la memoria encara roman fidel', *L'Avenç*, Mar. 1983, pp. 8–12.

[31] A typical report of the underground press referred to the bold action of some workers in the heavy engineering factory of Macosa in placing 22 flags of the Catalan Communist Party in different parts of the plant. 'An atmosphere of open enthusiasm for the Republic', wrote *Treball* in an issue dated 1947, 'reigns among workers in the factory.'

[32] C. Molinero and P. Ysàs, *'Patria, Justicia Y Pan'* (Barcelona 1985), 225–6.

[33] Ferri *et al.*, p. 89.

immediate task facing mothers of feeding their families. Francoist legislation penalized married women who stayed on at work by refusing them any family allowance, while those women who left work when they got married were rewarded with a so-called 'wedding bonus' (*Premio de Nupcialidad*).[34] These laws favoured a rapid turnover in the textile factories and enabled employers to take on younger and lower-paid women. Yet it is unlikely that in the forties such legislation could have entirely destroyed the traditions of collective organization among women workers in trades such as knitwear and cotton spinning. In both Manresa and Mataró, the textile industry had been strongly unionized in the thirties.[35] Moreover, the industry, in which women made up the majority of the work-force, was still enjoying a period of boom in 1946–7 that made it relatively easier for workers to win their demands.

The fact that strikes, considered treasonable by law, took place at all in this period can only be understood in the context of the euphoria prevailing after the defeat of the Axis powers. The regime was disconcerted, reacting to industrial action with a mixture of repression and negotiation. The employers gave way in many disputes, often conceding their workers' demands at the mere threat of disruption. Ignoring official channels, the management of many firms negotiated with strike committees and allowed the outlawed unions to organize on the shop-floor. Clandestine anarcho-syndicalist leaders are supposed to have reached a secret agreement with an important group of textile bosses.[36] The annual report for 1946 of the textile employers of Sabadell reveals that workers were seizing on the example of wage rises granted in other factories to force their bosses to do the same.[37] Indeed, the Civil Governor, referring in a public statement to the 'anarchy' prevailing in the wage structure of the textile industry as a result of these illegal concessions, threatened employers with severe sanctions if they broke the guide-lines.[38]

---

[34] R. Abella, *La vida cotidiana en España bajo el régimen de Franco* (Barcelona, 1985), 157.

[35] Brademas, *op. cit.*; and A. Balcells, *Trabajo industrial y organización obrera en la Cataluña contemporánea* (Barcelona, 1974).

[36] C. Molinero and P. Ysàs, *L'oposició antifeixista a Catalunya 1939–1950* (Barcelona, 1981), 118–19. See also *Solidaridad Obrera*, May 1946.

[37] Gremi de Fabricants de Sabadell, *Memoria*, 1946.

[38] Ferri *et al.*, p. 91.

THE LABOUR OPPOSITION IN THE FORTIES

Despite claims by the opposition to have initiated and led the strikes, the labour protest of 1946–7 was largely unorganized.[39] Undoubtedly, individual militants of the clandestine groups played a leading role in the strikes. Moreover, in the relatively less repressive climate of 1945–7, the underground organizations were able to rebuild old networks of members and sympathizers through which their press could be disseminated among workers. The first terrible years of the post-Civil-War period had been devoted to setting up a skeleton organization, and collecting money to aid gaoled militants.[40] The new confidence among workers in the aftermath of the Allied victory opened up fresh opportunities. By 1946, the old anarcho-syndicalist organization, the *Confederación Nacional del Trabajo* (CNT), which had dominated the union movement in Catalonia in the first three decades of the century, had reconstructed 14 trade unions in Barcelona with up to 10,000 due-paying members.[41] It is unlikely, however, that many took part in clandestine activities. The CNT organizer in La España Industrial before and after the Civil War admitted that in his factory '. . . there was no union, just members . . . the majority of workers joined up because I was there and for no other reason; they paid their dues and that's about all'.[42] For its part, the Socialist Union, the *Unión General de Trabajadores* (UGT), which had enjoyed a spectacular growth during the Civil War when it became compulsory to join a trade union, hardly got off the ground in the post-Civil-War period. It lacked the deep-rooted traditions of the CNT, and the conditions that had brought together the wide range of tendencies on which the Union had been based in the last years of the Republic had vanished.[43]

[39] See for example Cipriano Damiano, *La resistencia libertaria* (Barcelona, 1978), 152.

[40] Ibid.; M. García, *Franco's Prisoner* (London, 1972); A. Paz, *CNT 1939–1951* (Barcelona, 1982); Molinero and Ysàs (1981); C. M. Lorenzo, *Les Anarchistes espagnols et le pouvoir* (Paris, 1969).

[41] The lowest estimate among published CNT sources is 8,000: Casas interview in Fèlix Fanés, *La vaga de tramvies del 1951* (Barcelona, 1977), 130.

[42] Josep Calatayud, interviewed in L'Avenç, p. 27.

[43] Its control was now disputed by the remnants of the Socialist party, the *Partido Socialista Obrero Español* (PSOE), and the revolutionary party, the *Partit Obrer d'Unificació Marxista* (POUM), as well as by the Catalan Communist

The defeat of the Republic had bred bitter disputes among and within the organizations of the Left. The Communists were accused of treachery for having systematically stamped out the revolutionary movement in the belief that radical social change had to be subordinated to the defence of the Republican government. The Communists, in turn, blamed the Anarchists and the revolutionary party POUM for having created divisions within Republican ranks. Many CNT militants attacked their leaders for having joined the Republican government in defiance of the traditions of the movement. The Libertarian Movement, of which the CNT was the most important component, was still divided over whether to continue participating in political alliances with anti-Franco institutions in exile, or to return to its traditional apolitical line. Its militants in Spain, the majority of whom worked in Catalonia, supported the first option, while the leadership in exile favoured breaking off formal relations with other democratic organizations. An important section of the POUM broke away to found the Socialist Movement of Catalonia (MSC).

Indeed, while the first labour stoppages were breaking out, the energies of the Left were still consumed in polemics over the politics of the Civil War. The opposition, moreover, pinned unwarranted hopes on Allied intervention in Spain to restore democracy once the World War was over. The failure of the Western democracies to come to the aid of the Republic during the Civil War was forgotten in the atmosphere created by the anti-Fascist rhetoric of the Allied powers. Guerrilla warfare was seen as a means of paving the way for this intervention, and much of the activity of the civilian organizations in the interior was directed at providing logistic support for the military groups operating across the border and inland.

The strikes of 1946–7 thus tended to be seen by the exiled leadership as a prolongation of the Civil War and not so much as the resistance of the labour movement to the new conditions of work imposed by the victorious regime. Many of the leaders of the underground movements had returned to Catalonia clan-

party. For these parties in the post-Civil-War period, see H. Heine, *La oposición política al franquismo de 1939 a 1952* (Barcelona, 1983); J. Fabre, J. M. Huertas, and A. Ribas, *Vint anys de resistència catalana* (Barcelona, 1978); Molinero and Ysàs (1981).

destinely after several years in exile and were unfamiliar with the new reality. The opposition press of the time abounded in Civil War slogans and few echoes of the real conditions of working-class life could be heard.[44]

Skirmishes between the guerrillas and the civil guard would continue well into the fifties, but after the spectacular defeat of the Communist invasion of the Aran valley in the Catalan Pyreness in September 1944 they were no more than a nuisance to the regime. The failure of the guerrilla strategy was compounded by the evident reluctance of the Allies to move against Franco. Moreover, labour protest fell abruptly from mid-1947. The demoralization that ensued was intensified by the renewed confidence of the regime as it stepped up its repression of the underground oppostion. No less than five national committees of the CNT were dismantled by the police between 1946 and 1947 as informers and turncoats multiplied in the new *sauve qui peut* atmosphere.[45] Anarcho-syndicalist activists were rounded up in successive police raids and shot or tortured to death or jailed for years in appalling conditions. Deprived of their organizers, the clandestine union organization of the CNT collapsed. The remaining pockets of militants, cut off from each other and from their leadership abroad by repression and ideological division, were left to search for their own ways of surviving in the new dark age.

INFILTRATION AND COLLABORATION

It is from this period that the first significant shift took place within the underground opposition towards a strategy more in tune with the realities of post-Civil-War Spain. The most important realization was that the centre of resistance to the dictatorship was not the diminishing bands of *maquisards* but workers. The wave of strikes in 1946-7 had shown that only they had the potential to undermine the new order. It was clear, too, that the struggle to overthrow the regime would be a protracted one. Moreover, the effectiveness of secret police operations

---

[44] There were of course many exceptions: see e.g. the emphasis by *Solidaridad Obrera*, Feb. 1947, on the need to make wage demands.

[45] Damiano, pp. 133–65.

against the opposition had weakened the notion that it was possible to build clandestine networks of union members.

So it was that from 1947 onwards, increasing numbers of militants began to work within the rank-and-file structures of the State Union in the belief that they could use them to agitate and organize among workers. Officially, both the CNT and the Socialist UGT would maintain a boycott of the institutions of the regime throughout the dictatorship. Ignoring the stance of their exiled leaders, many individual anarcho-syndicalists in Catalonia began to take advantage of the limited opportunities of agitation that the OSE offered in its attempt to attract workers into the organization. For its part, the Communist Party abandoned the guerrilla strategy in 1948. Prompted by a suggestion from Stalin that they ought to work within the official Union, the Communists adopted the tactic of entrism into the OSE.[46] Characteristically, the new line was laid down by the leadership without consulting the members who had to carry it out. Stalin's advice about combining legal and clandestine work derived from the experience of the Bolsheviks more than 30 years earlier, yet the new strategy perfectly suited the conditions of struggle in Spain. Indeed, party militants in some areas had begun to work within the OSE before the directive came down from the leadership in exile.[47] The shift in strategy was the result not only of the consolidation of the regime but also of the new opportunities that were opening up after 1947 for agitation within the structures of the State Union. To understand the changing nature of the OSE, we need to look at the bizarre efforts of some of its officials during the first eight years of its existence to co-opt experienced trade-unionists of the thirties by threats and bribes.

The earliest attempts of the OSE to build an organized base can best be illustrated by looking at its experience in the textile town of Sabadell, some 15 miles to the north-west of Barcelona. Before the Civil War Sabadell had had the best-organized labour movement in Catalonia. It had also been the stronghold of the

---

[46] For a vivid description of the meeting between the leadership of the PCE (the Spanish Communist Party) and Stalin see F. Claudín, *Santiago Carrillo*, (Barcelona, 1983), 96–7.

[47] Molinero and Ysàs (1981), 50; interview with Bartolomé Baños, 11 Nov. 1985.

moderate unions that had temporarily left the CNT when the insurrectionist wing of the libertarian movement, the *Federación Anarquista Ibérica* (FAI), had taken control.[48] Two months after the fall of the town to the Nationalist armies, the OSE had set up shop in the former CNT headquarters. The leading Falangist and future Mayor, José María Marcet, was concerned to establish some measure of control other than coercion over a work-force with long traditions of union organization.[49] The first collaborators who came forward after appeals over the local radio were a handful of technicians and middle-class professional people who had joined the UGT during the Civil War when it became compulsory to be in a union.[50] Not content with this result, Marcet sought the help of the new Civil Governor of Barcelona, with whom he set up an operation called 'Red Leaders' to recruit moderate trade-unionists now in exile. Their plan was given a boost by the appointment of José Antonio Girón as Minister of Labour in 1941, and it is probable that his approval for the scheme was given in the course of a visit he made to Sabadell in the autumn of that year. Both Girón and Marcet sent secret agents to sound out exiled union leaders, some of whom had been interned in the French concentration camps set up to contain the flood of Republican refugees.[51]

Marcet's emissary came back empty-handed from his mission. The future Mayor of Sabadell had better luck closer to home. By using his extensive contacts among officials, he succeeded in getting a handful of former textile trade-unionists released from prison and gave them jobs in his factory, probably on condition they collaborated in the OSE. One of these protégés, previously the secretary of the Anarchist Youth in Sabadell, later became the powerful President of the local Textile Union, against whom the local labour opposition would campaign for many years without success.[52] Marcet claimed that the collaboration of former

---

[48] Balcells (1974), and Castells, vols. iv and v.

[49] Marcet, pp. 121–4.   [50] Castells, 26. 37.

[51] For evidence of Marcet's agent see Vicenç García Negrillo interview, Apr. 1973, AAS archives. See also Castells, 26. 36–9; and P. García Birlán (Andreu Castells), 'Operación mandos rojos para la CNS', *Can Oriach*, Apr.–May 1974. For Girón's efforts, see Lorenzo, pp. 337–8.

[52] Interview with Antonio Trives, 31 Oct. 1985. This is confirmed in a report by José Solís to the Civil Governor dated 16 May 1972, Civil Government (CG) archives no. 1425. The much-repeated claim that Marcet was able to get the collaboration of local leaders of the moderate Partido Sindicalista is only half true.

unionists was invaluable in maintaining social harmony in the local factories during his term of office from 1940 to 1960.[53]

The Minister of Labour's efforts in the same direction met with less success. Girón attempted to set up a collaborationist Labour Party (*Partido Laborista*) in 1944 but failed to draw in more than a handful of ex-unioists. By 1947, he had abandoned the project. The future head of the OSE, José Solís Ruiz, claimed to have made contact with 800 CNT militants during the course of 1942, of whom only a few agreed to collaborate.[54] Fresh efforts were made in 1947 to co-opt jailed CNT leaders. OSE officials visited Lorenzo Iñigo and Enrique Marco Nadal, who had been secretary-general of the CNT for a short while until his arrest in May, with the astonishing proposal that in exchange for the co-operation of leading anarcho-syndicalists the OSE, or, as it was also called, the CNS, would be renamed the CNT, and that all political prisoners would be freed once an agreement had been signed. They added, rather unconvincingly, that Franco was ready to sign the agreement with them in his office, after which a joint announcement would be made. needless to say, the proposal was turned down.[55] Eighteen years later, a similar offer would be floated with greater success.

It was significant that OSE officials sought to recruit mainly from moderate elements in the anarcho-syndicalist movement. They did so almost certainly in the belief that their offer of turning the OSE into a single non-political union confederation would appeal to the syndicalist ideology of many in the CNT. They may have been encouraged in this by the informal contacts that had taken place before the Civil War between the CNT moderates (the so-called *treintistas*) and the Falange.[56] Indeed, the anti-capitalist and workerist homilies of the Falange in its early days bore a certain resemblance to the political rhetoric of

Of the group around the ex-Partido-Sindicalista leader, Ricard Fornell, that attempted to make contact in 1940 with Falangists in the hope of collaborating in the OSE, only three seem to have been successful; Fornell himself was imprisoned on his return to Spain (Marcet spoke on his behalf at his trial). Paz, pp. 59–60; Castells, 27. 31; J. F. Marsal, *Pensar bajo el franquismo* (Barcelona 1979) 97.

[53] Marcet, p. 124.
[54] *Mundo*, 29 Jan. 1972.
[55] Lorenzo, pp. 273–7.
[56] Candel (1968), 121; Ellwood, p. 29.

some CNT leaders.[57] Moreover, unlike the Socialist Union whose ideological reference-point was Marxism, the CNT had deep ideological roots in Spanish soil. Yet the Falangists underestimated the political strength of anarcho-syndicalism. 'Operation Red Leaders' failed to lure any but a handful of old CNT leaders. Many others paid with their lives for refusing to collaborate.

The lengths to which OSE officials were prepared to go in their attempts to secure collaborators exposed the problems they were having in trying to draw workers into the organization. This was a serious failing, because, among the power groups or 'families' of Francoism, the Falange were rapidly losing influence from the early forties. The pure Falangists themselves would be displaced gradually within the State Union by a new generation of bureaucrats with very different political perspectives. Yet, throughout the dictatorship, the OSE would seek by rhetoric, patronage, and bureaucratic change to build a mass base among workers without losing control of the apparatus. The stream of reforms in the system of representation of the unions was an attempt to gain a constituency among workers in order to maintain some authority within the regime.

The first of such reforms was the creation in 1943 of the post of union branch delegate or *enlace*, and of *jurados* or works-council shop stewards in 1947, both to be elected by the shop-floor. The apparent democratic structure at the rank-and-file level, the so-called *línea representativa*, belied the fact that all full-time officials were designated by the regime and that the bureaucracy could veto candidates and remove a union representative's credentials at will. The first shop-floor elections in 1944 returned exclusively pro-apparatus delegates because all candidates had to be members of the Falange. It became customary among many workers for many years thenceforth to spoil ballot papers by voting for famous actresses of the day. In the 1947 elections, however, the political exclusion clause was dropped and for the first time it became possible for militants to stand as individual candidates. For CNT activists, the decision on whether to infiltrate cannot have been an easy one. To work

---

[57] I. Riera, in *Pàries, sindicalists, demagogs* (Barcelona, 1986), 17, notes similarities of language in the Franco period between *Solidaridad Nacional*, the paper of the OSE, and *Solidaridad Obrera*, that of the CNT.

within an institution of the Fascist State was to invite excommunication from the libertarian movement in exile. Some 25 years previously, the CNT, unlike the Socialists, had boycotted the official bargaining committees of the Primo de Rivera dictatorship. It had only been during the Civil War that the movement had overcome its ideological repugnance to the State by collaborating with the institutions of the Republic. For the leadership in exile this was now considered to have been a serious error.

Clandestine militants in Spain, on the other hand, were forced to be more pragmatic. For those who put themselves up for election from 1947 onwards, the benefits for working-class struggle outweighed their hatred of the system. In many cases, they may have been urged to stand by their workmates because they were skilled negotiators or were the only ones prepared to defy foremen. As shop stewards or union delegates, they acquired a limited protection from managerial reprisal. Deprived of organization by police harassment, CNT members went their different ways according to personal philosophy or to the exigencies of their workplace. In Mataró, for example, one group of anarcho-syndicalists infiltrated the OSE and rose to important positions, which they used to defend the interests of textile workers; another group in the same town steadfastly boycotted the OSE elections.[58]

There were other ex-CNT members who entered the OSE and rose in its hierarchy with less honourable motives. A position in the upper echelons of the 'representative' structure of the State Union offered material advantages as well as power. For example, a secret police report of 2 May 1972 on the President of the Sabadell Textile Union, an ex-CNT member, pointedly noted a greater level of luxury in his home than that compatible with his job as stock controller in a warehouse.[59] Some may have started their careers in the OSE as infiltrators but ended up collaborating to one degree or another. By creating a system of patronage and maintaining a militant rhetoric, a number of ex-

---

[58] The first group included the President of the local Textile Union, who supported the Workers' Commissions in the sixties: José Luis López Bulla interview, 14 Nov. 1985.

[59] Jefatura Superior de Policía de Barcelona (henceforth JSPB) report, CG archives no. 1418.

anarcho-syndicalists were able to build a moderately large rank-and-file base in the OSE that the labour opposition would have some difficulty in displacing in the coming years.

WORKING-CLASS LIVING STANDARDS

The decision by militants to infiltrate the State Union was an admission that the Civil War was over and that the Franco State could not be overthrown by guerrilla struggle. At the beginning of the new decade, the regime was further strengthened by *rapprochement* with the USA, which was anxious to incorporate Spain into its new Cold War alliance. However, the autarky was crumbling. The worst problem was the chronic shortages of raw materials, energy, and capital equipment. The cost was borne by the working class. Bereft of union organization, workers could not easily defend their living standards or working conditions. Basic wages were driven below subsistence level in many a workplace, forcing people to work long hours of overtime and throughout the short holidays. Nor was there any significant improvement at the end of the forties. Meat consumption in Spanish cities in 1950 was still only half that of the period 1922–6, and the working-class population ate half the amount of bread it had consumed in 1936.[60] According to official figures, the cost of living in 1949 was 447 points above the 1936 base rate, while wages had risen only 250 points in the same period.

The regime's statistics must be treated with extreme caution, however. The rates of pay fixed for each industry were distinctly out of step with the rise in prices. The employers were forced to make up the difference between official rates and merely subsistence wages by all kinds of bonuses and allowances. In 1943 these made up some 20 per cent of total wages in Barcelona; by 1950 they accounted for up to 50 per cent of the pay-packet in some firms.[61] When a new wage rise was decreed, workers were no better off, because the bonuses they had previously won were not consolidated into the new level of pay. They were forced therefore to renegotiate bonuses in order to maintain their real wages. The result was that take-home pay in

---

[60] *OPE*, 25 Aug. 1950.   [61] Molinero and Ysàs (1985), 166–250.

firms where workers could exert collective pressure was about 30% higher than the legal rates. In response to this pressure, some Sabadell employers undertook to pay an extra week's wages every quarter, using the pretext of a Nationalist feast-day.[62]

Nor did official price indices afford an accurate picture of working-class living standards, because they concealed the scarcity of basic foodstuffs and goods available at controlled prices. If take-home pay was higher than that indicated in official statistics, so was the price of food on the black market. The clandestine bulletin *OPE* estimated the daily wage of male textile workers with two children as follows (the pound sterling being worth at that time around 30.66 pesetas):

supervisor	47	ptas
skilled worker	32	"
semi-skilled	29	"
unskilled	23	"

while an unskilled woman worker in the same industry who did not receive a family allowance earned only 11 ptas.[63] A more accurate picture of real wages, taking into account overtime earnings, can be gained from the accounts of the Sabadell firm of Corominas. The weekly wage of a male wool-weaver in 1950 was 343 ptas and for a woman 182 ptas, a daily wage, that is, of 57.16 ptas and 30.33 ptas respectively over 6 days.[64] Compared with the official prices of foodstuffs this kind of take-home pay seems meagre indeed. However, if rationing is taken into account a direr picture emerges. In 1950 each person was limited to the following daily rations:[65]

0.033	litres of oil
0.15	kilos of bread
0.024	kilos of potatoes
0.009	kilos of rice

Working-class families were therefore obliged to resort to the black market to make up for the scarcity of goods at pegged prices. In the open market, prices were often more than double. Working from family budget accounts of the time, Fèlix Fanés

---

[62] Castells, 26. 44–5.   [63] *OPE*, 12 Jan. 1951.

[64] Calvet i Puig, p. 84.

[65] In 1951, a ration of 0.073 eggs per day was added. Fanés, op. cit.

has reconstructed the prices of some basic foodstuffs in Barcelona as follows:[66]

1 dozen eggs	29 ptas
1 litre of oil	30 "
1 kilo of rice	11 "
1 kilo of potatoes	4 "
1 kilo of bread	12–17 ptas

At this rate, a semi-skilled male textile worker had to work a full 8-hour day to purchase a dozen eggs, while an unskilled woman worker could barely earn enough to buy a loaf of bread. It is not surprising, therefore, that theft and pilfering were rife. The fact that the Catalan Communist Party, the PSUC, was forced to launch a campaign against the practice among its own members of stealing from their firms is a measure of the desperation of the times.

THE 1951 GENERAL STRIKE

This brief survey of living standards at the beginning of the decade sheds some light on the extraordinary reaction of the people of Barcelona to the announcement in February 1951 that tram fares were going up by 20 céntimos, one-fifth of a peseta. During the first week of March, the overwhelming majority of the city's population refused to travel by tram, the only public transport available at the time. In the early hours of the morning each day huge processions of workers filed into the capital on foot. Empty trams protected by armed guards and patronized by the occasional die-hard Francoist circulated the crowded streets. Knots of people gathered to demonstrate their protest and were charged at by the riot police. More serious clashes occurred in various parts of the city. Trams were stoned or set on fire. Despite the bad weather and a stream of threats from the Civil Governor, the boycott continued until 7 March. On that day, after seeking approval from the government, the authorities announced the cancellation of the rise in fares.

Twenty-four hours before, an official meeting of 2,000 union delegates had issued a call for a general strike in protest against

66 Fanés, op. cit.

the arrests made during the week. On 12 March, some 300,000 workers came out on strike, paralysing the city. The stoppages spread to most of the industrial towns of the hinterland. Violent clashes broke out between demonstrators and police. The action continued into the next day, and the work-force of many factories refused to work for a third day also. On the 17th, the Civil Governor himself, Eduardo Baeza Alegría (who had replaced Barba Hernández), was removed from his post, following the earlier fate of the Mayor of Barcelona. The commander of the Armed Police was also replaced, and the local head of the OSE was relieved of his responsibilities.[67]

Stated thus baldly, the March 1951 events in Barcelona seemed to spring out of nowhere. The only precedents for such a widespread protest were the smaller-scale strikes of Manresa and Mataró in the mid forties. Nor would such action be repeated in the subsequent history of the region during the dictatorship, save in the more modest student-led tram boycott of 1957 and in the localized mass mobilizations of the early seventies. The causes of the 1951 protest were many and diverse, but they converged at a specific moment in the history of the dictatorship that would not be repeated.

The most important motive was the latent anger among the Catalan working class after 11 years of unremitting oppression and exploitation. The rise in the tram fares was the latest in a series of price increases that had followed the first liberalization measures urged by the US government in exchange for its recent 62.5 million dollar loan to Spain. The rise in the price of raw materials as a result of the Korean War had also worked its way into price increases in the shops. Unrest has been reported in markets and the police had stepped up their patrols in the vicinity from September 1950.[68] The real wages of many workers had also been undermined by a sudden increase in power cuts. In the two months preceding the strike, between three and four working days a week had been lost owing to the shortage of

[67] For a description of the tram boycott and general strike see Fanés, op. cit.; García de las Heras, op. cit.; Ferri *et al.* pp. 148–74; J. Ll. Taberner and A. Oset, 'La Huelga General de 1951', *Destino*, 29 Dec. 1976.

[68] According to García de las Heras (pp. 68–73) the price of potatoes and vegetables had risen by 300–400%, rice had increased by 10–12 pesetas a kilo, and between October and November there had been a 14% rise in the price of 40 items in the family basket of goods.

electricity. The effect of the cuts had been mitigated only partly by the generators (some of them constructed form outboard motors) that companies had installed in their plants.[69] Since workers were not generally paid for lost production, the ensuing drop in take-home pay must have put an unbearable strain on the family budget.

The boycott of the trams was not only a working-class protest. It was also supported on a mass scale by other sections of the population. Students played a prominent role in the action. Middle-class citizens went to work on foot. Shopkeepers, bartenders, and owners of small workshops and the like showed their discontent at the burden of local taxation imposed by the central government on small businesses by shutting up shop. Many employers were disgruntled by the constraints of autarky and more recently were particularly hit by the sudden rise in the price of cotton on the world market following the outbreak of the Korean War. Not only did many of them ignore the order issued by the authorities during the general strike that each employee should have to sign a new work contract, but they also paid their workers for the days lost by the action.[70] A delegation of leading employers negotiated with the head of the Provincial OSE and with the authorities for the repeal of the fare rise.

Another surprising source of support for the boycott came from within the Falange itself. Rank-and-file members had been frustrated at the growing sclerosis of the organization, whose bureaucratic power was not matched by its political influence. Their relations with the Civil Governor, Baeza Alegría, nominally the local head of the Movement, had been growing worse. He was considered not only a dubious Falangist, having joined only at the end of the Civil War, but also a weak and ineffectual Governor. Despite almost hysterical pressure from the hierarchy of the party, the vast majority of Falangists in Barcelona joined in the action. One of their meetings to discuss the boycott was interrupted by the Civil Governor's secretary, who burst in with the dramatic announcement: 'Comrades, the Communists have taken over the streets', only to be greeted by a wave of laughter

[69] García de las Heras Ibid., p. 92
[70] Ibid., p. v.

and the remark that it was the people, among them the Falangists, who were demonstrating in the streets.[71]

The most important feature of the tram boycott, however, was that it was a protest against Madrid. The capital of Spain was not only the heart of the regime but the symbol of centuries of absolutist oppression of Catalonia. Even before the latest rise had been announced, tram fares in Madrid had already been lower than those in Barcelona. The 20-céntimo increase in Barcelona made local fares one and a half times as high as those in the capital. The leaflet that sparked off the action called on the each inhabitant of Barcelona, as a 'good citizen', to boycott the trams until parity with Madrid was achieved. It was, indeed, as much a protest againt the regime's discrimination against Barcelona, against its commerce, culture, and language, as a revolt against price rises. Throughout the clandestine press and in the anecdotes surrounding the boycott, there is a repeated emphasis on 'citizenship' that is in sharp contrast to the demonstrations of popular feeling in the mid seventies that mobilized under the banner of Catalan autonomy. The tram boycott had a strong nationalist content, but it was also the gesture of a city community, rooted in old traditions and struggles. This sense of collective identity would be undermined by the urban and social tranformation of Barcelona that was to take place in the sixties.

Several further explanations of the success of the boycott can be given. The first is that the action did not expose anyone to reprisals, for the obvious reason that there was no legal obligation for people to use the trams. Secondly, popular feeling against the tram companies had always run high. The key to successful strikes in the city, ever since the late nineteenth century, had been to block the trams and thereby paralyse the movement of police and troops. Anarchist workers had launched the General Strike of 1917, for example, by trying to set fire to a tram and tearing down the overhead cables.[72] 'The trams', as one writer noted, 'were a problem of law and order.' They were also

71 Fanés, pp. 77–90.

72 The blockade of the trams had been an important tactic in the General Strike of 1919 that had centred on the dispute at the La Canadiense plant; also during the 'Tragic Week' of 1909. See J. M. Huertas Clavería, *Obrers a Catalunya* (Barcelona, 1982). For the 'Tragic Week' see J. C. Ullman, *The Tragic Week* (Cambridge, Mass., 1968).

something of a juggernaut in the crowded streets of Barcelona. In 1950, no fewer than 21 people had died and 491 had been injured in accidents involving trams.[73]

A unique feature of the general strike was that it was launched within the State Union itself. The head of the Provincial OSE had called a meeting of 2,000 delegates on 6 March to discuss the boycott of the trams. According to an eye witness, he

made a sermon enjoining them to return to work and to advise their workmates to do the same. He ended by singing *Cara al Sol* [the Falangist hymn], and told the audience to go home because the meeting was over. But nobody moved from their seats. Then the real meeting began. For four hours, the workers remained in the hall, one speaker after another coming forward to give an improvised speech. They demanded the release of students and workers arrested as a result of the protest against the trams, and made other demands of an economic nature.[74]

Other accounts refer to the insults showered on the OSE head when he called on the delegates to start using the trams again.[75] But before the assembled representatives could be ejected from the building by the Armed Police, they issued a call for a general strike on 12 March.

Now it was by no means the case that the opposition had been so successful in their new tactic of entrism that they commanded a majority among the union delegates of Barcelona. Communist militants had only taken part on any scale in the union elections of 1950 after the Party's switch of policy in 1948. Among the people present at the meeting, they must have had only a handful of members. Alongside the Communists there were also activists of the *Hermandades Obreras de Acción Católica* (HOAC) or Workers' Brotherhoods of Catholic Action, one of the lay organizations of the Church that was adopting an increasingly militant stance on labour and social questions. It was certain, too, that among those calling for action were CNT activists. But the decision to call a general strike was more a reflection of the prevailing mood in the city and among workers after the extraordinary victory of the tram boycott than a result of the influence of the labour opposition.

[73] Fanés, pp. 63–6.
[74] Marsal, pp. 98–9.
[75] Fanés, pp. 112–14.

The call for a general strike on 12 March was answered by workers in all the main industries in Barcelona. By the afternoon, the stoppages had spread to nearby towns. The withdrawal of labour was not organized. Many people reported for work, only to down tools when news of strikes in neighbouring factories filtered through. In the absence of any form of co-ordination, the action began with wildcat strikes in workplace after workplace and was spread by pickets who toured factories in their area. In the wool town of Terrassa, the action began in the electrical firm Electra Industrial. From there, militants set out towards other factories. 'Using a pre-arranged signal,' one of the strikers recalls, 'we showered pebbles on the windows of different workshops to call their workers out.'[76] The general stoppage in the capital was boosted by the confusion of many employers and OSE officials, who had received hoax phone calls made by CNT militants at the end of the working day on Saturday purporting to come from the Union headquarters and announcing a General Strike on the following Monday.[77]

At the height of the action some 300,000 workers were on strike in Barcelona alone. Cinemas, restaurants, cafés, and retailers closed down. Women workers played an important role in persuading bars and shops to pull down their shutters. There were numerous demonstrations that were brutally attacked by the police. The Civil Guard were also reported to have entered factories. The strikes continued on the next day, and on a smaller scale into Wednesday. It was only on Thursday that the city returned to its old routine, though the atmosphere which reigned among its population could hardly be described as normal.

The authorities were so alarmed by the extent of the protest that battleships were sent into the port of Barcelona and 4,000 marines were marched through the city in a show of strength. The Falangist paper of Terrassa inveighed against the local populace: 'What has happened in our town during the last 48 hours can only be described as pitiful. Pitiful the lack of civic spirit displayed by our citizens . . . Pitiful the lack of decision and civic responsibility shown by those in charge of our factories . . .' In common with most of the press in the province, however, the paper was forced to concede that the strike was not just the work

---

[76] Baños interview.   [77] García de las Heras, p. 112.

of 'professional subversive elements' but was the result of economic deprivation and rising prices.[78]

The regime reacted to the protest in a way that would become familiar throughout the dictatorship. On the one hand, the supply of food to Barcelona was increased. Meat made its first appearance in the markets for a long time. The supply of electricity was increased. Rationing began to be phased out in 1952. For the first time since the Civil War conditions began to improve for the working class. On the other hand, the authorities directed their wrath against the clandestine opposition. Sixty-five CNT militants and 34 members of the Catalan Communist Party, the PSUC, were rounded up in mass police raids during the weeks following the action.[79]

The General Strike of March 1951 has been seen by some historians as marking the end of Civil War resistance and the beginning of the anti-Franco struggle.[80] If this is true, it is difficult to explain why there was nothing comparable until the strike movements of the early seventies. Even in these cases, moreover, the character of the protest would be different. Although the working-class movement of the latter part of the dictatorship would be immeasurably larger and better organized, labour protest was to have a more sectional or localized character. In reality, the social and economic transformation that took place in the late fifties and sixties would give rise to a new working-class movement that shared few of the preoccupations of workers at the turn of the forties. The 1951 strike was a protest against a uniformly exploitative system rooted in a stagnant autarky, while the new movement would arise in conditions of economic growth and wage bargaining.

It is true, however, that aspects of the new labour movement were already evident in the 1951 strike. It was the first expression of a new kind of indirect wage bargaining that became widespread in the mid fifties until a formal system was introduced in the early sixties. In so far as they concerned pay, the strikes of the fifties aimed at forcing the government to raise the basic rates on which real wages were calculated. In a sense, they were the equivalent of the eighteenth-century 'collective

[78] *Tarrassa*, 14 and 15 Mar. 1951.
[79] García de las Heras, p. 140.
[80] Fanés, p. 172; and Paz, pp. 374–86, for example.

bargaining by riot' in Britain.[81] The success of this pressure in 1951 (basic wages were raised by 25 per cent in the same year) would be confirmed by subsequent decrees in the fifties that followed closely on the heels of mass strikes. The 1951 General Strike was also the first occasion in which the State Union was deployed to launch actions of protest. The strategy of infiltrating the OSE was vindicated in the union meeting of 6 March. Although many years were to elapse before even smaller-scale strikes could be initiated from within the official Union, the 1951 events showed that it could be used successfully to agitate and to organize against the regime.

It was also evident that new forces besides the traditional opposition were at work in the labour movement. The anonymous leaflet of 8 February that set off the tram boycott was typical of the chain letters by which the Catholic workers' organization HOAC used to spread social and spiritual messages.[82] HOAC workers had been active in the OSE since the elections of 1947. In many places, the headquarters of the Church's lay organization were used to give advice to workers over labour problems.[83] The Catholic association also afforded legal cover for more irregular forms of union work. Militants of clandestine organizations joined the HOAC without confessing their political allegiances, even if they were prepared, in order to provide themselves with deep cover, to confess their 'sins' and take Holy Communion.[84] Another of the Church's lay groups, the *Juventud Obrera Católica* (JOC) or Young Catholic Workers (the youth section of Catholic Action), was already active among apprentices and in the slums of the industrial towns of Barcelona province.

Many of the Catholic activists who participated in these groups were imbued with a sense of moral indignation at the disparities of wealth in Spain. Their social concern was mixed with an

[81] Eric Hobsbaum, *Labouring Men* (London, 1964), 7..

[82] Fondo de Documentación para la Información Anarco-sindicalista, *Apuntes para una historia del movimiento obrero español de la postguerra* (n.p.; 1976), Arxiu Nacional de Catalunya (ANC archives). García de las Heras, p. 97.

[83] In Valencia, according to J. Picó, *El moviment obrer al País Valencià sota el franquisme* (Valencia, 1977), 86, it was called the 'Catholic Trade Union' by many workers.

[84] Baños interview; Molinero and Ysàs (1981), 50–2; and Fondo de Documentación, op. cit. 27–9.

evangelical zeal to restore Christian values into a society corrupted by oppression. During the sixties increasing numbers of them would turn from devotion to revolution as the Church hierarchy itself began to criticize the regime. The new labour movement that arose in the following decade would be based on a tacit alliance between Catholics and Communists that had no precedent in the history of modern Spain.

The tram boycott and General Strike of 1951, therefore, stood on the threshold of a period of transition in the history of the labour movement. Both were, in part, an expression of an old antagonism, exacerbated by the post-Civil-War oppression. The tram boycott itself renewed a form of dissent that had been a tradition in Barcelona. The strike was also a protest against those harsh conditions of life in post-Civil-War Spain that had already stung the workers of Manresa and Mataró, and of the Basque Country in 1946–7, into defying the authorities by downing tools and taking to the streets. But the mass action also contained the seeds of new forms of labour agitation that were to characterize industrial relations over the next 25 years.

THE LABOUR OPPOSITION AND WORKING-CLASS PROTEST IN THE FIFTIES

Official sources announced to the foreign press that the March strike had been organized by the Catalan Communist Party, the PSUC, and financed by local industrialists with a grudge against the regime.[85] The attribution of all social unrest to Communist subversion was to be a constant refrain throughout the dictatorship. It would help to give the Party the reputation of being the only organized opposition to the regime. Rank-and-file Communists may have played an important part in organizing action in their workplaces, but they cannot have numbered more than a few score. Yet it was evident by the mid fifties that, alone among the opposition groups, the Communists were beginning to rebuild their network of militants after the police raids of 1947–8. At first, the only contact with the Party for many members was the broadcasts of the *Radio Pirinaica* or *Radio Española Independiente* (REI), the Spanish Communist

---

[85] Paz, p. 378.

programme beamed to Spain from Bucharest. A Barcelona militant recalls, 'A group of us got together, some who had once been active but had lost touch, and others who had never been involved but were friends . . . and guided by Radio Pirinaica . . . we got organized without having any contact with the Party.'[86] The Communists had suffered few of the internal divisions that so debilitated the other working-class organizations of the Left in the aftermath of the Civil War.[87] This was largely because they had a highly centralized organization. Orders from the central committee in exile were obeyed without question. Even the abrupt tactical switch from guerrilla struggle to entrism was decided, as we have seen, without consultation among those who had to carry out the new line. Lack of internal debate gave the Communists a tactical flexibility that no other organization possessed, but it was to have negative consequences in the years to come. By the early fifties, the main strength of the PSUC's labour organization lay in Barcelona, where it had groups of militants in some of the main metal and textile factories. In the heavy engineering plant of Macosa, in Poble Nou, there was reported to be a branch of 40 members. Several thousand copies of *Treball*, the PSUC's underground paper, were distributed monthly in the factories of the capital.[88]

In the industrial hinterland, contacts were more difficult. The reconstruction of the Party there was the work mainly of immigrant workers, whose only contact with the organization was also the REI broadcasts. The new Party line on entrism was conveyed across the air waves to small groups of members huddled over their radio sets. Intense police vigilance made contacts between party nuclei very hazardous. The state of terror that reigned in Catalonia can be illustrated by the case of the Sabadell Communists. In the textile town to the north-west of Barcelona, two groups of Party members functioned without any knowledge of each other. The first consisted of a handful of survivors of the Civil War who met irregularly in the town centre and were in contact with the Party leadership. The second group

---

[86] Interview with Angel Rozas, 17 May 1983.

[87] The dispute over the national question that led to the expulsion in 1949 of the Secretary-General of the PSUC, Joan Comorera, seems to have had no repercussions among Communist workers. For details, see M. Caminal, *Joan Comorera*, vol. iii (Barcelona, 1984); Molinero and Ysàs (1981), 156–60.

[88] Molinero and Ysàs (1981), 150–6.

was formed among immigrant workers living in the caves above the river Ripoll, who had fled the post-war repression in Andalusia. Such were the problems of clandestine communication that contact between the two groups was made fortuitously when a Sabadell immigrant resident in Paris met a member of the second group when on holiday in his home town and reported its existence to the French Communist Party. The French, in turn, relayed the news to the PSUC. The first meeting between the two nuclei took place only in 1955.[89]

The largest group of Party members among immigrant workers was in Terrassa. The local Communist Party was reorganized independently of the Catalan leadership and in the name, not of the PSUC, but of the Spanish Communist Party, the PCE. Its first contact with the Catalan central committee was made only in 1953. Party militants in Terrassa had zealously applied the instruction to infiltrate the institutions of the regime. Some had joined the local branch of the *Requetés*, the right-wing Carlist militia that had been among the Nationalists' most fervent troops during the Civil War.[90] In the union elections of 1953 several local Communists reached the second level of the OSE representative structure, the local *Juntas* of the main industries in the town, a feat unparalleled elsewhere in Catalonia at that time.

The growing influence of the Terrassa Communists in the local labour movement was highlighted in January 1956 during the campaign of the so-called 'Cyclists' Army'. The Council had decided to increase the tax it levied on bicycles from 11 to 82 pesetas a year. The rise provided a focus for protest against the recent unprecedented increase in the cost of living. The push-bike was an essential means of transport for workers, most of whom lived on the outskirts of the town. On Sunday 22 January, 200 cyclists, led by Communist militants, gathered at the bottom of the main avenue of Terrassa and at a given signal began to distribute leaflets signed by the 'Cyclists' Army'. Brandishing posters in one hand calling for a minimum living wage, an 8-hour day, equal pay, and other economic demands, and pushing their

[89] Castells, 27. 22; and PSUC, *40 anys de lluita per la democràcia i el socialisme a Sabadell* (Sabadell, 1976).

[90] Baños interview; M. Ludevid, *El movimiento obrero en Cataluña* (Barcelona, 1977), 12; interview with Cipriano García, 25 Apr. 1983. Their presence in the ranks of the Franco faithful, however, was discovered during the general strike of 1951 and they were arrested.

bikes with the other, they made their way up the tree-lined avenue. By the time it had reached the top, the march had gathered some 2,000 demonstrators.[91] A squad of Civil Guards, hastily assembled to deal with the unexpected disturbance, assaulted the demonstration and led away many of its number, including eight members of the engineering committee of the local OSE. The cyclists' protest, however, achieved its main objective. The Town Council not only gave way over the increase in the bicycle tax but eliminated the tax itself. The action revealed the extent to which militants, mainly of the Communist Party, had penetrated the OSE and gained the support of groups of workers in the town. A few days before the demonstration a mass meeting of union delegates from all the industries in the town had voted to campaign against the proposed rise. The tactic of entrism was beginning to bear fruit.

The most important reason for the growing influence of Communist workers among a small circle of labour militants and conscientious shop stewards was their agitational work over bread-and-butter issues. From 1954 onwards the monthly issues of *Treball* were filled with reports from factories of small struggles over bonuses, speed-up, productivity measures, rationalization, and redundancies.[92] These reports reflected not only the growing confidence with which workers were beginning to defend their conditions but also the changes in the organization of work that were taking place in the mid fifties.

The Spanish–US agreement of 1953 which marked the beginning of the end of the autarky, was followed by a rapid freeing of prices, placing an unbearable strain thereby on many small firms that had mushroomed under the protectionist umbrella of the closed economy. The American loans and investment that began to flow into Spain were accompanied by unfamiliar measures aimed at increasing productivity. The effect of the new steps on real wages and conditions of work was drastic. The drive for greater productivity was not accompanied by a corresponding investment in machinery; higher production targets were therefore achieved by increasing the rates of

---

[91] *Treball*, March 1956; Ludevid (1977), 17–18; Cipriano García and Baños interviews.

[92] For example, the issues dated Jan. 1954, May–June 1954, and Feb., Aug., and Sept. 1955.

exploitation.[93] Some idea of the problems caused on the shop-floor by the new productivity drive may be gathered by the fact that in 1954, the engineering workers of Barcelona brought an average of 1,000 cases a month for arbitration by the local OSE.[94]

But the most urgent problem facing workers was the threat to their meagre living standards posed by inflation. Their purchasing power in 1954 was still considerably below what it had been in 1936. While prices were reported to have risen by 55.4 per cent during 1955–6, wages did not keep pace. The widespread unease over inflation among many sections of the population flowed into a renewed boycott of the trams in February of 1957 after the Civil Governor again imposed a fare rise. This time, however, it was not followed by stoppages in the workplace. One important reason, it could be argued, was that labour protest over wages was beginning to have some effect. The strikes, in particular in the Basque Country, Asturias, and Catalonia, were transforming the regime's mechanism of wage determination by periodic decree into an informal system of pressure bargaining. In response to strike movements in the three regions, the government was forced to decree three wage increases in four years, amounting to a total rise of 85–90 per cent.[95]

The turning-point came in 1956. The wave of strikes that spread that year from Navarra to the Basque Country and then to Catalonia was a clear sign that the regime's economic policies were not working. The government was forced to award two new rises. Wage increases, in turn, fed into the chronic inflation caused by the structural problems of Spain's semi-autarkic economy. On 27 February 1957 a new government was formed by Franco in which the proponents of a reformed economic framework for Spain would soon prevail over the obdurate supporters of the closed economy.

As in most of the shifts of offical policy during the dictatorship, the new economic policy that began to come into effect in the early sixties was the result not so much of political processes as

---

[93] J. Estivill *et al.*, *Apuntes sobre el trabajo en España* (Barcelona, 1973), 74–5. At a loss to describe the new system, *Treball* referred to it in its Aug. 1955 issue as the 'American method of production'.

[94] *Treball*, Feb. 1955.

[95] 25% in 1951, 14–17% in 1953, and 30% in 1954; Ludevid (1977), 16.

of working-class pressure. In contrast to the defensive struggles of the late forties, the strikes of the latter half of the fifties were informed, among the better-organized workers, by a fresh confidence in their industrial power. The voice of a new assertive generation of workers could be heard in the leaflet produced by the workers of the Barcelona engineering plant, La Maquinista, justifying their strike on 12 April 1956:

We have been deceived. The Government had promised us a wage rise to compensate for the rise in the cost of living, which had gone up by almost 30% since January. Some workmates even believed that we would get a rise of 50% . . . At any rate, the 16% rise now in force amounts to only a 2–3% rise for two reasons: first, because what they give us with one hand they take away with the other by raising social security contributions, and second, because the increase in wages is used as an excuse to raise prices which leaves us with hardly any rise at all. That is the reason for our strike.[96]

In the event, the 16-per-cent rise sparked off a wave of strikes in Navarra and Guipúzcoa that spread to Barcelona in mid April. The stoppages began in La Maquinista and extended to the largest engineering factories and later the textile factories in the Catalan capital. Armed police surrounded the factories on strike and detachments were sent in to make arrests.[97]

Two years later, it was the Asturian miners' strike that set the example. Their action was taken up by 50,000 workers in Catalonia demanding wage rises. It is noticeable, however, that the strikes of March 1958 in Catalonia were more organized than those of two years previously.[98] The pressure of the stoppages on government and employers alike was evident in their contradictory responses. *Treball* reported that some employers protested to the Civil Governor over the lock-outs and expressed their willingness to concede a wage rise. However, the local office of the Ministry of Labour issued a statement forbidding any modification of wages without due authorization. The next day, a new decree was announced by the Ministry flatly contradicting the statement by allowing firms freely to concede pay rises above the official ceiling.[99]

96 Quoted in *Solidaridad Obrera*, 24 Apr. 1956, from *France-Soir*.
97 *Solidaridad Obrera*, 3 May 1956; *Treball*, May 1956.
98 *Solidaridad Obrera*, 3, 10, and 17 Apr. 1958; *Endavant*, Apr. 1958; *Treball* Apr. 1958.
99 *La Vanguardia Española*, 30 Mar. and 1 Apr.

The confusion reflected the shifts that were taking place in government circles over labour policy. Only a month after the strikes, a new law was passed that fundamentally altered the framework of industrial relations in Spain. The Law of Collective Agreements sanctioned collective bargaining on a factory, local, or national level between workers' and employers' representatives within the State Union. Its avowed purpose was to stimulate productivity. A second less explicit objective was to let wages rise to their market level; employers were allowed, within certain limits, to raise wages according to the pressure of their work-force and their own economic situation. The new law was a recognition of two facts. Firstly, it recognized that the complexity of new techniques of production required greater flexibility in the fixing of wage and bonus rates, and that new technology could only be implemented effectively if working conditions and pay were negotiated on the spot. Secondly, the law was a tacit acknowledgement that the old method of establishing wage rates by government decree was socially disruptive. The new system was designed to take the steam out of wage regulation by allowing wage rates to find their own level through bargaining, thereby fragmenting the pay grievances of workers. Yet the State retained its right to intervene by continuing to fix the basic wages on which bonuses were calculated. Moreover, all collective agreements had to be approved by the Ministry of Labour, which could disallow pay awards if they were considered inflationary.

The new government seemed to have understood the nature of the strikes in the latter half of the fifties better than the opposition. Encouraged by the level of mobilization in the March strike, and by the spread of unrest in the universities in April, the Communists attempted to launch a nation-wide Day of Action on 5 May in support of their new anti-Franco, Popular-Front-style policy of 'National Reconciliation'. Their call for action aroused virtually no response.[100] Undaunted by these meagre results, the Communists planned a new national Day of Action for 18 June 1959. This time all the forces of the opposition, except the PSOE, joined the call. The 24-hour *Huelga Nacional Pacífica*, or Peaceful National Strike, was preceded by a massive propaganda

---

[100] *Treball*, July–Aug. 1958.

campaign on the part of the clandestine organizations. The Mayor of Sabadell, José María Marcet, noted that

For some two months there was a massive propaganda effort, unlike any other I had known in the 20 years I had been running the political life of Sabadell. Thousands of letters were sent to people of all social and political classes (including myself) from inside the country and from abroad . . . inviting them to strike on the 18th of June; every day for several weeks the municipal authorities collected vast quantities of leaflets scattered about, under cover of night, especially in the outskirts of the town. The campaign was backed up by a great deal of money and resources and perfectly orchestrated.[101]

Preferring to trust their clandestine press rather than their own judgement of fellow workers, militants had high expectations of 18 June. A Communist shop-floor leader in Terrassa later confessed, 'We thought that the regime would crumble as a result.'[102]

The 'Peaceful National Strike' of 18 June 1959, however, was a complete failure throughout Spain.[103] In Catalonia there were few stoppages in support. The handfuls of workers who tried to picket the entrances to factories were dissolved by the police. The only serious effect was a wave of arrests that decimated the opposition; 90 members of the PSUC were rounded up shortly after. The July issue of *Treball*, while claiming that the strike had 'mobilized the popular masses of Catalonia', contained more reports of arrests than of actions.

The failure of the Days of Action, however, should not lead to the conclusion that the strike waves of 1956–8 were purely concerned with economic grievances. They were political movements to the extent that they were directed against the State, and led to open and violent confrontations with the forces of law and order. They were also movements of solidarity with victimized workers or groups of workers such as the Asturian miners. In the stoppages of the latter part of the fifties can be discerned already the pattern of strikes that would characterize the new labour movement. When political protest and solidarity

---

[101] Quoted in Castells, 27. 60.   [102] Baños interview.
[103] See J. A. Biescas and M. Tuñón de Lara, *España bajo la dictadura franquista* (Barcelona, 1980), 327–9 for a nation-wide evaluation of the Day of Action, and R. Rossanda, *Un viaje inútil o de la política como educación sentimental* (Barcelona, 1984), 45–7 for a critical view from Madrid.

were linked to economic grievances, the response to calls for strike action would mobilize broad sections of workers. On the other hand, appeals for solely political protest found little echo, not least because no immediate benefit could be perceived from thus losing a day's pay. The Days of Action not only laid workers open to severe repression but bore little relation to the existing conditions of working-class struggle on the shop-floor.

Judging from the underground press, one can be forgiven for thinking that the leadership of the clandestine organization was guided by models derived from the quasi-insurrectionary period of the thirties. The image of the revolutionary masses, awaiting the opportune moment to take action, seems to haunt the rhetoric of the opposition bulletins. From the fiasco of the Day of Action on 5 May, the July–August issue of *Treball* drew the conclusion that 'the popular masses show a great desire for action. They have shown that they are ready to undertake peaceful actions on a widespread scale.' As if the 'masses' all read the clandestine press, instead of the heavily censored commercial newpapers, the Executive Committee of the PSUC declared that the Day of Action 'did not leave a sense of failure among the masses, and even less so when they learnt of the results of the Day of Action in Madrid and in other parts of Catalonia and throughout Spain'.[104]

Between the early thirties and the late fifties there lay an enormous gulf. Not only had social and economic conditions changed out of all recognition, but there was also a new and numerically larger generation of workers who share none of the traditions of the pre-Civil-War era. The gap between the two periods would be widened by the radical transformation of Spanish society that was shortly to take place.

The new period was ushered in by the Stabilization Plan of 1959. The decree was the culmination of a campaign, conducted within the government by the so-called 'technocratic' ministers of the Opus Dei, backed by the International Monetary Fund and the Organization of Economic Development and Co-operation, to shed the last vestiges of autarky. To carry out the measures that would lead to Spain's incorporation into the Western economy they had to overcome the hostility of many members

[104] *Treball*, June 1958.

of the Francoist establishment who still had dreams of splendid isolation. Franco, not without extreme reluctance, finally authorized the decree, persuaded by the argument that, if the economic problems facing the country worsened, the regime itself would be under threat.[105] The Stabilization Plan introduced a series of stiff measures designed to purge the less productive sectors of the economy. At the same time, it dismantled many of the restrictions that had barred free trade between Spain and the Western bloc. The new tone of austerity was set by the Minister of Commerce, Alberto Ullastres. Opening the Barcelona Trade Fair in June 1959, he insisted on making the toast with lemonade instead of champagne.[106]

The effect of the Stabilization Plan on the working class was drastic. The austerity measures plunged many firms into an immediate crisis. Some were forced to close down; in others, the work-force was pared down, overtime was eliminated, and bonus rates cut. The take-home pay of workers, which depended to a great extent on overtime and bonuses, dropped by as much as 50 per cent.[107] As unemployment rose, the flow of migrants from the countryside to the cities was temporarily redirected towards other European countries, whose booming industries were short of cheap labour. Many workers in the industrial centres were also forced to emigrate. Throughout 1960, queues of young people applying for visas filled the German consulate in Barcelona. In the main square the Plaça de Catalunya, crowds of unemployed people often gathered, only to be dispersed by the police.[108]

The Stabilization Plan inaugurated a period of economic development and social change without precedent in the history of modern Spain. Underpinned by tourism, foreign investment, and the remittances sent home by the million or more emigrants who found work abroad, the Spanish economy grew at a faster rate than that of any other country in Western Europe. But the human price of such a rapid expansion would be high. The dignitaries who launched the Barcelona Trade Fair in 1959 may

[105] J. A. Biescas, 'Estructura y coyunturas económicas', in Biescas and Tuñón de Lara, p. 64.   [106] Candel (1968), pp. 272–83.
[107] N. Sartorius and V. Díaz Cardiel, *Clase obrera y multinacionales* (Madrid, 1975), 26.   [108] Candel (1968), 282.

have had to do without champagne for the day, but for working-class and peasant families the sacrifice was going to be of a different order.

2
The Transformation of the Working Class

> Today . . . I must warn you of a danger: with the progress in the means of communication, the power of the radio, cinema, and television, the windows of our fortress are being prised open. The licentiousness of the air waves and the published word pervades the atmosphere around us, and breezes from foreign shores are blowing through our windows, corrupting the purity of our environment. The poison of materialism and dissatisfaction has reached the threshold of our homes, at the very moment when the dangers that threaten the world are greater than ever. . .
>
> (Extract from Franco's New Year message of 1956)[1]

Even more than the Civil War itself, the changes wrought by the economic development of Spain in the sixties broke the continuity of the labour movement. Within the framework of an authoritarian political system, a modern industrial society emerged, dominated by monopoly capital and tightly controlled by the State. Yet it was also a backward economy. Alongside the gleaming new industries lay thousands of small factories and workshops enjoying the protection of Spain's tariff barriers. The sustained growth that took place throughout the decade brought about a radical transformation of the working class. Entire rural communities moved from the countryside to join the swelling ranks of the proletariat as Spain was converted from a predominantly rural economy into an industrial society. Structural change was accompanied by a revolution in the values of workers as Spain was drawn into the consumer boom of the Western economy. It is as if the Spanish nation entered a crucible at the end of the fifties and emerged a decade later in a different form. This transformation completed the destruction of old allegiances and habits among workers that the regime had begun

---

[1] Quoted in *OPE*, 5 Jan. 1956.

by political means. Very few of the pre-war traditions carried through to modern labour movement. The new forms of collective organization that grew in the sixties were moulded by contemporary needs.

This extraordinary upheaval was not confined to Spain. The boom of the fifties and sixties changed the face not only of industrialized Europe but also those countries on its fringes and those with which it retained old colonial links. Millions of people, as a result, were uprooted from their village or native land and found a new home in the more prosperous cities or countries that needed their labour. The process of economic and social change in Spain resembled particularly that of Italy, and in

MAP 1   *Barcelona Province*

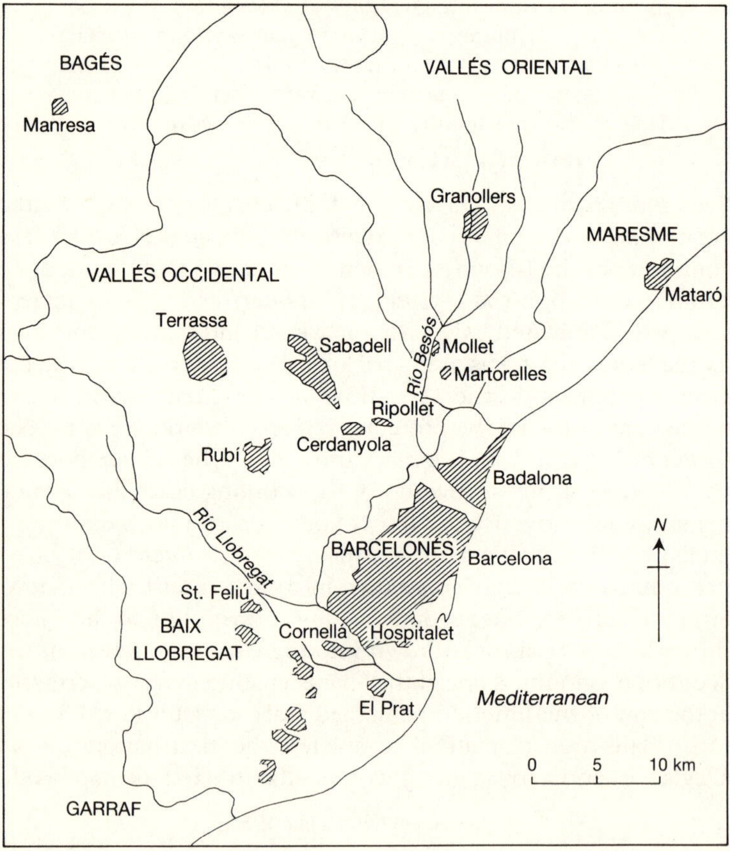

many respects the description of urban and social conditions in Barcelona that follows could be applied equally to Turin or Milan. As in Italy, Spain's immigrants came from the South and joined a working class that had been relatively small but highly organized until the victory of Fascism. Between the two labour movements in the post-war period, however, there were crucial differences that will be examined in the last chapter.

To understand the new labour movement that emerged in Barcelona and its environs, we need to trace the main outlines of the social transformation that took place in the sixties. The most visible change was in the shape of the cities. Over a 20-year period, from 1950 to 1970, the city of Barcelona grew from just over one million to one and three-quarter million inhabitants, while the population of the outlying towns of Terrassa, Sabadell, and Mataró amongst others trebled. This demographic increase was due almost entirely to immigration. By the end of the sixties, immigrants accounted for half or more of the population of several conurbations in the area. The only part of Barcelona that was still recognizable was the old city centre and the Eixample, the gridiron of tall residences and long avenues built for the bourgeoisis at the turn of the century. It is true that the city had not ceased to expand since 1900, absorbing nearby towns and villages on the plain like a spreading oil stain (see Map 2). However, the growth it experienced between the mid fifties and 1970 was more rapid than anything that had taken place in the first half of the century, equivalent to the creation each year of a city of 100,000 inhabitants.[2]

The city had grown outwards since the mid nineteenth century from its historic centre within the medieval walls around the port, crossed the barriers of the rivers Besós and Llobregat to the north and south respectively, and skirted the mountains at the far end of the coastal plain to penetrate into the valleys of the hinterland. The motorways were the pioneers of new urbanization and industrialization just as the rivers and later the railways had been in an earlier epoch. A modern metropolis emerged by the seventies that had drawn into its nexus all the urban centres within a radius of 50 kilometres. Newly harnessed to the provincial capital, the surrounding towns also underwent a rapid development.

---

[2] Círculo de Economía, *Gestión o caos* (Barcelona, 1973), 57.

MAP 2 *Urban Growth of Barcelona*

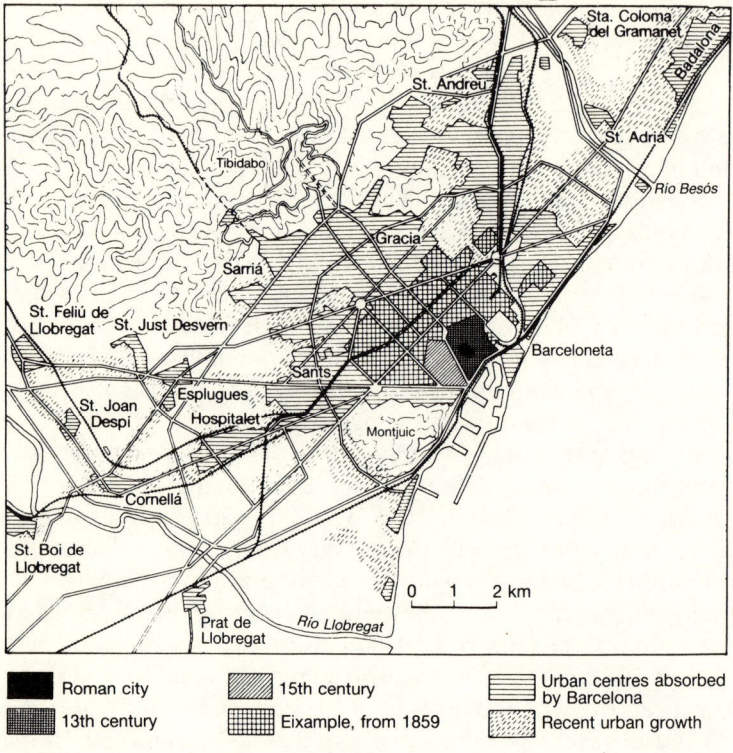

■ Roman city	▨ 15th century	▤ Urban centres absorbed by Barcelona
▦ 13th century	▦ Eixample, from 1859	▨ Recent urban growth

The stimulus of urban expansion was industrial growth. Until the sixties there had been no real transformation of the structure and location of modern Catalan industry. Textiles had remained the dominant if declining activity, whereas engineering and chemicals were rapidly expanding. Outside Barcelona, industry had been located along the Llobregat and Ter rivers, in the textile towns of Terrassa, Sabadell, and Mataró, and in towns of the interior. The new decade saw a rapid decline in the agricultural sector and the unprecedented development of engineering, chemicals, and construction alongside the old textile industry. By 1970, production was concentrated around these four industries, which together employed almost 70 per cent of the industrial workers in the province. The tertiary sector, especially banks, insurance, and transport, grew even faster, absorbing almost 36 per cent of the active population by the end of the decade.[3] This growth soaked up resources from the rest of Catalonia, concentrating the bulk of industry into the Greater Metropolitan Area of Barcelona, within which the capital gathered to itself most of the tertiary sector. Industry was progressively displaced from the centre to the periphery of the city through congestion and rising land values, leaving two inner industrial areas, the Zona Franca by the port and the San Andreu, Poble Nou, San Adriá triangle to the north. Almost all of Barcelona's industry was concentrated in these two districts, the Zona Franca estate alone providing 72 per cent of the city's industrial jobs.[4] However, small workshops of every trade abounded in the old working-class areas of the city, such as Sans and Gracia.

The new location of industry was governed by two criteria: proximity to the capital and the price of land. Industry in the sixties was attracted to the towns on the periphery and in the hinterland of Barcelona. By 1970 the provincial capital was encircled by two rings of industrial development, the closer one describing a semicircle linking Prat, Cerdanyola, and San Adriá, and the other joining Martorell, Terrassa, Sabadell, Mollet, and Martorelles (see Map 1).[5] Unlike industry in Barcelona, much of the new development was located in areas designated as residential or where planning allowed a combination of residential and industrial land use. In the inner ring, almost half of the firms of over 20 employees were located in zones of dual classification.[6] In these areas, factory and tenement block rubbed shoulders, and strikes sometimes spilled out into shopping areas.

As for the make-up of industry, Barcelona and its district or *comarca* (known as Barcelonés) took on a highly diversified structure.[7] While 43 per cent of jobs in the province were in the textile industry, only 11 per cent of these were situated in

[3] Centre d'Estudis de Planificació, *Reconocimiento territorial de Cataluña* (Barcelona, 1978) and *Industrialització a Catalunya 1960–1977* (Barcelona, 1982).

[4] M. Tarragó, Ll. Brau, and C. Teixidor, 'Planificación y crecimiento de Barcelona (1958–1971)', *CAU*, Nov.–Dec. 1973, pp. 93–105.

[5] A. Ferrer Aixala, *Presentación y estadística de los planes parciales de la Provincia de Barcelona* (Barcelona, 1974).

[6] J. Clusa Oriach, *La localización industrial en la comarca de Barcelona* (Barcelona, 1973).

[7] One of the territorial divisions of the province was the *comarca* or district, of which there were 38 in Catalonia.

Barcelonés. Most of the new industries, such as chemicals, food-processing, and pharmaceuticals, were drawn to the area around the capital. Many of them were multinationals. Indeed, by the end of the decade foreign capital had penetrated deep into industry in Catalonia, bringing new technology and methods of production. Of the 297 large-sized companies with their headquarters in Catalonia, 98 were multinationals and 75 were controlled by foreign capital.[8] In contrast, the old industrial centres of the province largely retained their traditional character as textile towns. This urban and industrial growth was not rationally planned but neither was it unavoidable. It was governed by speculation and the search for maximum profit with the minimum social expenditure. In the absence of effective instruments of planning or democratic accountability, private interests and local authorities colluded in the evasion of planning regulations in order to advance their mutual interests.[9] Barcelona thus grew in the image of Francoist society. Its new profile was the spatial expression of *laissez-faire* capitalism, corruption, and social exploitation.[10] The most important juncture in this process was the appointment of Josep María de Porcioles as Mayor of Barcelona in 1957. Porcioles' financial interests were centred on the newly-created Banco de Madrid, which, despite its name, brought together mainly Catalan capital accumulated in black-market operations and in the textile industry. One of the bank's leading shareholders was no less a figure than the Marquis of Villaverde, father of Franco's son-in-law. It was a mark of the growing integration of a section of the Catalan bourgeoisie into the national league of financial capital. The Banco de Madrid, followed by the Banco Catalán de Desarrollo, proceeded to launch into a vast real-estate operation that was responsible for much of Barcelona's urban growth.

Housing development in the sixties was spurred not so much by the needs of immigrant families as by their savings. In the previous decade, cheap housing estates had been built by

---

[8] J. M. Vidal Villa, 'La industria en Cataluña', *Ciudad y Territorio,* Apr.–June 1977, pp. 21–7. See also Francesc Cabana, *Les multinacionals a Catalunya* (Barcelona, 1984).

[9] For a history of town planning in Barcelona see Martin Wynn, 'Barcelona: Planning and Change 1854–1977', *Town Planning Review,* Apr. 1979, pp. 185–203; J. Borja, 'Planeamiento y crecimiento urbanos de Barcelona (1939–1958)', *CAU,* Nov.–Dec. 1973, pp. 86–91.   [10] Borja, ibid.

institutions of the government and the State Union, the OSE, but they had made little impact on the housing deficit, which by 1959 had reached up to 100,000 dwellings. In the sixties it became profitable for private companies, subsidized by the State, to build estates to accommodate families who had managed to scrape together the down payment for a flat through years of overtime or moonlighting. The waste land between the old city and the new industrial estates, previously dotted with small market gardens and shanty towns, began to be filled by massive tenement blocks. Rapidly the first ring of urban and industrial centres, such as Cornellá to the south and Badalona to the north, became joined to the capital in one massive urban sprawl.[11] Except, on the one hand, for the new bourgeois residential district in the west (stretching to the foothills of the Tibidabo mountain) and, on the other, the decaying inner-city enclaves, urban conditions deteriorated as one moved out of the city centre.

This transformation shattered the web of relationships that made up working-class communities inside and on the fringes of the city. Inner and outer boundaries became ill-defined. In the city centre, the old working-class districts such as Poble Sec, Sans, and Barceloneta declined as occupational communities, as industries closed down or moved out, and their population changed. The displacement of industry and the enforced geographical mobility of immigrant families broke the links between work and residence.[12] Giant urban projects, such as motorways and office blocks, dislocated old districts of the city. On the outskirts, communities were swallowed up by the spreading city, their space turned into huge dormitory suburbs without adequate infrastructures.

The town of Cornellá may serve to illustrate the consequences of this rapid growth. Measuring 6.9 square kilometres, the town grew from a population of 11,000 in 1950 to 76,387 in 1970. By

[11] There was a marked decline in the agrarian population on the fringes of the city. Thus the agrarian population in Cornellá dropped from 12% in 1950 to 1% in 1970, and that of Santa Coloma from 5% to 0.4% over the same period. J. Martín Moreno and A. De Miguel, *La estructura social de las ciudades españolas* (Madrid, 1978), 82.

[12] For a study of the effect of industrial displacement in Barceloneta, see Soledad García, 'Urbanisation, Working-class Organisation, and Political Movements in Barcelona', Ph.D. thesis (Hull, 1983).

that time, it had lost any recognizable boundaries, having become part of the continuous urban development that spread out of the city centre. The old town hall and the church were among the few landmarks that were a reminder of the former landscape. The massive new developments that were scattered among the factories, shops, and roads suffered from a severe lack of urban projects and social services. The local Economic and Social Council of the OSE, not normally given to voicing protest, noted that urban deprivation had created '. . . a deep social unrest among working-class families that affects the factories where they work. Moreover, the inhabitants are not integrated into the district in which they reside, nor are the districts connected with the urban centre.' The OSE report went on to complain about '. . . the complete subordination of the town to the metropolis. Its dependence is on all levels—work, leisure, equipment, services, tertiary activities . . . which means that Cornellá has become a mere suburb of Barcelona with all the problems that this entails . . .'[13]

For the majority of its working-class population, any urban and social cohesion that Barcelona had once enjoyed was now largely destroyed. The focus of social interaction was the neighbourhood and the workplace. New forms of collective identity would be shaped in the seventies around new districts or larger areas within the metropolis. The sense of belonging to a city-wide community that had been so evident in the 1951 tram strike seemed to have been lost like the city itself in the sprawl of Greater Barcelona.

Urban and industrial growth in the towns of the hinterland followed a different pattern. A distinction should be made here between the old textile towns of Terrassa, Sabadell, and Mataró, and the towns that sprang up in the sixties. Although the former experienced an unprecedented demographic growth, it was spread over a longer period and was cushioned by old traditions and resources. Thus Sabadell's population grew from almost 48,000 in 1940 to around 60,000 in 1950; ten years later there were 105,000 inhabitants and by 1970 the population had reached 160,000.[14] In contrast the new towns that appeared in

[13] Consejo Económico Social del Bajo Llobregat, *Informe sobre las necesidades más urgentes de la comarca de Cornellá,* 14 Apr. 1972 and *Plan de necesidades urgentes de la comarca de Cornellá,* May 1972.

[14] Figures rounded from those of COCIS, *Memorias,* 1960–74.

the Baix Llobregat valley and in the Vallés Occidental and Oriental area grew in the space of a decade. In the twin towns of Cerdanyola and Ripollet that straddle the motorway from Barcelona to Sabadell, the population shot up from 5,000 and 6,000 respectively in 1960 to over 20,000 each ten years later.

The old towns also kept their traditional industrial character. Although in steady decline, the woollen industry still dominated the activity of Sabadell and Terrassa, employing over a third of the working population in 1970.[15] Newer industries sought to set up their plants on the outskirts of Barcelona or in the newly industrialized areas of the Vallés Oriental and Baix Llobregat. The service industries tended to be located in the metropolis. Hence, these three towns preserved an industrial homogeneity, sharing their activities between engineering, construction, and above all the different branches of the textile industry. Moreover, their urban growth was less traumatic than that of Barcelona and periphery, or that of the new towns. Mataró grew outwards from the old quarter, which remained the nerve-centre of the town.[16] Unlike Barcelona, many of Sabadell's and Terrassa's factories stayed within the conurbation; a continuous chatter of textile machines and the stench of chemicals and oil issued from the small factories scattered about the centre of both towns. But while Terrassa kept its urban and industrial development within the expanding boundaries of the town, Sabadell spawned new industrial conglomerations on all four sides, separated from the town by a few kilometres of waste land.

Both towns saw the construction on their outskirts of huge tenement blocks accommodating immigrant families from the shanty towns built in the forties and fifties. Land values were lower than in Barcelona, however, enabling many immigrant families to rent or buy small plots outside the towns, on which they built their own houses. Unauthorized barrios grew up on the outskirts without electricity, transport, or drains. Towards the end of the fifties, the Mayor of Sabadell calculated that out of a total of 200 kilometres of streets in Sabadell, 48 km were unpaved and without drains. 'The growth of the suburbs', he wrote, 'was completely uncontrolled. They looked like . . . the

---

[15] For the industrial structure of Sabadell see Consejo Económico Sindical del Vallés Occidental, *Informe al Primer Consejo*, 13 May 1970.

[16] For the growth of Mataró see P. Lleonart, P. Macías, and R. Ardèvol, *El Maresme: les claus de la seva contínua transformació* (Barcelona, 1981).

far West'. Indeed, some of the new barrios were given nicknames such as Kansas City.[17] Often separated from the town outskirts by a stretch of no man's land, they marked the division between the immigrant and Catalan populations.

The social structure of the urban centres in the province also varied considerably, as can be seen in Table 1. The municipality of Barcelona contained a more heterogeneous population, reflecting the greater spread of the occupational structure. The older towns, though they had lost some of their autonomy owing to the magnetic pull of the metropolis, still retained a certain balance in their class structure. The new towns and the urban conglomerations on the fringes of the city, in contrast, were overwhelmingly working-class areas.

TABLE 1   *Socio-economic Categories as Percentages of Total Population in Five Towns*

	Barcelona	Cornellá	Ripollet	Sabadell	Terrassa
Employers, managers, higher professionals	8.8	2	3	5.5	4.1
Professional, white-collar, technicians, self-employed	35.7	18.3	14	26	25.4
Manual	30.6	65.5	67.7	53.6	50.9

Source: author's calculations from the Municipal Census of 1970.

The above figures do not include a number of occupational categories, such as agricultural workers, but these are too small to affect the overall distribution of figures. The percentage differences are made up overwhelmingly by the inactive population.

In the upheaval of the sixties, then, only Sabadell, Terrassa, and Mataró retained a relative social and urban cohesion. Even for the immigrant population living on the outskirts, their centres were a vital reference-point. It is true that a sense of separateness from the towns' mainly Catalan residents seems to have persisted among immigrant families. It was common among Terrassa immigrants living on the outskirts to say, on going to the town

[17] Marcet, pp. 313–14 and 292–3.

centre, 'I'm going to Terrassa.'[18] But the commercial and bureaucratic centre was still accessible on foot or by bicycle; and the population was still small enough for a certain provincial intimacy to persist. The local centres of power—the Town Hall, the police station, the headquarters of the State Union—were focal points in the lives of immigrant workers. In contrast, Barcelona must have been too vast to comprehend and decidedly more anonymous to the rural immigrant. There were several layers of power in the city, for it was also the capital of the province. The colossal OSE building in the Vía Layetana, for example, was the headquarters of both the local and the provincial Unions; it must have seemed all the more impenetrable.

The social, urban, and industrial changes briefly touched on in this chapter all helped to shape the emerging labour movement of the sixties. Their impact on the development and character of the labour movement will be examined in greater detail in Chapter 4. An equally important influence on its character was the massive influx of immigrants into the towns of Barcelona province. The incorporation of hundreds of thousands of rural workers into the industrial work-force not only helped to break the tenuous hold of past traditions but also brought new values and demands. The single most important feature of this new largest ever wave of immigration was that it was drawn into the area by the economic boom. The migration of the forties had been a flight from rural poverty. The settlers who began to arrive from the mid fifties onwards came with higher expectations.

By the early seventies, some 40 per cent of the population of Catalonia were of immigrant origin. The majority of them were from the South, in particular from eastern Andalusia, where many had been employed as agricultural labourers, miners, fishermen, charcoal-burners, and construction workers. There were also rural migrants from Galicia, Castile, and Aragon who had been smallholders and whose only common ground with the former was their condition as settlers. Indeed, there is no simple picture of the occupational origin of the immigrants, nor of a common historical or cultural experience. Among the first

[18] J. Ricart Oller, *Egara: una parroquia obrera bajo el franquismo* (Terrassa, 1979), 18.

leaders of the new labour movement were experienced militants from the mines and building-sites of the South. There were also highly literate immigrants among the white-collar workers in the banks and insurance companies. And there were many illiterate seasonal workers who got jobs as hod-carriers in the construction sites burgeoning in the capital and along the coast.

For the incoming migrants there were three sources of livelihood: industry, services (in particular transport and, for women, domestic service), and self-employment as bartenders, taxi-drivers, street hawkers. The building trade was for many an unskilled immigrant a stepping-stone to a better job. Factory employment was valued as it gave greater security than construction and a higher chance of moving up the occupational ladder; the larger the firm the greater were the possiblities of acquiring skills. However, of a sample of immigrant workers in a survey conducted in Catalonia in the early seventies over 70 per cent worked in construction and transport. Conversely, only 16 per cent of building workers were Catalan in origin.[19] Indeed, the immigrants filled the lower-paid manual jobs. 82 per cent of unskilled and semi-skilled workers in a 1970 sample in the Barcelona *comarca* were non-Catalans.[20] The balance of immigrant to indigenous workers, however, depended on the industry. In the textile trades the bulk of unskilled or semi-skilled workers were Catalan in origin and mainly women. In the engineering and chemical industries there was probably a balance between the two groups, but indigenous workers tended to occupy the more skilled jobs. Transport workers were largely immigrants. On the other hand, in the service sector such as banks and hospitals in which status and pay were higher, the majority of the work-force were Catalan.[21]

For all the opportunities that economic growth offered them, most immigrant workers continued to fill the less skilled and lower-paid manual jobs. The further down they were on the occupational scale, the fewer their chances of self-advancement and the wider the gap between them and indigenous workers. Conversely, the wave of immigration enabled many local

[19] E. Pinilla de las Heras, *Estudios sobre cambio social y estructuras sociales en Cataluña* (Madrid, 1979), 138, 145, 550, 563.

[20] Centre d'Estudis de Planificació (1982), 116.

[21] Pinilla de las Heras (1979), 551. See also R. Ferras, *Barcelone: croissance d'une métropole* (Paris, 1977), 202–25.

workers to make a rapid ascent of the professional ladder. New skills could be acquired and there were plenty of opportunities to move on to jobs with a higher status and better pay. Even within the same occupational category, indigenous workers tended to enjoy higher rates of pay.[22] There were several reasons why Catalan workers had the edge on the majority of the immigrant labour force. Firstly, they were generally better educated. A sample of workers in 1970 in the Barcelona area indicated that while 27 per cent of Catalans had completed their secondary education at least, only 10 per cent of immigrants had had more than a rudimentary schooling and among the rest there can be assumed to have been a high level of illiteracy.[23] Even by the eighties, over 10 per cent of the population in the largely immigrant communities of Badalona, Cornellá, and Santa Coloma were still illiterate.[24] A second important factor that placed immigrants at a disadvantage was their ignorance of Catalan. While the language of the mass media and officialdom in general was Castilian (the 'Christian' language of Spain according to the Nationalist invaders of 1939), the native language of Catalonia was common currency in the streets and shops, in many factories, and in the lower echelons of administration. If the Francoists looked down on Catalan as a subordinate language, Castilian Spanish rapidly became, in the Catalonia of the sixties, the language of the less educated. Notwithstanding the efforts of the regime, Catalan grew to be perceived by immigrants as a means of social advancement.[25] Thirdly, Catalan workers were in a better position to defend their pay and conditions of work than immigrants. Not only did they have an old tradition of union organization but they enjoyed a more secure and self-assured position in society.

A far greater obstacle to integration was residential segregation. Immigrant families were concentrated in ghettos, whether they were shanty towns or estates. This was not a new phenomenon.

---

[22] Pinilla de las Heras (1979), 581, found a differential of 1.3 in rates of pay between immigrants and Catalans in the skilled manual and administrative grades. For evidence of the occupational mobility of indigenous workers see ibid. 327–34.   [23] Ibid. 118.

[24] Riera (1986), 67–85.

[25] In a survey of immigrant workers in Cornellá at the beginning of the seventies, 97.3% wanted their children to learn Catalan. A. C. Comín and J. M. García-Nieto, *Juventud obrera y conciencia de clase* (Madrid, 1974).

Tales were told in the thirties of signs put up at the entrance to shanty towns warning people that at that point Catalonia ended and Murcia began.[26] But the scale of immigration in the fifties and sixties was greater than any known previously. Moreover, immigrant families, it they had any choice at all, sought to live among people from their own communities. Many shanty and self-built towns housed entire communities who had deserted their villages *en masse*. In one such place on the outskirts of Sabadell, the old Mayor and Councillors continued quite unofficially to exercise their office.[27] As shanty towns in Barcelona were cleared, many people from these communities found themselves in the same overspill estates built to attract the savings of the shanty-dwellers. Amidst the high concrete blocks of these buildings it was difficult to preserve the sort of existential links that bound village communities. Moreover, many immigrant families were forced to take overcrowded sub-let accommodation wherever they could find it. According to the Urban Commission of Barcelona in 1970, some 30,000 families were housed in flats already occupied by the legal lodgers.[28]

Nevertheless, sub-let accommodation and shanty towns offered immigrants an important advantage—that of mobility. The purchase of a flat, even though it represented a step upwards, tied them down to high monthly repayments and narrowed their options even further.[29] Home-ownership also reinforced the geographical concentration of immigrants. In the great tenement blocks of Satellite City (Ciudad Satélite) in Cornellá, one of the most densely populated districts in Europe with only 10 square metres of space per person (compared to 290 in London), 90 per cent of residents were immigrants.[30] The shanty towns of the immigrants were exchanged for the 'vertical ghettos' of the new estates.

The more immigrants were able to take advantage of the opportunities offered by the boom, the more they were drawn into the cash nexus that tied them down to jobs and residence.

[26] F. Candel, *Els altres catalans* (Barcelona, 1963), 9–10. See also Castells, 27.
27.   [27] Castells, ibid.
[28] J. M. Alibés *et al*., 'La Barcelona de Porcioles', *CAU*, Sept.–Oct. 1973, pp. 29–104.
[29] For a discussion of this question see M. de Solá-Morales *et al*., *Barcelona: remodelación capitalista o desarrollo urbano en el sector de la Ribera Oriental* (Barcelona, 1974).   [30] Comín and García-Nieto, p. 72.

Upward social mobility may have compensated to some extent for the destruction of the social network of village life. But when it became clear that there were limits to individual progress, more critical attitudes emerged and found expression in community struggles over poor housing, social services, and the degraded surroundings. Two contradictory tendencies were thus at work. On one hand workers and their families were encouraged by the capitalist environment and the structures of Francoist society to seek individual paths of self-improvement. Seductive models of affluence (largely American) were portrayed on the screens of cinemas and television sets and in the pages of magazines and comics. Exultant advertisements promised a quick accession to a brand-new life that was in stark contrast to the poverty and displacement that had been the lot of most immigrants. On the other hand, the experience of collective struggles at work and in the community was nourishing a new sense of mutual dependence.

Although there are virtually no surveys of attitudes covering this period, it is possible to identify from a number of sources the changing perceptions of immigrants. The first years of the newly-arrived immigrant were devoted to the struggle to obtain a stable job and a decent dwelling. The initial difficulties of adaptation to urban life were innumerable. It was even a problem, as one immigrant said in an interview, to get used to the fact that one did not say 'Good morning' to people in the streets. But the difficulties were not confined to relations with the outside world. Immigration radically altered family life. The new settlers had been forced, as a commentator has written, to move from 'an open family in a closed society to a closed family in an open society.'[31] The strains this caused can only be understood in the individual life stories of immigrants.

A miniature survey carried out in the mid sixties by the priest Pedro Negre Rigol affords a vivid sketch of attitudes in a largely immigrant working-class neighbourhood of Barcelona.[32] He observed considerable prejudice among Catalan residents towards the new immigrants, but noted that this feeling was even more marked among those immigrants who had settled in the

---

[31] J. Botey Vallés, 'Cinquanta-quatre relats d'immigració', *Perspectiva Social*, Jan.–June 1980, pp. 34 and 39.

[32] P. Negre Rigol, *El obrero y la ciudad* (Barcelona, 1968).

area some time previously. Among the long-established settlers he found a greater sense of identification with the city and with Catalan culture than among the newly-arrived whose only reference-point was the neighbourhood itself. The longer their stay in Barcelona, the more critical was the attitude of immigrants towards conditions in the neighbourhood and the more frustrated their aspirations of social advancement. He also noted that immigrants tended to become less religious as a result of their assimilation into the urban environment. Another Catholic writer asserted that attendance at mass in Barcelona dropped from 15 per cent in 1950 to only 8 per cent in 1970.[33] Pedro Negre claimed to have found an almost complete lack of class-consciousness among his respondents, though a strong feeling of social injustice was expressed, especially by the more skilled and longer-established immigrants.

In contrast, a survey conducted some seven years later in Cornellá suggested a new more radical consciousness developing among young workers of both immigrant and local origins.[34] A study of dyers and bleachers in Barcelona in 1971 also indicated a growing class-consciousness among better-paid immigrant workers.[35] These partial findings confirm the more general evidence, which will be examined in Chapter 5, that immigrant workers, as they became more integrated in employment and in the community, increasingly moved from individual self-reliance to collective action. There is an evident time-lag between the arrival of immigrants in the fifties and sixties and their involvement in the working-class movement on any mass scale towards the beginning of the seventies.

The important point was that the immigrants and slum-dwellers of Barcelona were not generally a lumpenproletariat. They made up a majority of the work-force in the new engineering and chemical factories; they manned the building-sites and drove the buses.[36] It was above all the experience of work that shaped the changing perceptions of immigrant

[33] J. Castaño i Colomer, *Memories de la JOC a Catalunya 1932–1970.* (Barcelona, 1974), 180. See also the survey in the estate of Can Serra in Botey Vallés, pp. 49–87.   [34] Comín and García-Nieto, op. cit.

[35] J. R. Logan, 'Bases socials de la consciència de classe a Barcelona', *Papers*, no. 12 (1979), pp. 55–71.

[36] According to the Catholic centre, Caritas Diocesana, 43.75% of the population of the shanty towns were gainfully employed (over 5% above the

workers. For the factory worker, it was not only the acquisition of an industrial skill that brought new values, but also the experience of collective work and organization. Domestic service in middle-class Catalan families helped to change the values of many immigrant women and facilitated their integration into the new society. There were others who, because of their trade or economic activity, lived on the fringes of the society they had adopted. The street hawker and the older construction navvy on an isolated building-site, among others, tended to remain only partially assimilated into the surrounding community.[37] Just as the background of the settlers varied widely, so the experience of migration was by no means uniform.

Indigenous workers and their families were no less affected by this social transformation. The most obvious sign of change was the general rise in living standards. Per capita income in Spain grew by 383 per cent between 1950 and 1975. That this increase in wealth was not equally distributed was borne out by the fact that living standards, as measured by the satisfaction of basic needs, rose by an average of 232 per cent in the same period. Nevertheless, the change in the quality of life for working-class families was real enough. Over a 20-year period, the infant mortality rate was halved and the index of nutritional levels doubled.[38] Hunger and disease no longer ravaged the homes of the poor. The caves and shanty towns in which the first immigrants had made their home gave way to massive tenement blocks equipped with at least running water and proper heating. The damp, cold, and overcrowded apartments in which

Spanish average). Of these 63% worked in industry and 36% in the tertiary sector (above all in domestic service and transport): Equipo de Estudios de Caritas Diocesana, *Visión sociográfica de Barcelona* (Barcelona, 1965), 223–4.

[37] M. Siguan, 'L'assimilació dels immigrants en la societat catalana: el punt de vista del psicoleg', in A. Jutglar *et al.*, *La immigració a Catalunya* (Barcelona, 1968), 33–66.

[38] Servicio Sindical de Estadística, *Bienestar social en España* (Madrid, 1976), 70–186, and FOESSA, *Informe sobre la situación social de España* (Madrid, 1970). For further evidence of transformation of living standards see *Reseña estadística de la Provincia de Barcelona,* in Molinero and Ysàs (1985), 258; Instituto de Estudios Sindicales, Sociales y Cooperativas (Delegación de Barcelona), *Estudio sociológico sobre el trabajador y su medio en la ciudad de Barcelona* (Madrid, 1969); and J. Clusa i Oriach *Estudio-informe de los barrios de Can Oriach, Plana de Pintor, Torrent de Capellà* (Sabadell, 1967).

indigenous workers had lived were exchanged for bright modern flats that they would eventually own.

However, living standards varied widely within the working class. The poor were being replaced constantly by new immigrants. There were still shanty towns in the late eighties, stretching along the railways to the north and south of the city. But the better-paid skilled workers, including the many who had worked on the production lines in Germany and Switzerland, had managed to accumulate a substantial amount of savings. Not only had they bought their own flat and car, but they were looking in the early seventies to invest their savings in plots of land, second homes, or smallholdings outside the city. A spot check of pupils in a secondary school in the working-class area of Cornellá in 1984 revealed that the families of almost half of them owned some sort of property with a plot of land; and a similar conclusion was drawn from a survey of workers in the Siemens and Pirelli multinational companies.[39] By the early seventies, small estate agents were setting up stalls in the markets of Barcelona and organizing free Sunday excursions with wine to view plots of land outside the city. Beneath the vast operations of banks and property developers there swarmed a host of small and sometimes crooked real-estate speculators intent on profiting from the old agrarian instinct of land ownership still strong in the new working-class.[40]

This picture of relative affluence must be set against the total inadequacy of social services, the poor quality of housing, and the lack in working-class areas of educational, cultural, and recreational facilities; in short, the poverty of the social wage. Even though most workers paid obligatory national insurance contributions, they were poorly served by the health services. There were no hospitals for miles in the densely populated working-class districts that ringed the city. In contrast to the wealth of plush private clinics in the centre of Barcelona, the outlying areas had a totally inadequate provision of doctors' clinics.[41] Health checks in the poorer districts of the city revealed severe problems among its population. Sixty-five per cent of

---

[39] Riera (1986), 74 and 81.

[40] Interview with José María Alibés, 13 Nov. 1985.

[41] For a study of health provision in Barcelona, see N. Acarín and C. Sans, 'Equipamiento, organización, y gasto sanitario en Barcelona', *CAU*, May-June 1976, pp. 64–72.

children in the Verdun district in the northern outskirts of Barcelona showed symptoms of rickets, another 68 per cent suffered from tonsilitis, and almost half needed fillings in their teeth.[42] Many new working-class estates lacked paved streets, proper lighting, nurseries, parks, and schools. The houses themselves were generally badly constructed. The surroundings were often bare and polluted. The playing-grounds of the local children were muddy waste lands filled with broken glass and rusting machinery.[43] Educational provision was so bad that many parents chose to pay modest fees to send their children to Catholic-run schools for working-class children. Yet even these schools hardly offered an adequate education. In the municipality of L'Hospitalet, the average size of their classes was 46 compared to 56 in the State schools. In contrast to the minimum space of 8 square metres for each pupil laid down in 1971 by the EEC, the private schools in the area had only 1.75 square metres and the State schools 1.96.[44]

Moreover, in order to achieve a decent living wage, workers were forced to toil long hours at work. A survey of blue- and white-collar workers in 1969 found that a majority worked over 55 hours a week, while a 1971 study of the working-class district of Sant Ildefons revealed that three-quarters of workers interviewed spent over 12 hours a day at work and more than a third over 14 hours.[45] For all the Francoist laws protecting employment, many workers had a precarious hold on their jobs. Illegal blank work contracts abounded, which applicants were required to sign without knowing their terms. Jobs were particularly insecure on the building-sites, where some subcontractors were explicit about the terms on which workers were hired, as the following extract from a labourer's contract

---

[42] *Nueve Barrios,* Apr. 1974.

[43] For case studies of urban deficiencies see M. J. Olivé, 'Crecimiento urbano y conflictividad en la aglomeración barcelonesa', *Revista de Geografía,* Jan.–Dec. 1974, pp. 99–127; F. Miguélez, G. Alvarer, and J. J. Santolaria, 'Planificación y conflictos urbanos', *CAU,* July–Aug. 1975, pp. 29–34; M. G. Wynn, 'San Cosme, Spain: Planning and Renewal of a State Housing Area', *Journal of the American Planning Association,* Jan. 1980, pp. 76–87, and 'The Residential Development Process in Spain—a Case Study', *Planning Outlook,* xxiv. 1 (1981), 20–9. For a more descriptive and vivid portrait of conditions in the new working-class estates see F. Candel, *Apuntes para una sociología del barrio* (Barcelona, 1972).

[44] Miguélez, Alvarer, and Santolaria, op. cit.

[45] Instituto de Estudios Sindicales, Sociales y Cooperativas, op. cit.; the results of the second survey are quoted in Riera (1986), 43.

reveals: 'If work has to be suspended partially or totally as a result of lack of materials or for any other reason, the holder of this contract will consider himself automatically dismissed as soon as work is halted, without any claim or compensation being due.'[46] The problem of long hours of work and job insecurity was compounded by the absence of proper safety measures at work. Indeed, the cost workers had to bear in order to achieve living standards that were taken for granted by industrial workers elsewhere in Europe was high. Despite the considerable improvement in take-home pay during the sixties, Spanish workers were considerably worse off in 1970 than their counterparts in Europe, as Table 2 indicates.

TABLE 2   *Comparison of Prices in Hours of Work Between three Countries in 1970*

Product	Germany	Italy	Spain
Bread (500 grammes)	8 min	10 min	11 min
Veal (1 kilo)	1 h 51 min	3 h 48 min	5 h 43 min
Cheese (100 grammes)	10 min	17 min	1 h
Eggs ($\frac{1}{2}$ dozen)	12 min	22 min	31 min
Potatoes (1 kilo)	4 min	8 min	9 min
Woollen skirt	7 h 43 min	12 h 54 min	21 h 18 min
Electricity (50 kWh)	3 h 27 min	5 h 19 min	12 h 42 min
Television	103 h 42 min	225 h 55 min	494 h 10 min
Refrigerator	37 h 50 min	65 h 28 min	142 h 22 min
Washing-machine	161 h 40 min	180 h 16 min	944 h 46 min
Private medical treatment	2 h 6 min	3 h 53 min	5 h 36 min
Car	1075 h 29 min	1716 h 53 min	4065 h 3 min

Source: EEC Office of Statistics, quoted in *Luchas Obreras,* 17 Mar. 1974. Figures are based on average prices and wages.

By the end of the sixties, therefore, the working class of Barcelona bore little resemblance to that of the post-war period. It was not only immeasurably larger but its composition was more complex. Subsequent chapters will look at the workers of different industries and districts of the conurbation. What needs to be stressed here is that by the mid seventies the majority of

[46] Quoted from *Juventud Obrera* in Candel (1968), 297.

working-class families had achieved a measure of dignity and hope that sharply contrasted with the hardship of the first 15 years of the dictatorship. Although their stake in the new society was small, workers would not lightly give up the benefits and opportunities that they had acquired through immense effort and not without considerable suffering.

Over half the working class in the Barcelona area were immigrants, many of them segregated residentially from their Catalan counterparts. Few had experienced factory work and none shared the traditions of unionism in Catalonia. In any case, a new generation formed the majority of workers; by 1965, only 40 per cent of the working population could remember the Civil War and even fewer had had experience of unionism or collective association. Moreover, the propaganda of the regime and the fear that kept older people silent about the past combined to produce a largely apolitical generation of young workers. Economic growth and integration into Western Europe were providing new opportunities for social advancement. The breakup of communities through urban expansion and immigration reinforced the individualism so encouraged by the regime. The main instrument of this self-improvement was money, accumulated through overtime, moonlighting, and collective pressure on the shop-floor.

As living standards rose, new patterns of consumption typical of advanced capitalist societies began to appear. In a characteristically patronizing tone, the OSE commented in 1970,

The Barcelona working-class family is singularly accessible to the lure of advertising, inviting them to buy the greatest number of very varied consumer goods. The television, which dominates households, gives easy access to advertising and there are psychologically suitable ways of fulfilling these needs—an increase in bonuses and overtime. It is therefore easy for these people to think they can rise to a higher level of consumption than their take-home pay permits.[47]

How far was the labour movement shaped by this new working class? To what extent were militants able to articulate the aspirations of ordinary workers? These questions will be examined in the chapters that follow.

---

[47] Organización Sindical de Barcelona, *Informe socio-económico de la Provincia de Barcelona,* Sept. 1970, CG archives no. 1425.

3
The Growth of the New Labour Movement

Without a united union, we would regress to the social struggles of yester-year that divided workers and pitted them in bloody conflict against the employers instead of uniting all in concord and dialogue.

(Extract of speech by Franco in 1967, quoted in Manuel Vázquez Montalbán, *Los demonios familiares de Franco* (Barcelona, 1987), 139–140)

The 'economic miracle' shored up a dictatorship that had seemed to falter in the mid fifties. By the early sixties, the regime was projecting an image of confident progress. The besuited, mild-mannered figure of Franco, now approaching old age, could be seen on the newsreels talking earnestly with experts as he opened a dam or visited a new hospital. It seemed as if the 'fortress' of Spain had been converted into a great factory. Foreigners were now welcome on its shores—between 1960 and 1966, the number of tourists rose from 6 to 16 million a year. And while many Spaniards bore deep scars of resentment against the regime, it was easy to believe the propaganda, so assiduously laid on by the media, that the government was responsible for the boom. The years of widespread penury now lay behind. The era of television, Real Madrid, and the rags-to-riches bullfighter, El Cordobés, had begun.

Labour unrest continued to plague the regime, however. In the spring of 1962, a wave of strikes swept through the country from the Asturian mines and across the main industrial centres of Spain. At the beginning of May a state of emergency was declared in Asturias and in the Basque provinces. By the middle of the month, the strikes had spread to most of the engineering and textile factories in the province of Barcelona. It was the biggest strike movement so far in the history of the regime. In a triumphant speech in June, the exiled leader of the Spanish

Communist Party, Santiago Carrillo, declared, '. . . the strikes of April and May are the first wave of a series of struggles that will drown the dictatorship . . .'[1]

Yet the exultant accounts of the opposition misunderstood the nature of the new labour protest. The spontaneous and generalized outbursts against government wage norms that characterized strike action in the second half of the fifties gave way in the next decade to a more regular pattern of disputes. The 1958 Law of Collective Agreements shifted the target of workers' grievances from the State to the employer. It also fragmented disputes in time and place. As a result, labour dissent no longer took on the same political dimension. The scale and vehemence of the strike movement of spring 1962 owed not a little to the erosion of take-home pay and the lingering effects of the recession brought on by the Stabilization Plan. But it was also the first time that the new system of wage bargaining between workers and employers began to take effect, because the government had just lifted the wage freeze imposed at the end of 1959. The context of the strikes was the negotiation or renewal of factory and industry-wide agreements that normally took place in spring. It was no coincidence that three and a half times as many agreements were being negotiated in 1962 as in 1961.[2]

For the first time, the government was forced to acknowledge the existence of conflict between employers and workers. Following the unrest of spring 1962, a Law of Collective Disputes was promulgated in September 1962 that recognized, albeit ambiguously, the legality of strikes motivated by 'economic' demands. For all its restrictions, the new law gave the more organized workers a greater possibility of winning their claims. The new official policy was adopted not entirely under protest. For the more far-seeing members of the government, the new mechanism of labour relations not only provided a safety-valve for militancy but also forced firms to be more efficient. Furthermore, the increase in take-home pay that would result from a less controlled labour market would generate a domestic market essential for capitalist development.[3]

[1] *Mundo Obrero*, June 1962.
[2] Organización Sindical, *Información de convenios colectivos sindicales*, 1969.
[3] For an interesting discussion of this question see A. C. Comín, *Per una*

Nevertheless, the 1962 spring 'revolt' marked a watershed in the post-war history of Spain. The introduction of bargaining created a new dynamic that would in the long run undermine the institutions of the regime. The government was faced by a dilemma: how to modernize the economy without changing the political system. The new policy of economic development was shot through with contradictions. The job protection by which the regime hoped to compensate workers for the loss of their right to organize collectively ran against the capitalist imperative of restructuring and job flexibility. If plant-level bargaining was necessary in order to introduce new technology and work methods requiring the co-operation of the work-force, it also raised the demand for democratic shop-floor representation and strengthened the confidence and autonomous organization of workers. More generally, the regime ran the risk of losing legitimacy when it was unable to satisfy the rising economic and social expectations fuelled by integration with Western economies.

While it was a means of modernizing industry, collective bargaining became an effective channel of social grievances. It gave militants an opportunity to agitate and organize around recurrent negotiations. The inability of the official structures of the State Union to deliver satisfactory agreements led to the creation of unofficial committees that drew up demands, negotiated with management, and led strike action. Agitation over collective agreements became the most effective point of contact between militants and rank and file. Indeed, much of the labour protest that ensued during the remainder of the dictatorship would originate from these negotiations. The forms that militant organization would take were moulded largely by the shape of collective bargaining. It is essential, therefore, to look in some detail at its structure and at its effect on the emerging labour movement of the sixties.[4]

estrategia sindical (Barcelona, 1970), 50–2, and F. Claudín, *Documentos de una divergencia comunista* (Barcelona, 1978), *passim.*

[4] Despite its importance, there have been few analyses of collective bargaining in Francoist Spain. For the sixties, see Amsden, op. cit,; for bargaining in Barcelona in the last years of the regime, see F. Miguélez Lobo, 'La negociación colectiva 1969–1975: el caso de Barcelona', *Revista de Estudios Sociales*, no. 17–18 (1976), pp. 205–22; and for a case-study of the engineering industry, Ll. Fina, 'Convenios y salarios en el sector metalúrgico español 1960–1975,' Ph.D.

COLLECTIVE BARGAINING

The most striking characteristic of the structure of collective bargaining was its fragmentation. The OSE was divided into 28 trade unions, each of them subdivided into branches. For example the Textile Union was made up of 12 branches, of which the most important were Wool, Cotton, Dyeing and Bleaching (the so-called Water Branch or *Ramo del Agua*), Knitwear, Silk, and Dressmaking. In the Wood and Furniture Union, there was even a branch for walking-stick and umbrella-handle makers. Each branch was organized separately within the Union and had its own collective agreement. In every industry, bargaining took place on different levels: there were plant-level, company-wide, and area agreements (the latter covering towns, districts (*comarcas*), or provinces), and finally nation-wide contracts. The decision over which level the negotiations took place depended on a number of factors: the characteristics of each industry, the balance of forces between management and workers, the size of the units of production, and even the whim or ambition of full-time union officials.

In the sixties, the only meaningful bargaining—where workers were able to exert pressure on the employers—took place in plant-level negotiations and, in a few instances, local negotiations. The hundreds of thousands of people who worked in small firms were covered by provincial contracts over which they had no influence whatsoever. Indeed, the minimum conditions laid down in these agreements were often ignored in small plants because there was neither the will on the part of the OSE nor the machinery to put them into effect. For the majority of workers, therefore, the introduction of collective bargaining meant little change from the wage-fixing mechanism of the fifties through State decree. In theory, workers in the larger firms that had their own contracts were also covered by local or provincial contracts, but they could afford to ignore them because their own pay and conditions were invariably better. Some local agreements, however, were subject to the collective pressure of

thesis (Universidad Autónoma de Barcelona, 1979). The main sources for the following analysis are the publications of the Barcelona Provincial OSE, which can be found in the archives of the Crown of Aragon in the *Depósito Regional* at Cervera University, and in the archives of the Civil Government.

workers in small factories, either because of the peculiar structure of the industry concerned (as in the case of the dyers and bleachers, which will be discussed in Chapter 5) or because the geographical concentration of factories affected by them gave them an accumulative social significance (as in the cases of the Cornellá and Sabadell engineering agreements, and the Terrassa textile contract).

The structure of collective bargaining was thus highly divisive. The lines separating the different units of bargaining described not merely differences of skill or trade but divisions between larger and smaller plants, militant and unorganized work-forces. The most important effect of this was to widen the wage differentials among workers of the same skill in the same industry but from different-sized plants. When the figures for agreements across all industries are compared, the pay differentials were even wider, amounting in the case of skilled workers from different industries to a ratio of 2.38.[5] If we consider that the wages paid in the small workshops that were not covered by provincial agreements were often below the minimum established for each industry, the differentials among workers of the same skill must have been even greater.[6] Yet within the plants with their own agreements, collective bargaining helped to reduce the divisions of professional grading that were such a marked feature of the regulations established for each industry by the Ministry of Labour. Rates of pay were as much a function of where you worked as of your skill; a labourer in a militant work-force that was able to negotiate its own agreement might earn more than a skilled worker in a factory covered by the provincial contract. Thus bargaining laid the basis for greater unity and greater division at the same time.

One of the main aims of collective bargaining was to increase productivity through the introduction of incentive schemes. By the end of 1963, over 77% of agreements contained productivity clauses that workers' negotiators accepted in exchange for higher wages and the opportunity to make more money through bonus

[5] Organización Sindical (OS) de Barcelona, *Análisis de 22 convenios en 1962 y 1963 en 13,385 firmas con 190,296 trabajadores*, 1964 and 1965, CG archives no. 1243.

[6] The differential of 35% noted in Madrid by Sartorius and Díaz Cardiel (op. cit. 16) between a semi-skilled worker in a small workshop and his counterpart in a large factory was therefore similar to that found in Barcelona.

schemes.[7] The fixed bonuses of the fifties were replaced by ones that were measured by the amount or speed of work carried out and whose value amounted to up to half the wage-packet. There were two main effects. First, work conditions tended to deteriorate. The OSE noted in 1966 that '. . . productivity in many cases takes the peculiar form of a general reduction of the times stipulated for the work carried out by the work-force or an increase in the intensity of human effort required'.[8] Second, productivity bonuses increased the pay gap between workers in the more dynamic companies and those in the less innovative factories or workshops. In turn, widening differentials of pay and bonuses created wage drift.[9] The most militant work-forces created the breach through which other well-organized workers in the same industry were able to pass on to higher wages. Their struggles set the pattern of wage rises and legitimized action to achieve a similar level of pay.

However, the ability of workers to win favourable agreements, as we have seen, depended on the level of bargaining. Plant-level and local bargaining was more susceptible to the organized pressure of workers. In the firms with plant agreements, the workers' negotiating team was made up of members of the *jurado*, the works council of the OSE. By the early sixties, militants in many of the big engineering firms had succeeded in getting themselves elected to the works council, despite the obstruction of management and the officials of the State Union. Where they were not able to control the works council, they agitated on the shop-floor to put pressure on the negotiating team to come up with a good deal. On a provincial level, on the other hand, bargaining was in the hands of OSE stalwarts, elevated to the provincial committee by the electoral machinery of the State Union, whose interests were not necessarily those of the workers they were supposed to represent. According to the secret police, for example, not one member of the negotiating team for the provincial engineering agreement of 1963 worked in firms affected by the agreement.[10] Moreover these firms were

7 OS, *Informe sobre convenios colectivos*, 30 Sept. 1964, CG archives no. 1243.

8 OS, *Informe sobre la contratación colectiva*, 25 Jan. 1966, ibid.

9 See for example *El Economista*, 5 Sept. 1964.

10 Jefatura Superior de Policía de Barcelona (JSPB), *Nota Informativa*, 4 July 1963, CG archives no. 1245.

small and difficult for militants to organize, and their owners were under no pressure to make concessions. The reports of the secret police during the negotiations refer constantly to the 'meanness' of the offers made by the employers and the resulting unrest among workers. 'But the atmosphere of disgust among workers does not mean that there is a danger of any disputes arising because the firms in which they work are too unimportant. On the other hand, it has created a psychosis of social injustice that is generating a spate of demands in the Provincial Engineering Union.'[11]

The atomization of collective bargaining encouraged corporatist tendencies among those groups of workers who were able to organize to achieve better pay and conditions. Taking advantage of the new bargaining system and a booming economy, they rapidly pushed up their take-home pay. While average wages conceded in collective agreements in the province of Barcelona rose by just under 45 per cent between 1962 and 1965, skilled workers in the most militant engineering factories were able to win the same rise in just one year.[12] The rise in take-home pay, however, was paid for in part by worsening conditions of work in the form of increased work speeds, and other productivity measures. The militant work-forces also paid less attention in the sixties to health and safety, job grading, and problems relating to contracts and company rules than to matters of wages and bonuses. The consequences will be examined in Chapter 5.

To sum up, the introduction of collective bargaining, while it stimulated organization and militancy among groups of workers who could use it to their advantage, created functional divisions within the working class. The labour movement that took shape in Barcelona in the early sixties was deeply marked by this contradiction. It lay at the roots of the formation of the Workers' Commissions or Comisiones Obreras, the first co-ordinated movement of workers in the post-war period.

---

[11] Jefatura Superior de Policía de Barcelona (JSPB), *Nota Informativa,* 4 July 1963, CG archives no. 1245.

[12] OS, *Informe sobre la contratación colectiva,* 1962–4 and 1966, CG archives no. 1243.

THE RISE OF COMISIONES OBRERAS

The origins of Comisiones Obreras are to be found in the rank-and-file committees set up to organize strike action in the Asturian coalfields during the second half of the fifties. Similar committees sprang up elsewhere in the heat of disputes, only to disappear once the strikes were over. They were spontaneous forms of collective organization, supplanting unrepresentative works councils with a democratically elected leadership. Their nature was as varied as the different conditions of each strike demanded. In Barcelona, such committees were formed in the late fifties and early sixties in several of the big engineering plants. The introduction of collective bargaining, however, created the need for more durable forms of organization. The new factory committees that developed from 1962 were set up by militants to lead campaigns over the recurrent process of wage negotiations.

It was in Madrid in autumn 1964 that the first attempt was made to organize on a broader and more permanent basis. Normally, union delegates of each industry met sporadically when summoned to the local headquarters of the State Union. During the course of one such official meeting in the Spanish capital, the idea arose of creating a co-ordinating committee of engineering shop stewards. Once a week thereafter, delegates from the main engineering plants of Madrid gathered in order to draw up a common platform of demands for the forthcoming negotiations over the provincial agreement. Among the most prominent militants in their ranks were Communists and Catholic activists, but supporters of the new committee included Falangists. On 2 September, in the presence of OSE officials, 600 delegates met to elect the *Comisión Obrera del Metal de Madrid*, the Engineering Comisión Obrera of Madrid.

There were two remarkable aspects about the event; the first was that it was in practice the first democratic broadly based union organization to be set up in Spain since the Civil War, and the second, that it was set up with the approval of local full-timers of the OSE. The point was that it arose organically out of the bargaining process and must have seemed, even to the officials of the State Union, an efficient way of conducting union business. The document that was approved during the course of the meeting related primarily to economic questions affecting workers in the industry. Yet, in cautiously expressed terms, reflecting the breadth of opinion represented in the meeting, the statement challenged the economic policy of the government and denounced the absence of any effective right to strike.[13]

Over the next few months, the example of the Engineering Comisión spread to other industries in the capital. Alarmed by the growth of these new rank-and-file organizations, the top officials of the OSE finally took action. Meetings of the different Comisiones were banned from the Union headquarters and they were forced to use a variety of venues, ranging from church halls to Carlist clubs and even Falangist centres. This diversity of meeting-places revealed the broad support that the new organization was attracting in Madrid. Indeed, the Engineering Comisión Obrera included a Communist, a Falangist, a Christian Democrat, and a Socialist.[14]

The creation of the first Comisión Obrera in Barcelona followed a very different path. To trace it, we may start with the police report of April 1963, mentioned earlier, that noted the disgust of engineering workers in the small factories over the conditions of the provincial agreement. This unrest was exacerbated by the unfavourable terms of the new contract signed in July.[15] The police reported attempts among the shop stewards affected by the agreement to co-ordinate opposition.[16] The difficulty of organizing action among the dispersed and small factories covered by the provincial contract has already been pointed out, and no common protest resulted. At the same time, a handful of delegates from the major engineering firms were meeting unofficially to discuss their respective plant agreements. In an attempt to bridge the two groups three workers from the motor-cycle firm Montesa tried to convene a meeting of branch delegates on 2 October to discuss the forthcoming negotiations over the 1964 provincial agreement. They managed to bring

[13] J. Ariza, *Comisiones Obreras* (Madrid, 1976), 89–92.

[14] Biescas and Tuñón de Lara, p. 365.

[15] Alianza Sindical Obrera (ASO), *El convenio colectivo siderometalúrgico Provincial de Barcelona*, Aug. 1963, CG archives no. 1243.

[16] JSPB, *Nota informativa*, 4 Oct. 1963, ibid. See also Candel (1968), 247–8.

together only 13 people in the OSE headquarters, where, to make things worse, they were refused permission to hold a meeting.[17]

'We then decided, with some Communists, to create a common platform [for the negotiations],' recalls one of the Montesa workers, a UGT member, 'and to do this we had the idea of forming a Comisión Obrera in Barcelona. We got in touch with Catholics of the JOC and HOAC, and a meeting was organized by word of mouth in a parish church in Cornellá.'[18] The clandestine meeting attracted 40 workers from different industries and a committee was elected to prepare for a secret congress to launch the new organization. The historic event took place on 20 November 1964 in the church of San Medir in the Sans district of Barcelona. Of the 200 or so people who came, the majority were engineering workers, many from the well-organized factories of the city, such as Hispano Olivetti, SEAT and La Maquinista. There were people also from the textile, construction, chemical, print, and wood industries, as well as bank employees. According to the police reports, most of those present were activists from clandestine organizations and Catholic groups. In fact, the organizing committee was made up of 5 Communists, 2 Catholics, and one independent. A programme of political and economic demands was approved that included a minimum wage of 200 pesetas for an 8-hour day, an escalator clause to be attached to wages, the right to strike and form unions, and the recognition of the Comisión Obrera.

Nine days later, watched closely by the police, some of the engineering workers who had participated in the meeting met in the Zoo by the elephant enclosure to plan the creation of the

[17] JSPB, *Notas Informativas*, 4 Oct. 1963 and 3 Oct. 1964. Interview with Josep Pujol, 30 Oct. 1985.

[18] Pujol interview; among those present was a police informer, a worker with Nazi sympathies from the Cumbre engineering factory in Baix Llobregat. There are therefore many details about the activities of the first Comisión Obrera of Barcelona in the numerous police reports sent to the Civil Governor between 1964 and 1965; CG archives no. 1243. One of these found its way into opposition hands and was published in J. A. Díaz, *Luchas internas en CCOO Barcelona 1964–70* (Barcelona, 1977), 72–84. For other accounts see J. Pujol, 'El naixement de CC.OO. a Barcelona', *Debat*, 5 July 1978, pp. 52–5; J. Fabre and J. M. Huertas, 'La fundació de CCOO a Barcelona', *L'Avenç*, Sept. 1982, pp. 12–15; T. Bonet, 'El moviment de les Comissions Obreres a Catalunya', *Nous Horitzons*, 1–2 quarter 1965, pp. 29–40. Further details and corroboration were obtained in interviews with Josep Pujol and Tomás Chicharro.

Barcelona Engineering Comisión. The police, at a loss to describe this new phenomenon in their reports, could find no better designation for the group than the 'Elephants' and they named their investigation 'Operation Elephants'. Oddly enough, they were convinced at first that the new movement was an operation, led by Catholics with the support of Christian Democrats and even Opus Dei elements, to set up 'Free Catholic Unions'.[19]

The history of the creation of the Comisión Obrera of Madrid and that of Barcelona reveals something about the structures within which the labour movement of the early sixties operated. Summarizing the two different experiences, it can be seen that the first Madrid Comisión developed out of the collective bargaining process and was founded within the OSE with the support of the majority of engineering union delegates. The first Barcelona Comisión, on the other hand, was a clandestine organization, created by activists outside the State Union and with no organic connection to any industrial struggle. This divergence was not the result of different labour strategies. In fact, the leadership of both was broadly speaking the same: a novel alliance of Catholic activists and Communists (with the additional participation in Barcelona of Catalan Socialists.)

In reality, the most important cause of the disparity lay in the different relevance of the bargaining structures in the two cities, and this, in turn, embodied a different industrial base. The Madrid engineering workers' contract was a focal point for the interests both of workers from the large firms that had their own agreements, and of those from medium-sized and small firms that did not. In Barcelona, as we have seen, bargaining in the engineering industry was more fragmented: the provincial agreement vied with plant bargaining and local area contracts. Under the Sabadell engineering agreement of 1963, for example, a skilled worker was assigned up to one and a half times as much pay as one covered by the provincial award.[20] Underlying this difference was the greater complexity and dispersion of the industry in the province of Barcelona. The Spanish capital had grown into an industrial city only recently; most of its large and

---

[19] JSPB reports, Nov. 1964, 19 Jan. and 23 Feb. 1965, and 10 Aug. 1966, CG archives no. 1243.

[20] OS, *Cuadro comparativo de salarios resultantes de diversos convenios de la industria siderometalúrgica* (1963).

medium engineering factories had been set up in the fifties. Barcelona's metallurgical industry, on the other hand, consisted of brand-new firms as well as old companies with long traditions of plant bargaining and industrial relations. Though both cities had many small factories and workshops (95.1 and 95 per cent of engineering firms in Barcelona and Madrid respectively employed under 50 workers), Madrid's engineering work-force was more concentrated; 66 per cent of workers were in firms of over 100 compared to 47 per cent in Barcelona, the difference being even greater in firms of more than 500 workers.[21] While the industry was geographically more dispersed in Greater Barcelona, engineering firms in Madrid were concentrated in newly-built industrial estates encircling the city. Moreover, the latter shared a similar technological base, having been established during the previous decade by largely multinational capital. It has been argued, for example, that the spread of skills in the engineering industry was greater in Barcelona than in Madrid, where a majority of the manual work-force in the big factories were semi-skilled production-line workers.[22]

Thus the structure and history of the engineering industry of Barcelona generated centrifugal tendencies in the already atomized bargaining process. This strengthened in turn the corporatist tendency among engineering workers in the large plants of the city that led their militants to take less interest in provincial elections and bargaining than in the struggles of their own plants. These differences help to explain the more political nature of the Barcelona Comisión Obrera, in contrast to the industrial origin of its Madrid equivalent.

THE ACTIVISTS OF COMISIONES

The perplexity of the Barcelona branch of the Spanish secret police as to what the new movement was about was quite understandable. After 15 years of divisions, Communists, Catholics, and Socialists were working together. Contacts were invited to meetings of the Comisiones Obreras, in the words of

---

[21] CONC, 'Informe sobre el sector del metal' (unpublished study, 1978); Sartorius and Díaz Cardiel, op. cit.

[22] Sartorius and Díaz Cardiel, op. cit.

the police, 'irrespective of their tendencies or political affiliations'.[23] To add to the confusion of the authorities, the participants seemed all to be shop stewards or union delegates and their discussion was not political but confined to labour questions such as forthcoming agreements and elections. The police were quick, however, to detect any internal tensions. They noticed an apprehension on the part of some of the participants, clearly the Catholic activists, that the organization might take on a political dimension. They also observed a muted struggle between the Catholics and Socialists, on the one hand, and Communists on the other for control of the leadership.[24]

Yet the foundation of the Comisiones Obreras was remarkably free of the political divisions that had hitherto separated the Left. One of the founders of the Barcelona Comisión later wrote, 'I have never known such determination for united action as at that time, in the midst of severe repression; Socialists, Communists, and Catholics working together in a common industrial struggle . . .'[25] This was in sharp contrast to the anathemas poured on each other by the leadership-in-exile of the left-wing organizations. The aspiration for unity among the earliest participants of the Comisiones Obreras stemmed from the necessary unity of the shop-floor, where there was no other protection against victimization. Moreover, none of the organizations of the Left had any large rank-and-file base. The new organization offered the potential of becoming a mass movement, because it was attracting a generation of militants who had cut their teeth in the recent wave of industrial protest and were suspicious of the old parties and unions. For many labour activists of the clandestine groups, the need to build a united front of militants irrespective of their political beliefs or creeds overrode the ideological divisions so cherished by some of the exiled leaders, living still in the political world of the Civil War.

Among the new militants in the early Comisiones Obreras two groups need to be distinguished: workers from the labour organizations of the Church, and a new political grouping, the Catalan Workers' Front, the *Front Obrer de Catalunya* (or FOC). Of the labour organizations of the Church in Catalonia, the

---

[23] JSPB, *Nota Informativa*, 20 Nov. 1964, CG archives no. 1243.
[24] JSPB report, 10 Aug. 1966, CG archives no. 1243.
[25] Pujol, p. 54.

Young Catholic Workers (JOC) had enjoyed a spectacular growth over the previous ten years. By 1964, there existed some 200 small branches of the JOC (with about 7 members in each) in the diocese of Barcelona alone. Its paper, *Juventud Obrera*, sold around 12,000 copies every month in Catalonia. According to the secret police, 'The paper of the Young Catholic Workers . . . is being handed out in some profusion in the most important workplaces,' and 'There is a noticeable rise in the demand for this paper among groups of workers and it is being read more and more.'[26] The evangelical mission of the earliest groups had rapidly given way to a temporal commitment to social justice that was beginning to worry not just the authorities but the Church hierarchy itself. The changing values of the young members of the JOC were part of a new dynamic within the Church all over the world and were articulated by Pope John XXIII in the early sixties in the two encyclicals, *Pacem in Terris* and *Mater et Magistra*. But the call against oppression and exploitation had a special resonance in Spain. Indeed, by the sixties the alliance of the Church and the regime was beginning to crumble. Among the most outspoken critics of the dictatorship were the Catalan clergy led by the Abbot of Montserrat, whose denunciation of the regime in an interview in *Le Monde* in 1963 earned him exile.[27] Under the legal protection of the Church, JOC members were able to voice criticism of social conditions and of the lack of political freedom that would not have been tolerated were it not for the special relationship between the regime and the Spanish episcopacy. Their growing social commitment was encouraged by the priests of many of the poorer parishes, who were undergoing a similar conversion.

There were several reasons for the JOC's appeal to young workers of both sexes. It offered a variety of social activities, organizing surveys of working conditions in factories, local meetings about problems on the working-class estates, and courses on labour history, collective bargaining, the role of union representatives, and so on. Many of the efforts of its young

[26] JSPB reports, 23 Apr. and 9 May 1964, CG archives no. 1252.
[27] For the Church in Catalonia in the early part of the dictatorship see J. Benet, *Catalunya sota el regim franquista* (2nd edn. Barcelona, 1979), especially pp. 411–53; for an overall view of the Church's relations with the regime see J. Chao, *La iglesia en el franquismo* (Madrid, 1976).

militants were directed towards fighting discrimination against women workers and apprentices, both of whom suffered harassment and appalling conditions of work on the shop-floor.[28] The growing tension between the JOC, the authorities, and the Church hierarchy came to a head in May 1964. The occasion was the successful campaign organized jointly by members of the JOC and the FOC to boycott the buses in Sabadell on the 2nd of the month in protest at the poor service offered. Among the people arrested by the police as a result of the action were 17 leading members of the local JOC. Their arrest and the terrible beating sustained by one of them in the police station aroused heated protest among the parish priests. Even the Archbishop of Barcelona, under the pressure of events, made a veiled defence of the campaign. In a letter to JOC branches he suggested that such a boycott might be justified where 'the laws and the doctrine of the Church are in open contradiction'.[29]

However, the Church hierarchy's patience with the growing radicalization of its labour organizations was coming to an end. Throughout 1965, the latter were criticized in a succession of declarations by the bishops of Spain. In the following year the Church suspended the organizations until new statutes were promulgated that gave the hierarchy greater control of their activities. The crack-down against the Catholic rank-and-file groups by both the Church and the authorities hastened the radicalization of their activists. Two beneficiaries of this process were the Communist Party, which was able, over the next ten years, to recruit many of their leaders, and a new clandestine union, the *Unión Sindical Obrera* (USO), or Syndical Workers'

---

[28] Candel (1968), op. cit.; Castaño i Colomer, op. cit. The authorities were particularly worried by the apprentices' night school in the Barcelona district of Clot run by the Jesuits and filled with JOC activists. Here, according to a secret police report, 'The boys are being trained ideologically in open opposition to the regime. The latter is described as reactionary, conservative, and capitalist, and contrary to the social doctrine of the Church that calls for the freedom of association, which, they are taught, does not exist in Spain. One of the aims of this association [the JOC] . . . is the constitution of a union outside the existing Unions . . .' (JSPB report, 26 May 1964, CG archives no. 1252). Several leaders of the Comisiones Obreras in Barcelona were trained in the school. For more details see J. Dalmau, *La crisi del P.S.O.E. vista des del conflicte Pallach-Reventós* (Barcelona, 1979), 54.

[29] *Nous Horitzons*, 4th quarter. Interview with Juan Molas, 14 Nov. 1985. For an account of the boycott see A. Castells, 'El FOC i la vaga d'autobusos de Sabadell', *Debat*, 4 July 1978, pp. 102–7.

Union, formed by JOC militants in Asturias in 1960 and established five years later in Catalonia. Neither the JOC nor its adult equivalent the HOAC would recover from the crisis of 1964–6. They would play little role thereafter in the history of the working-class movement.[30]

Nevertheless, the culture of the Church's labour organizations had a profound influence on the character of the movement. It was carried into the clandestine organizations by their newly politicized militants. It was kept alive by the scores of parish priests who lent their Church halls for secret meetings of Comisiones Obreras and denounced the authorities from their pulpit. The hand of the JOC can be found in the struggles of the seventies over living conditions in the barrios. Its influence can be seen at work in USO's emphasis on shop-floor work and labour education. And an echo of Catholic evangelism can be detected in the zeal of some of the left-wing groups of the sixties, of which the most important was the Catalan Workers' Front, the FOC.

The FOC was a small political organization that was to play a role within the labour opposition out of all proportion to its size. Unlike the national front to which it was federated, the FLP (Popular Liberation Front), it was able to build a small working-class base mainly from among the most radicalized ex-members of the Catholic organizations. Notwithstanding its title, the FOC counted many students and intellectuals among its activists. The story of the FOC's political evolution during the sixties is as complex as its internal documents are prolix. The stages of its ideological journey until its collapse at the end of the decade will be charted later. However, we are more concerned here with its role in the working-class movement than with its internal disputes. Suffice to say that its ideological origins were characteristic of the New Left in Europe at the time: a hybrid of Castroist and Christian socialism, a rejection of Stalinist dogma and democratic centralism, and a conviction that the traditional parties and unions of the Left were obsolete if not treacherous.[31]

---

[30] For the crisis of the JOC see Castaño i Colomer, op. cit., and by the same author, J. Castaño Colomer, *La JOC en España* (Salamanca, 1978).

[31] For the history of the FOC see P. Maragall, 'Un instant de reconstrucció de la historia del FOC', *Debat*, no. 4 (July 1978), pp. 81–98; also J. Sanz Oller (José Antonio Díaz), *Entre el fraude y la esperanza* (Paris, 1972); and Díaz, op. cit.

The earliest political formulations of the FOC shared the same analysis of the situation in Spain as the small group of critics, led by Fernando Claudín, who were expelled from the Communist Party in 1964: that is, the Franco regime represented the interests of the bourgeoisie, who would be forced eventually to liberalize the State. In contrast to the Communist strategy of building a broad alliance of democratic 'anti-feudal' forces, the FOC called for the creation of an independent working-class movement to ensure that the terms of the liberalization would be as democratic as possible.[32] Comisiones Obreras was precisely this kind of movement, and the FOC's handful of working-class militants played an active part in spreading the example of the first Comisión Obrera.

The idea of creating a rank-and-file organization was not new, of course. Communists, Anarchists, and Socialists had set up their own fronts in an effort to attract the new generations of militants. Because they were illegal organizations or because they functioned as recruitment agencies for the party, these rank-and-file groups failed to extend beyond the closest contacts of party members. Comisiones Obreras, on the other hand, belonged not to the opposition but to the wider labour movement, having grown out of the spontaneous strike committees of the fifties and sixties. Furthermore, it enjoyed a semi-legal status, at least initially, because it was made up of shop-floor union delegates. The earliest police operations were directed at the political elements in the movement.

Of the traditional working-class organizations, the Communist Party was the first to recognize the potential of the Comisiones Obreras. As early as 1954, the PSUC had been calling for the creation of United Committees (*Comisions d'Unitat*) in the workplace, modelled on the rank-and-file committees elected during strikes. In 1957, *Treball* had proposed the setting up of committees (*comisiones obreras*) either to advise those works councils dominated by militants or to act as an alternative leadership where they were management-oriented.[33] The party

[32] For the most lucid exposition of this line see Claudín (1978). Claudín's support in Catalonia came from Communist students in Barcelona University, where the FOC ideologues also worked: conversation with Fernarndo Claudín 11 Jan. 1985. Thus the resemblance in their analyses was no coincidence as Maragall claims (op. cit. 86).

[33] *Treball*, July and Aug.–Sept. 1954. See also S. Carrillo, 'En torno a la encuesta sindical de Nuestra Bandera', *Nuestra Bandera*, 4th quarter 1962.

had attempted to set up its own rank-and-file organization, the Workers' Syndical Opposition (OSO). Despite a widespread propaganda campaign in the early sixties, however, it failed almost everywhere to attract anyone who was not a member or a fellow-traveller.[34] The emergence of Comisiones Obreras made OSO obsolete. The new movement gave the PSUC a twofold opportunity: to reach a wider audience of unaffiliated militants, and to break out of the political ghetto in which it had found itself since the Civil War. The Party's journal confidently asserted in 1965,

The Communists support this movement because it is a living organization that has emerged out of struggles and that unites workers. We are striving and will continue to strive to ensure that Socialists, Catholics, militants, and all anti-Franco workers join forces in this movement. It must not be subordinated to any party or political group but must be led and run by the workers themselves.[35]

The newly created Comisión Obrera of Barcelona represented the first occasion in the post-Civil-War period in which Socialists and Anarchists formed a united front with Communists. They did so without the blessing of their leadership in exile. The Socialist union in Catalonia was largely controlled by members of the *Moviment Socialista de Catalunya* (MSC), a moderate breakaway from the revolutionary party POUM, the *Partido Obrero de Unificación Marxista*. Together with Catalan Anarchists, and a small underground Catholic union, they had formed a united-front labour organization, Alianza Sindical Obrera (ASO), in 1962 in an attempt to attract the new generations of militants who fought shy of the old working-class organizations. The united front was denounced by the exiled leaders of the UGT and CNT in France, and the activists in Catalonia were violently disowned.[36] The main bone of contention was the decision of militants in Catalonia to participate in the structures of the State Union. More in touch with the reality of the class struggle in

[34] The police reported that OSO distributed some 55,000 leaflets between 1962 and 1964 in Barcelona alone. JSPB report, 30 Jan. 1965, CG archives no. 1243. According to a broadcast by the Communist exiled station, *Radio España Independiente*, in 1964, the OSO 'is not a clandestine union, nor a political party. It contains all workers who are fighting for higher wages, the right to strike and form unions. It was not invented by the Communists. It belongs to all workers.' (Ibid.) [35] Bonet, op. cit.
[36] *Boletín de la UGT*, Dec. 1962.

Spain than their exiled leadership, they understood that they could have no influence unless they took part in collective bargaining and union elections. One of their leaflets, dated 25 April 1963, proclaimed '. . . there is an urgent need to prepare working-class action by incorporating shop stewards into the common struggle . . . The cold parlours of the trade unions must ring with the sound of rebellious demands . . . breaking with inertia and passivity.'[37]

The quarrel came to a head when, in 1964, the banned ASO militants began to make contact with the Communists, the *bête noire* of the UGT and CNT in exile, contacts, as we have seen, that would lead to the creation of the first Comisión Obrera of Barcelona. This *rapprochement* also upset the exiled leadership who maintained a decidely anti-Communist line.[38] Even the United States Embassy took a hand in the matter. One of the founders of the first Comisión, an MSC militant, was invited to the house of a top American official, together with some workers from the FOC. There they were offered financial support on condition that they kept the Communists out of the new organization. The proposal was turned down.[39] The division between the social democratic leaderships in exile, deeply influenced by Cold War politics, and their increasingly radical membership in the interior finally ended in scission and the collapse of the short-lived united labour front.

The Anarchists had their own internal problems. In addition to their continued susceptibility to police raids, the CNT committees in Spain were weakened by perennial divisions. The most damaging split resulted from the unsuccessful attempt of the Madrid committee to come to some sort of accommodation with the State Union in 1965. Eighteen years after OSE officials had tried to cajole two imprisoned CNT leaders into collaborating with the new State Union (see Chapter 1), the same two, together with ten others from the organization in the

[37] CG archives no. 1243. See in contrast the *Boletín de la UGT* of July 1963, which reiterates the UGT's abstentionist line and calls on workers to follow the official *Alianza Sindical*.

[38] For example Josep Pallach, 'Nosaltres i els Comunistes', *Endavant*, July 1959.

[39] Pujol interview. According to the same source, American officials also had a meeting with HOAC militants and maintained regular contacts with CNT members.

capital, were holding talks with Falangists over a five-point programme to co-opt the CNT into a reformed State Union.[40] Although their initiative, prompted as much by demoralization as ideological confusion, came to nothing in the end, it did much to erode the reputation of the CNT.

In reality, the old anarcho-syndicalist organization had been reduced virtually to a memory. Repression and internal divisions had combined to disperse Anarchists into small uncoordinated groups reacting on their own initiative to the changing political situation around them. The vast majority of the old union members of the CNT, of course, had long ceased to belong to the organization. Nevertheless, it still held some prestige among the older workers in Catalonia, as the ex-CNT collaborators in the State Union well knew. Among the handful of Anarchists who continued to meet, minimal contacts were maintained by a series of skeletal regional committees (whose lease of life before the police tracked down their members averaged 4 months), but no decision-making apparatus existed to guide their policies.[41] But the failure of the CNT to regain its hegemony among workers was due less to repression than to the difficulties of reconciling traditional anarcho-syndicalist methods of struggle with the conditions imposed by the regime. The kind of direct action and decentralized organization that were the essence of the CNT were hardly suitable to the underground struggle against Francoism. During earlier periods of clandestinity, as under the dictatorship of Primo de Rivera, Anarchists had shown themselves unable to function effectively when deprived of open channels of agitation.[42] The new forms of struggle in the sixties around collective bargaining and shop-floor representation went against the tradition, long held by the libertarian movement, of boycotting the structures of the State. Moreover, the constant refrain of the regime that Communists were to blame for social

[40] For the so-called *Cincopuntista* affair see Ll. Ferri, 'Traidores a la CNT', and L. A. Edo, 'Trampa a la CNT', in *Mundo*, 11 and 18 Dec. 1976 respectively. See also Damiano, op. cit., and Lorenzo, op. cit. There is an extensive file on the talks in CG archives no. 1387.

[41] José Cases interview. For details of the different tendencies among Catalan CNT members, see the report of the police, who had two informers with top positions in the Anarchist movement: JSPB, *Informe sobre la situación del Anarco-Sindicalismo en el interior y grupos clandestinos del mismo*, Feb. 1963; also JSPB, reports of 17 Oct. 1963 and 15 Sept. 1966, CG archives no. 1260.

[42] Brademas, op. cit.; Albert Balcells (1974).

unrest served to give them, and not the Anarchists, the reputation of being the most decided opponents of the dictatorship. When the CNT resurfaced in 1976, it would be a pale shadow of its former self. George Orwell's prediction in 1938 that 'Anarchism is deeply rooted in Spain and is likely to outlive Communism when Russian influence is withdrawn' was not borne out.[43]

The first Comisión Obrera, therefore, drew on a wide spectrum of anti-Franco forces who saw its potential as a united rank-and-file organization capable of articulating the aspirations of many workers. But the fact that the Comisión was formed largely by political activists outside the structure of the OSE made it especially prone to police repression. The first attempt by the new organization to come out into the open was swiftly pounced on by the police. Seventy-two hours before a demonstration planned by the San Medir meeting for 23 February 1965, the police struck, arresting the whole of the executive committee of the Comisión. On the day of the demonstration, several thousand people gathered in the Antonio López square in front of the main post office. From there they attempted to make their way to the OSE headquarters in the Vía Layetana to present the programme of demands of the Comisión to Union officials. The march, however, was scattered by the repeated charges of the riot police and many demonstrators were arrested.[44] The dissolution of the first Comisión Obrera by the police left the new movement without leadership. Individual comisiones existed in a number of factories, there was a committee linking militants in the dyers' and bleachers' Union, and in dozens of plants militants formed *ad hoc* committees to draw up demands for the forthcoming round of bargaining. But none of these activities were co-ordinated.[45]

It was only in the summer of 1966 that a new occasion arose to rebuild the organization: the Union elections for the works councils and the local and provincial committees of the OSE. The 1966 elections represented an extraordinary event in the history of the regime, when workers were presented with the opportunity to choose from among different union options, one

[43] Orwell, op. cit. 61.
[44] *Le Monde*, 25 Feb.; JSPB report, 25 Feb., CG archives no. 1243.
[45] See for example Bonet, op. cit.

of which, in veiled terms, advocated the abolition of the State Union itself. The campaign and the election results need therefore to be examined in some detail, for they throw light on the support enjoyed by militants among the working class of Greater Barcelona.

UNION ELECTIONS AND THE GROWTH OF COMISIONES OBRERAS

The 1966 elections were held at the climax of the campaign of political reform launched by the government in 1957. The period of liberalization or *apertura* of the first half of the sixties was intended to consolidate the regime by stimulating economic growth, integrating disaffected sections of the bourgeoisie, and laying the institutional foundations for the continuation of the regime after Franco's death. The measures culminated in the apparently successful referendum of December 1966 over the so-called Organic Law of the State.[46]

For the duration of the referendum and electoral campaign, the authorities slackened their harassment of the labour opposition. For the Falangists of the OSE bureaucracy, the elections represented an opportunity to build a new social base to shore up their power, eroded by the rise of the Opus Dei technocrats. The officials of the State Union were hoping, like the opposition itself, to attract a new generation of workers. But they were banking on the assumption that collective bargaining and improved wages had produced a more economistic working-class who would reject the political overtures of anti-regime elements. The head of the Catalan OSE stated in an newspaper interview, 'I have full confidence in the common sense of workers who know how to distinguish between those who speak with honour and sincerity and those whose only aim is to provoke disunity.' He went on to refer to '. . . a new type of worker who knows which side his bread is buttered on, who can tell what's fair and what isn't. The greatest achievement of our

---

[46] For a fuller discussion of the *apertura*, see A. Vidal, 'Peligros y posibilidades de las Comisiones Obreras', *Cuadernos de Ruedo Ibérico*, Aug.–Nov. 1968, pp. 35–45; J. Roig (Francesc Viçens), 'Veinticino años de movimiento nacional en Cataluña', *Horizonte Español*, vol. ii (Paris, 1966), 127; and R. Soler, 'The New Spain', *New Left Review*, Nov.–Dec.1969, pp. 3–27.

organization is in having produced a change of mentality, a new syndical culture, an ability to negotiate.'[47] In a similar burst of confidence, the Minister in charge of the OSE, José Solís Ruiz, in an electoral rally in Barcelona, called on workers to 'vote for the best', a slogan that was taken up with enthusiasm by the opposition.

Even the police displayed a new mood of tolerance, at least for the duration of the campaign. One of several secret meetings held by Comisiones militants to draw up an electoral platform was interrupted by a police patrol. After being told that the meeting concerned the elections, the inspector went off to get further instructions, leaving two armed police to guard the 90 men and women in the school hall where the meeting was being held. On his return, he announced that the meeting could continue as long as public order was not disturbed.[48] However, the growing activity of militants around the campaign did not escape the notice of the police. Almost every day, reports reached the desk of the Civil Governor from the police headquarters warning about the support militants were gaining on the shop-floor. One such report stated, '. . . there is a fear among supporters of the regime that these elements may get a high enough number of their people elected to begin their erosion of the policies of the Unions, as a first step towards . . . converting them into an powerful and effective tool against the regime . . .'[49]

The space provided by the authorities gave activists of the labour organizations a unique opportunity to rebuild Comisiones Obreras and to campaign for its programme among a wide audience of workers. During the autumn, the Barcelona Comisión was relaunched in a series of clandestine meetings that attracted a growing number of militants. An electoral programme was drawn up in which agitational issues such as wages were combined with political demands intended more to raise consciousness than to mobilize. This mixture of propaganda and agitation would be a common feature of all the platforms of Comisiones Obreras.[50] Important decisions were also made

[47] *Tele-Exprés*, 5 Sept. 1966.

[48] Sanz Oller, p. 74; Centre de Treball i Documentació, 'Debat: Comissions Obreres, 1968–69; repressió i crisi', *Quaderns* (Barcelona, 1981), p. 100.

[49] JSPB, *Nota informativa*, 15 Sept. 1966, CG archives no. 1249.

[50] The seven-point platform consisted of the following demands: the

about the structure of the movement. Comisiones would be organized according to industry. The basic unit, the workplace comisión, would be co-ordinated by industry-wide committees (or *coordinadoras*) for each area, from which delegates would be elected to the Barcelona Comisión or its equivalent in the towns surrounding the city. The movement, therefore, was modelled on the structure of the OSE, which was in turn that of the collective bargaining process. It gave the fledgeling movement a strong trade-union orientation, in contrast to the district-wide structure advocated by the revolutionary Left. In less than two years a bitter polemic would be fought over this question.

Nevertheless, for all the grand plans of the political activists, Comisiones Obreras remained a movement without any well-defined structure. Industry-wide co-ordination was informal and each workplace committee relatively autonomous, because police harassment prevented closer contacts. In any case, the point of reference for many workers was not the embryonic organization, nor even its programme, but a charismatic leader who stood up to management or to OSE officials voicing common demands for better conditions. The absence of democratic unions lent an extraordinary importance to the role of leaders. It was their prestige that enabled the new organization to attract groups of militants and spread its programme to increasing numbers of workers.

In the towns of the industrial belt, the elections also provided the rallying-point for the setting up of local Comisiones Obreras. A handful of militants from the Barcelona Comisión, in an initiative nicknamed Operation Rake, toured the industrial centres of Catalonia, encouraging their contacts to set up branches of the organization.[51] The genesis of each branch varied according to the configuration of forces in the labour opposition. The commonest pattern was the united front between Communists and Catholics that had lain at the root of the first Barcelona Comisión. The meetings of the new branches were

construction of a united democratic union, the recognition of the right to strike, a minimum wage of 300 pesetas for an 8-hour day, the attachment of an escalator clause to wages based on a genuine cost-of-living index, the release of jailed militants, workers' control of Social Security, and full pay during sick leave and upon retirement.

[51] Interview with Angel Rozas, 27 April 1983; Tomás Chicharro interview.

generally held in the countryside in a usually vain attempt to evade the notice of the authorities. The Terrassa Comisión Obrera's meetings in the woods outside the town were attended by a plain-clothes policeman, who used to spend the time propped against a tree-trunk reading a newspaper.[52] The Sabadell Comisión was emboldened by the tolerance shown by the authorities towards its first meetings on the outskirts of the town to move the venue to a parish hall and a school near the centre of Sabadell. Its meetings thus became almost public rallies. One of them, held to oppose the December Referendum, was packed by uniformed and plain-clothes police, who were treated to a speech by a militant about how bad policemen's pay and conditions were.[53]

In meetings such as these, we get a glimpse of the potential of the earliest Comisiones Obreras to draw together not just labour activists of all generations but also many shop stewards and workers of no political party or underground union. Undoubtedly, the relatively tolerant climate of the period encouraged the less committed but serious union delegates to attend the meetings of Comisiones Obreras and to participate in drawing up a programme. The electoral campaign also gave many workers their first contact with an organized opposition within the OSE. Although Comisiones militants did not present themselves as such, their programme was recognizably opposed to that of the bureaucracy. In numerous authorized shop-floor meetings and rallies in the State Union headquarters, militants were able to address the kind of audience they could never have reached in normal circumstances. An official meeting of 3,000 employees of the Telephone Exchange was addressed by workers supporting the Comisiones programme; and in the ballot, the anti-official platform received a vast majority of the votes.[54] Even more remarkable were the weekly meetings held in the Terrassa headquarters of the OSE against the wishes of the local officials. An attempt by riot police to evict workers

---

[52] Baños interview.

[53] Ginés Fernández interview in AAS archives, 15 Dec. 1974. For the foundation of the Sabadell Comisiones Obreras see Castells, 28. 61–4 (who mistakenly dates its first meeting as October 1965 instead of 1966). A short report by the Mayor to the Civil Governor on this meeting can also be found in the CG archives no. 1319. For that of Badalona see *Unidad*, Aug. 1966.

[54] Interview with Fernando Almendros, 21 Mar. 1983.

attending one of these unauthorized meetings led to four of their number being taken hostage until the officials agreed to let everyone go without arrests.[55]

The electoral battleground did not merely divide the bureaucracy from the anti-official camp. In the no man's land between stood a number of groups who belonged to neither. To understand the inner workings of the OSE within which militants chose to campaign over the elections, we need to look briefly at the different interest groups that had grown in its crevices.[56]

In their concern to develop some kind of rank-and-file base, the top officials of the State Union tolerated the existence of clans that competed against each other for influence within the organization. By the mid sixties, the power that the Falange had once enjoyed over the machinery of the OSE had weakened. The Falangists themselves were divided between reformists and 'purists', though neither were organized tendencies but currents of opinion. While the latter wished the OSE to remain in the hands of the ideologically pure, the reformists favoured its renovation by incorporating a new generation of apolitical workers.[57]

Competing with these two groups for control over the bureaucratic machinery was a clan of ex-CNT members who had reached powerful positions within the delegate structures of the State Union since the late fifties. Using patronage and populism, they had built a network of influence in the engineering and textile unions that ensured their re-election. This group, rather than the Falangists of either hue, enjoyed the tacit support of the Ministry of Labour, which had always encouraged the co-optation of old CNT members as a means of building a rank-and-file base (see Chapter 1). Significantly, their leaders continued to maintain that they were supporters of the CNT, knowing the rich vein of support which the name still possessed among many workers. Nor were they unswerving supporters of the regime, despite the backing of official circles. A police report on the

---

[55] Baños interview.

[56] Most of this information is taken from police reports about the electoral campaign, in particular the *Nota informativa* of 26 Sept. 1966, CG archives no. 1386. Some corroboration was obtained in interviews with Jośe Alcaina Caballero (28 Oct. 1985), Trives, and López Bulla.

[57] For more details, see Ellwood, pp. 221–45.

elections of 1966 faithfully conveys the ambiguities and opportunism of one of these leaders:

He is efficient in union matters, although a bit of an unscrupulous rogue . . . Apart from personal qualities or defects, he is a typical unionist, quite a materialist and unwilling to make any personal sacrifices, but a fighter. He will not oppose the regime unless he is forced to by his own interests; and in fact he is caught in a highly compromising position. His avowal of CNT ideology is partly to win prestige among workers because of the strength of CNT traditions, and partly because he genuinely believes in it.[58]

In an effort to get militants elected, the labour opposition was not averse to reaching tactical agreements with some of these groups. By doing so they were able to split the votes of official candidates and muster support for their own.[59] However, the electoral slates which the labour opposition put forward in the 1966 elections were usually anti-official alliances made up of militants who identified with the Comisiones programme and others who were concerned to represent workers but steered clear of the semi-clandestine movement.

Among the underground groups, few disputed the need to participate in the 1966 elections. Answering the charge that the elections merely strengthened the OSE, the Communists argued that participation was the only way of ensuring that the union hierarchy could not rejuvenate the organization on their own terms. The elections, they maintained, were a means of reaching masses of workers and building a new movement capable of destroying the OSE and creating an authentic union.[60] Only the UGT kept to its policy of boycotting the union elections, but it had no organized presence in Catalonia.

The 1966 elections in Greater Barcelona registered not only the highest poll ever for a union election (with a rate of participation of between 86 and 95 per cent of the labour census)

[58] JSPB, *Nota Informativa* of 26 Sept. 1966.

[59] Thus engineering militants in Sabadell combined with a leading leftist Falangist to oust the right-wing leadership of the local Union: Trives and Molas interviews. In the Transport Workers' Union of Barcelona, militants supported a right-wing railway worker in his bid to reach the National Committee of the OSE in exchange for support from his group for Comisiones candidates to the Provincial Committee: interview with Nicolás Albéndiz, 19 May 1983. For the PSUC line on tactical alliances see *Unidad*, Aug. 1966.

[60] *Treball*, July 1966.

but an unprecedented turnover of delegates. The secret police, who had direct access to the OSE records, reported that less than a quarter of shop-floor representatives were re-elected, and that among the new delegates some 75 per cent were young workers born after 1936, many of whom, so the police believed, belonged to the Catholic or left-wing organizations. A study of the election results in 30 major factories by the Social and Political Brigade revealed that few of the new representatives were on the files of the police. Thus, only 9 were identified as CNT members, 13 as Communists, 16 as Comisiones militants, 12 as 'strikers', 5 as 'demonstrators', and 8 as 'rebels'. Yet, as the police observed, 'There is no doubt that among this mass of workers without a record there are large numbers who support the Comisiones line. They will reveal their hand soon, especially when the collective agreements run out.'[61]

The results of the first round of elections showed massive support for the anti-official platform. In the big factories of Barcelona, Comisiones militants swept the board. The daily paper *Tele-Exprés*, in a veiled reference to the Communists, noted on 19 October, 'It is significant that the Comisiones candidates, many of whom hold an unmistakable political position, have won a major triumph, especially in the largest factories in Barcelona.' Adding together the number of delegates in each factory in the city, the police calculated that half of the votes in the engineering, construction, textile, and transport industries went to supporters of the anti-official platform, while the rest were shared among the ex-CNT and official slates. In other industries, however, the majority of the votes went to the latter two.[62] Successes were reported by the Communist paper *Treball* in Baix Llobregat, Sabadell, and Terrassa, where anti-official candidates were said to have won almost all the 300 positions up for the vote.[63] In the second round of elections for the local and provincial committees, the results were patchy. While they achieved some remarkable victories in the Telephone

[61] JSPB, *Notas Informativas*, 3 and 18 Oct. 1966, and Dirección General de la Guardia Civil, *Relación nominal de los individuos elegidos sindicales en las recientes elecciones y de los que se supone pueden representar un problema para el futuro por sus antecedentes desfavorables al régimen*, 22 Dec. 1966, both in CG archives no. 1386.

[62] JSPB, *Nota Informativa*, 28 Oct. 1966, CG archives no. 1386.

[63] November 1966.

and Transport Workers' Unions, on the dyers' and bleachers' provincial committee, and on that of the Sabadell engineering union, the anti-official candidates failed to penetrate to any degree into the higher reaches of the OSE.[64]

The elections of 1966, none the less, were a vindication of the clandestine organizations' strategy of using the structures of the regime to build an opposition movement. Far from lending credibility to the OSE, the campaign underlined the failure of the bureaucracy to win over the new generations of workers through a rhetoric of renovation. The shop-floor posts were filled by a new layer of shop stewards who may not have had the political beliefs of the party activists but who shared their opposition to the State Union. The boldness of these new militants, as they set about organizing unauthorized meetings on the shop-floor and challenging OSE officials, made many an older trade-unionist blanch, who remembered the repression of the forties and fifties.

The results of the ballot showed a rising tide of support among thousands of workers for a programme of wage militancy and union democracy. Previous elections had registered growing support for militant candidates only among the best-organized work-forces. The electoral campaign of 1966 found an echo among a new and much wider audience. Several reasons for this shift in opinion can be put forward. The most obvious explanation is that for the first time a radical alternative to the bureaucracy was being widely broadcast. More importantly, the concrete evidence of economic growth since 1962 had given a new confidence to workers in their ability to push for higher wages. Economic expansion and the rise of a new generation of workers had broken the crust of fatalism that had led to such high levels of abstention and spoiled ballot-papers in the elections of the fifties. Another reason for the tide of anti-OSE opinion was disillusionment with the lukewarm efforts of the bureaucracy to defend living standards. A secret police report of 26 April, warning of the erosion of support for the State Union, referred to '. . . a process of decomposition that began with the loss of the deferential respect workers once had for the political and administrative leadership of the Union Organization'.[65] The

---

[64] Centre de Treball i Documentació, op. cit. 106. Other information is from a police report of 3 Nov. 1966, CG archives no. 1386, and from interviews with Manel Pagés (17 Oct. 1985) and Antonio Trives.

[65] JSPB report, CG archives no. 1249.

support for the demand for union democracy, a central plank of the Comisiones programme, was not a mere political aspiration. Rather, it reflected the need on the factory floor for effective representation in the collective bargaining process.[66] The two main demands of the Comisiones programme, then, keyed in with the immediate preoccupations of growing numbers of workers.

It would be wrong, however, to see this support or indeed the level of political consciousness among sympathizers of the new movement as uniform. The police, for example, noted that the pro-Comisiones candidates in the telephonists' union were '. . . more professional and economistic than other more political Comisiones groups . . .'[67] The strength of the organization's campaign during the elections rested on its ability to bring together different strands of the labour movement around a common fighting programme. It was another matter, once the elections were over, to weld a common strategy out of them.

The weakness of the electoral alliance of 1966 can best be illustrated in the area where its results were most spectacular. The Comisiones campaign in Sabadell had been run clandestinely by a handful of Catholic and Communist workers from a bar opposite the headquarters of the local OSE.[68] Their campaign was directed mainly at workers in the engineering factories, because the local textile union was largely controlled by an ex-CNT worker who had risen to the rank of president and who had built a powerful electoral base. With a programme modelled on that of the Comisiones Obreras of Barcelona they conducted a vigorous campaign, spreading leaflets throughout the local factories, organizing meetings every week in a left-wing labour lawyer's office, and making contact with old CNT militants, Catholic activists, Socialists, and unaffiliated militants. The open meetings over the electoral campaign of the newly-formed Comisión Obrera of Sabadell have already been mentioned. A leading leftist Falangist was promised support in his bid to

---

[66] See *Treball*, Dec. 1968, and *Poder Obrero*, Sept. 1968, for further comments on the political benefits of collective bargaining. The 8th Congress of the PCE in 1972 referred to the struggle over shop-floor conditions as 'the great political and revolutionary school of the working people': in HOAC (ed.), *CCOO en sus Documentos 1958–76* (Madrid, 1977).

[67] JSPB report, 3 Nov. 1966, CG archives no. 1386.

[68] The following details are from interviews with Juan Molas, Antonio Trives, Manel Pagés, and Ginés Fernández (9 Nov. 1985).

become president of the local engineering committee in order to oust its right-wing leadership.

The results of the poll exceeded the expectations of the opposition. While the local bureaucracy retained control of the textile unions, it was swept aside in the engineering committee, having failed to build a strong enough base among local metallurgical workers. Of the 36 new union delegates on the committee, 33 were anti-official candidates and Comisiones supporters. Most of the new representatives, however, lacked experience of work within the OSE. Among them were a group of Catholic activists who disapproved of any permanent involvement in the State Union. Their desertion of the committee, and the manoeuvres of the new president to obstruct and isolate the majority group, having won his position thanks to the votes of Comisiones supporters, combined to undermine the effects of the electoral victory. The damage was completed by the first wave of arrests launched by the authorities at the end of 1966. It was no coincidence that they chose Sabadell as their first target.

PROSCRIPTION AND RECESSION

It was police repression, as much as inexperience and internal divisions, that checked the advance of the new movement. The relatively uninhibited atmosphere of the electoral campaign was succeeded by a witch-hunt of the leaders of Comisiones. The police had clearly gathered together a lot of evidence as to who were the ringleaders of the new organization. In their first operation in Sabadell, they went for the three main architects of Operation Rake.[69] The arrest of militants was not a new phenomenon in the sixties. What was unusual was the scale of repression. A sample of police and Civil Guard reports during 1967 gives some idea of the extent of the crack-down; 35 militants arrested in Sabadell in March, 40 in Cornellá (including 9 women) in April, a further 11 in Sabadell in May, 8 in Santa

---

[69] Angel Abad, Tomás Chicharro, and Angel Rozas. The police had evidently done their homework. A report of 20 May 1967, for example, lists the names, addresses, and workplaces of 17 leaders of the Baix Llobregat Comisiones Obreras. JSPB report, CG archives no. 1382.

Coloma in September, 37 in Terrassa in October, 10 in Mataró and 8 more in Terrassa in November. At the same time the ruling of the Supreme Tribunal in the same year that Comisiones Obreras was not only illegal but subversive, in that it aimed to overthrow the State, ensured the severity of sentences against convicted militants in the Public Order Tribunal. The Law of Banditry and Terrorism of 1968 completed the panoply of proscriptions against any form of opposition to the regime. The wave of repression culminated in the three-month State of Emergency in 1969, which empowered the authorities to round up suspected opponents without legal restraint.

It was no coincidence that the crack-down occurred soon after the Referendum on the new Constitution, the climax of the institutional shake-up carried out by the government since 1957. It also followed close on the union elections of the autumn of 1966. Both signalled the end of the liberalization period that the regime had considered necessary to achieve a greater respectability abroad and a new consensus at home. It was clear, also, that the attempt of the OSE leaders to build a new base among the young generation of workers had failed dismally. Moreover, the cycle of economic growth on which the government's policies of institutional reform depended was coming to a close. After averaging an annual rate of growth in GNP of 8.6 per cent in the early sixties, the economy registered less than 2 per cent growth in 1967, a problem made more acute by the continued deficit in the balance of payments.

The scale of the repression against Comisiones Obreras took most militants by surprise. The relative freedom allowed by the authorities during the union elections had raised hopes that the new movement could agitate openly, at least on labour matters. Some of the opposition, mistakenly, had seen the relaxation of police harassment as a sign of the weakness rather than the strength of the regime. According to the Communists, the problem lay more in the inertia and fear created among workers by years of repression. 'In the past 27 years,' wrote *Treball* in July, 'the struggle of the working class has been so hard it is no surprise that there are workers who do not realize that the enemy can be fought with less clandestine, more open methods and sometimes even in full daylight.' In the first national meeting of Comisiones Obreras, held in Madrid on 9 October 1966, the local engineering workers' leader, Marcelino Camacho, had attributed the success of the movement to the fact that it agitated openly. It was not possible, he had said, for the mass of workers to co-ordinate in secrecy.[70]

The earliest definitions of Comisiones had stressed that it was a mass movement, open to all workers opposed to the OSE, irrespective of religious or political beliefs. The declaration of the Madrid organization in June 1966 had warned against the danger of divisions within the working class: '. . . in the future, we may enjoy the freedom to organize but it will be only a theoretical freedom if we are divided into different unions. We have to struggle right now to achieve a single union movement if we are to be united in freedom and democracy.'[71] Unity, openness, mass participation—these were aims formulated in the heyday of the electoral campaign, when the nascent organization had been relatively free of harassment from the authorities. In the period of repression and economic crisis that followed it would be difficult to sustain any of them.

Emboldened, however, by the success of the elections and the growth of the movement, the different branches of Comisiones launched a series of demonstrations throughout 1967. The first, a 'citizens' demonstration' on 17 February, called jointly by the Barcelona Comisión Obrera and the Democratic Union of Barcelona University Students (SDEUB), was set upon by the police and dozens of militants were arrested, including several shop stewards of the Hispano Olivetti factory. A solidarity strike by their fellow workers led to further victimization and at a stroke the leadership of what was reputedly the strongest factory committee in Catalonia was almost obliterated.[72]

The largest action was launched on 27 October by Comisiones Obreras as part of their first nation-wide demonstration. In Madrid, the protest began in the big engineering factories of the industrial belt; from there, thousands of workers converged on the centre of the city, battling with the police on the way. It was an extraordinary demonstration of support for the new movement, but it was marked by a wave of arrests; in the week

---

[70] The minutes of the meeting are in Díaz, pp. 104–6.

[71] 'Declaración de las Comisiones Obreras de Madrid', in Delegación Exterior de CCOO (ed.), *Documentos básicos de Comisiones Obreras* (n.p., n.d.).

[72] See *Treball*, March 1967, and Díaz, pp. 147–9.

preceding the action, over a thousand people were detained.[73] The demonstration in Barcelona was also attacked by the riot police and, among other militants, leaders of the Maquinista factory committee in their turn were taken into custody. In Terrassa, thousands of demonstrators gathered on the main avenue. The police charges were met with showers of stones and the riot continued until the early hours of the morning. Thirty demonstrators were arrested, including the leaders of the local Comisión.[74]

The mounting toll of arrests during the year cast doubt on the wisdom of Comisiones' policy of keeping a high profile. One of its leaders later justified this policy: 'It was a race against the clock . . . We couldn't just sit around doing nothing . . . At that time workers were constantly under threat and their rights were being constantly trampled on . . . Any movement claiming to represent workers has to come out in their defence at times of struggle.'[75] However, the offensive against militants by the OSE bureaucracy, the employers, and the police was bad enough without exposing them to indiscriminate arrest on a street demonstration. In the space of a year some 30 to 40 Comisiones leaders in Greater Barcelona were sacked. Throughout the country over the same period, over a thousand trials were held of Comisiones members. Thousands of union delegates had their credentials removed by officials of the State Union.[76] By the end of 1967, most of the workers who had come to the fore as militant shop stewards since 1962 had been plucked from their places of work, or deprived of their representative status. The labour movement had lost a generation of shop-floor leaders.

The effect on the less committed but serious stewards who formed the base of Comisiones after the 1966 elections is not hard to imagine. Even in the traditionally militant dyers' and bleachers' Union, 'the situation became difficult for the more honest and combative union representatives who, if they tried to confront the management or the OSE bureaucracy, found themselves isolated to some extent from other stewards and from

---

[73] Instituto de Estudios Laborales, 'El conflicto obrero en España 1960–70' (unpublished, 1972). For the earlier demonstration in Madrid on 27 February see F. Jáuregui and P. Vega, *Crónica del antifranquismo* ii (Barcelona, 1984), 218.

[74] *Treball*, Nov. 1967, *Diario de Barcelona*, 28 Oct. 1967, Cipriano García interview. [75] Chicharro interview.

[76] Albéndiz interview. See also Biescas and Tuñon de Lara, p. 406.

the workers.' Demoralization spread among the new delegates; as the year went by, more and more gave up their positions or simply abandoned any struggle. The Communist journal *Nous Horitzons* commented, 'It is as if the edifice built upon the victory of the syndical elections has come tumbling down.'[77]

The open offensive of Comisiones was also brought to a halt by an acceleration of the economic crisis. The government declared an austerity package in November 1967 that included a total wage freeze for one year. Collective bargaining, the main point of contact between militants and the rank and file, was suspended. The number of disputes in the province of Barcelona recorded by the Ministry of Labour fell from 82 in 1967 to only 31 in the following year.[78] Registered unemployment rose by 50 per cent between 1966 and 1967 as firms closed down or were given permission by the government to shed labour.[79] 'Worries are growing among the mass of workers,' reported the police at the end of 1967, 'ever since the announcement of the wage freeze, because of the fall in pay which it implies; because of the disappearance of overtime in almost all the factories; and because of the total absence of offers on the job market.'[80] Apart from a few sharp conflicts over redundancies, there was a marked retreat of the labour movement in contrast to the wage offensive of 1962–66.

The new situation posed a dilemma for the labour opposition. Police harassment made the task of drawing workers sympathetic to Comisiones into an organized and underground movement even more formidable. Reports reaching the desk of the Civil Governor from the Civil Guard and the secret police record a steady drop throughout 1967 in the numbers of workers attending the clandestine meetings of Comisiones branches until few but the politically active members remained. Moreover, economic crisis and wage freeze robbed militants of the tools of agitation (except in so far as they were able to mobilize workers against redundancies).

The new predicament was well expressed in a document

---

[77] Both quotes from *Nous Horitzons*, no. 21 (1970).

[78] Ministerio de Trabajo, *Informe sobre conflictos colectivos*, 1968.

[79] JSPB, *Nota Informativa*, 2 Nov. 1967, CG archives no. 1378. Firms were obliged by law to seek permission from the Ministry of Labour through a 'crisis report' (*expediente de crisis*) if they wished to close or make redundancies.

[80] JSPB report, 11 Dec. 1967, CG archives no. 1387.

produced by the Barcelona Comisión in the summer of 1967. Since the elections of 1966

. . . things have changed. The employers and the government have brutally stepped up their repressive policies with the intention of snatching our victories from us, and of separating the leaders and the vanguard from the masses . . . Comisiones has declined in effectiveness and doubts and divisions have arisen over what to do about the employers' and government's counter-offensive . . . When the mass meetings [of Comisiones] came to an end, the leaders lost a vital link with the rank and file; and as factory meetings also declined, the most organic link with workers was severed or at least damaged . . . The shop-floor leaders have certainly found it more difficult to relate directly to the mass of workers. In these circumstances, not only did the work of the industrial comisiones [the *coordinadoras*] become more difficult but the factory comisiones ceased to be as representative as they had been during and immediately after the elections before the repression began.[81]

Police harassment and economic downturn both struck at the roots of the movement. The growth of Comisiones Obreras as an organized movement between 1962 and 1966 had depended on a number of balances: between the spontaneous activity of thousands of rank-and-file workers and the leadership of militants; between the construction of unofficial shop-floor and industrial committees and the penetration of the official structures of the OSE; between movement and organization. The new conjuncture upset these fragile equations, putting a premium on the two extremes of legal and clandestine agitation, and cutting the movement from under the feet of militants. Increasingly, Comisiones Obreras was thrown on to the resources of the labour opposition. Before there was time to build on the successes of the 1966 elections, the fledgeling organization found itself isolated from the rank and file that had voted for its programme of demands. While previously Comisiones had been anchored to the labour demands of a working-class movement on the offensive, the direction that it took between 1967 and 1969 was influenced increasingly by the strategies of the labour opposition. These three years were marked by a fierce polemic between the clandestine organizations over the identity of Comisiones. Although the

---

[81] The document is published in full in Díaz, pp. 157–69.

dispute involved only a few score militants and was centred almost entirely in Barcelona, it left a profound mark on the movement in Catalonia as a whole.

THE CRISIS OF THE LABOUR OPPOSITION

The divisions revolved around several interrelated questions. Should Comisiones go underground in the new repressive context? Should militants continue to agitate in the OSE in view of the increasing harassment of militant union delegates by employers and bureaucracy alike? What sort of political role should Comisiones have? What balance should be struck between this political involvement and its role as a labour movement? Should Comisiones organize by area or by industry? These matters were argued with a passion that is difficult to grasp now unless two assumptions that were held in common by almost all the organizations of the Left are taken into account: the first was that the Franco regime was about to collapse, and the second that the working class, at the head of a popular movement, could be mobilized to overthrow it. From this sense of urgency flowed the need to ensure that Comisiones had the 'correct' policies and leadership. Political control of the apparatus of Comisiones thus became an essential objective of the Left. For, beyond this conviction of the imminence of radical change, there was little agreement about the nature of the regime and what should replace it.

The strategy of the Communists in the sixties rested on the belief that the Francoist State represented a narrow alliance of landowners, monopolies, and Falangists, opposed to the interests of the vast majority of Spaniards. The task of the Left, it followed, was to build a broad-based opposition front to overthrow the dictatorship and install a democratic State. This meant reconciling some of the class antagonisms that had led to the Civil War; the new line was called the Policy of National Reconciliation. The democratic revolution, in turn, would sweep away the remnants of feudalism, and complete the tasks of the bourgeois revolution, giving rise to the conditions for a socialist transformation of society. The shock troops of this alliance between the 'progressive' classes would be the labour movement, and its tactical weapons were the General Strike of workers, backed by a so-called Popular or Peaceful National Strike. In the Seventh Congress of the Spanish Communist Party in 1965, the Secretary-General, Santiago Carrillo, maintained that a revolutionary situation was approaching and even predicted that a General Strike might occur by the autumn of that year.[82] In the eyes of the Communist leadership, Comisiones Obreras had a crucial political role to play in this process. '. . . Comisiones Obreras can be not only the main instrument . . . of the National Strike but also the organization that will ensure that the working class leads the conquest . . . of democracy . . .', wrote the PSUC journal *Nous Horitzons* in 1965.[83]

The strategic implication of their analysis in 1967 was that Comisiones should continue to maintain a high profile. Mass mobilizations, according to some leaders of the PSUC, were a way of keeping the momentum of the 1966 movement going in a period of general retreat. They were also a means of consolidating the nascent anti-Franco alliance in Catalonia by forcing moderate political parties to adopt a more radical position. But within the Party this policy was increasingly challenged by some leaders of Comisiones Obreras.[84] They questioned the wisdom of launching street actions that resulted in the arrest and dismissal of militants. Unlike their comrades in Madrid, Comisiones leaders in Barcelona were often caught by the police not because they were known to be militants but because they were detained during the course of a demonstration. The criticism was echoed by some workers in a mass meeting in the Hispano Olivetti factory after the arrest of four of their shop stewards in the 17 February demonstration.[85] These Comisiones leaders also called for a greater emphasis on union work on the shop-floor and among OSE delegates.

[82] Carrillo, *Después de Franco, ¿que?* (Paris, 1965). See also Claudín (1983), 181. As Claudín points out, there was a marked shift in Carrillo's thinking after 1965 towards the analysis first put forward by Claudín. In his report to the Central Committee, later published as *Nuevos enfoques a los problemas de hoy* (Paris, 1967), Carrillo foresaw the possibility of an agreement between reformist elements of the regime and the opposition for a non-revolutionary transition to democracy: Claudín (1983), 182–3.   [83] Bonet, op. cit.

[84] López Bulla interview. See also X. Vinader, 'Angel Abad, o l'enyorança del FLP', *Arreu*, 21–7 Mar. 1977, pp. 28–9, and Centre de Treball i Documentació, op. cit. 89–122.

[85] JSPB report, 20 Feb. 1967, CG archives no. 1387.

The polemic divided those that saw Comisiones Obreras as a political vanguard, whose task was to lead the 'democratic revolution', and those that felt it was primarily a labour movement with a political role to play in the struggle for democracy. In the period between 1967 and 1969, the difference was resolved in favour of the former. Symptomatic of the downgrading of union work was the disbanding of the PSUC's union fraction, the *Núcleo Sindical*, which had been meeting regularly to discuss the labour policies of the Party. One of the critics within the Party commented later,

. . . when this fraction threatened, not so much to split away, but to concentrate on agitating among shop stewards, works councils, rank and file, the shop-floor, disputes, the OSE, collective bargaining, it was seen as going against other more political tasks. When there was a risk that the pendulum might swing towards union work, the fraction was dissolved and disappeared.[86]

Though bitterly divided among themselves, the organizations of the revolutionary Left shared the belief that the regime represented the interests of the bourgeoisie as a whole (though they disagreed about the composition of this class). The fight against the dictatorship, therefore, could not be separated from the struggle against capitalism; likewise, democracy could only be achieved through the victory of revolutionary socialism. Here their paths diverged. The most important of these small groups, the Catalan Workers' Front, the FOC, adopting a Leninist position in the mid sixties, argued that Comisiones should become an anti-capitalist movement leading an alliance of all exploited classes and led itself by a revolutionary party. The task of the FOC activists was to agitate within Comisiones to transform the struggle over economic issues into an offensive against capitalism through 'transitional' programmes of action that bridged the gap between bread-and-butter claims and revolutionary demands.[87]

The FOC, indeed, saw itself as the anti-capitalist tendency within Comisiones, opposed to the 'reformist' tendency represented by the PSUC. In contrast to the Communists' form of

[86] Angel Abad in Centre de Treball i Documentació, op. cit. 112.

[87] 'Declaración política de la Tercera Conferencia del FOC 1969', in *Cuadernos de Cultura Socialista de Vallés Oriental*, 20 Mar. 1969, *Poder Obrero*, March 1968, and *Estatutos del FOC* (2nd edn), Aug. 1968 (ANC archives).

organization for Comisiones based on the co-ordination of militants in the same industry, the FOC proposed the building of area comisiones, led by factory branches but including neighbourhood and youth branches as well. This was based on a revolutionary model derived from the experience of the Soviets in the Russian Revolution. As for labour strategy, the FOC sought to return to the roots of working-class struggle, the factory floor, and hence to greater clandestinity and less public exposure of Comisiones Obreras. It moved uneasily, however, between the two extremes of shop-floor agitation and revolutionary propaganda, failing to establish, in its publications and still more in its practice, any kind of relationship between the two.[88]

A second group of the revolutionary Left, the *Partido Comunista Internacional* (PCI), derived different strategic conclusions from its analysis of the 'crisis' of 1967–9. The PCI was the result of the split from the PSUC in 1967 of a Maoist tendency, the second such schism in three years. It argued for abandoning the delegate structures of the OSE and the process of collective bargaining on the grounds that they strengthened the regime and impeded the building of a revolutionary alternative. Faced by the domination within Comisiones of the Communists and the FOC, the new party created its own rank-and-file organization, the ultra-clandestine *Comisiones Obreras Revolucionarias*, which had a spectacular but ephemeral growth in the SEAT car factory, where, for the duration of a few months, it all but captured the factory committee.[89]

The sharply contrasting analyses of the Communists and the revolutionary Left created another division: whether Comisiones Obreras should support the movement for national rights in Catalonia. The polemic was short-lived, for by the early seventies most of the groups to the left of the PSUC had taken on board the aspirations of Catalan autonomy. In the sixties, the revolutionary

[88] An example of the FOC's approach to industrial work is the second issue of the FOC-dominated print-workers' bulletin, *Comisión Obrera de Artes Gráficas (COAG)*, which combines advice on how to organize office staff in the industry with an article on the philosophy of Georges Sorel and ends with a call for the formation of a 'TRULY REVOLUTIONARY UNION'. For a model factory struggle (Blansol in 1968) according to the revolutionary Left, see J. Dalmau, *Crónica d'un combat obrer* (Barcelona, 1977).

[89] For details of the PCI line see *Unidad*, issues 1–5 (May–Oct. 1967), and *El Proletario*, issues 1–6 (1968–9).

Left asserted that national self-determination could not be achieved without socialism; the demand for national rights, therefore, had to be linked to the struggle against capitalism. Any nationalist alliance with the local bourgeoisie, they argued, entailed the subordination of the working-class movement to the class enemy. Addressing the workers of Catalonia, a leaflet of September 1967 of the engineering Comisión Obrera of Barcelona, dominated at the time by the FOC, declared, '. . . your Catalonia will be either the Catalonia of the working class, without exploiters or bourgeoisie, or just one more bourgeois trap to keep you down . . .'[90]

The Communists, on the other hand, argued that support for the national movement was one of the conditions for the creation of a broad alliance of democratic forces that could overthrow the dictatorship. The PSUC's stance on the question, in any case, had its origins in the Party's foundation in 1936 as a result of a merger between Communists, Socialists, and radical nationalists.[91] The pre-Civil-War leadership of the labour movement, under the hegemony of the CNT, had shunned nationalism as a petty bourgeois phenomenon. By contrast, the PSUC argued that the national movement 'has always been a progressive force, a factor of economic and political renovation'.[92] The Communists claimed that the regime had alienated an important section of the Catalan employing class, which could be drawn into support for democratic as well as national rights; and that, in fact, the Catalan middle bourgeoisie had most to gain from restoration of these rights, because its interests were blocked by the economic stranglehold of foreign and State monopolies.[93]

[90] The leaflet is published in Díaz, pp. 185–7.

[91] For the formation of the PSUC see R. Vidiella, 'Com va neixer el PSU de Catalunya', *Nous Horitzons*, 2nd and 3rd quarter 1976; and for the connections between the PSUC and the radical nationalists of the Estat Català in 1936, E. Ucelay Da Cal, 'Documents (1936): els nacionalistes catalans al PSUC', *Arreu*, 25–31 Oct. 1976.

[92] PSUC, *El problema nacional català* (1971), quoted in J. M. Colomer, *Espanyolisme i catalanisme* (Barcelona, 1984), 294.

[93] Ll. Rebert (Pere Ardiaca), 'La burguesía nacional catalana i la unitat antifranquista', *Nous Horitzons*, 4th quarter 1964. For further details of the polemic over the national question see J. Solé-Tura, *Catalanismo y revolución burguesa* (Madrid, 1974); Colomer (1984); I. Riera, 'Comunistes i catalans', *Nous Horitzons*, Dec. 1977, and by the same author, 'Moviment obrer i qüestió nacional sota el franquisme', *Taula de Canvi*, Mar.–Apr. 1977.

It was true that the Catalan employing class was divided in its support for the regime. The most important financial and industrial groups in the region began to enter the mainstream of the Spanish ruling class at the end of the fifties. But a smaller section of the middle bourgeoisie, at the hub of which was the Banca Catalana, gave increasing support to cultural and political manifestations of Catalanism.[94] They were hardly a significant force within the financial and industrial nexus of Catalonia, however. Industry was dominated by Spanish and foreign capital and administration and the mass media were in the hands of non-Catalans. Nor would they play a significant role in Catalan politics until the period of transition to democracy after Franco's death.

The PSUC were on surer ground in arguing that nationalist aspirations could lay the basis for some degree of unity between the labour movement and influential sections of the middle class, such as students, professionals, intellectuals, and priests. The enormous expansion of the services industry had created a new class of white-collar workers, the majority of whom were Catalan-born and therefore likely to be drawn into the anti-Franco movement as much by the demand for national rights as by that for workers' rights. According to the Communists, these social groups together consistituted '. . . the present *Catalan national movement*, which is both a cultural, social, and political phenomenon; a movement which is deeply anti-Francoist and genuinely democratic'.[95] The active participation of working-class organizations in the national movement would make it easier to unite national aspirations with demands for amnesty for imprisoned militants, the reinstatement of workers sacked for union activities, and the recognition of free unionism.

An equally important reason for supporting national demands was the urgent need to unite indigenous and immigrant workers. The history of the labour movement in Catalonia before the Civil War had been marked by a strong undercurrent of tension between Catalan and non-Catalan workers. It had been common practice among employers to use regional and linguistic

[94] A secret police report on this group's activities and the finances of the Banca Catalana was submitted to the Civil Governor in March 1971: 'Notas sobre la situación político-social en Cataluña', CG archives no. 1567.

[95] From 'Declaració del Comite Executiu del PSUC', *Nous Horitzons*, 4th quarter 1964. Underlined in the original.

differences to divide their work-force.[96] In some areas the splits in the anarcho-syndicalist movement in the thirties had separated Catalan from immigrant workers.[97] The Radical Party of Alejandro Lerroux had based its populist appeal on the distinct interests of immigrant as opposed to indigenous workers.

There were important historical reasons why most immigrant workers came to support the demand for Catalan autonomy in the seventies, and these will be examined in Chapter 5. But the role played by the PSUC in the forging of a united national movement cannot be ignored. The Communists went to great pains to bridge the gap among its sympathizers between Catalans and immigrants. The Party weekly, *Treball*, had been written since the forties in Catalan, despite the fact that half or more of Party members could not speak the language, though many might have been able to read it. A crucial role was also played by workers' leaders of immigrant origin in encouraging their rank and file to identify with Catalan aspirations. And the consistent support for national demands which the PSUC ensured in the propaganda and activities of Comisiones Obreras was responsible in no small measure for the failure of any nationalist union option on the lines of the Basque ELA-STV to emerge successfully.

The polemic over whether Comisiones Obreras should support nationalist demands rose to the surface each year from 1966 on the occasion of the celebration of the national day of Catalonia, the *Diada* of September 11. The issue came to a head at the end of 1967 when PSUC militants in Comisiones Obreras unilaterally gathered together all the local branches (and indeed some newly-improvised ones) that they controlled in the region into a Catalonia-wide organization, the *Comissió Obrera Nacional de Catalunya* (CONC). The title of the new organization indicated the determination of the Communists to give the movement a decidedly nationalist identity. Of the 40 or so branches which formed the CONC, however, few were anything more than a handful of Communists or fellow-

---

[96] R. Vidiella, 'El veritable problema no son els immigrants', *Nous Horitzons*, 1st quarter 1967.

[97] In Sabadell, for example, the moderate labour movement of the so-called *treintistas* was almost exclusively Catalan and spoke that language, as opposed to the CNT members who used only Castilian: Calvet i Puig (1982), 40.

travellers, as FOC militants were quick to point out.[98] The new organization hardly resembled the original model, the Madrid Engineering Comisión Obrera; it neither had roots in the factories, nor brought together the different groups of the labour opposition. As the main architect of the CONC later admitted, 'There was a gap between the reality in the factories and all this machinery we were setting up.'[99] The formation of the CONC thus reinforced the political and voluntarist nature that had characterized the movement in Catalonia since the formation of the first Comisión Obrera in 1964.

To sum up, there were two main divisions within the Barcelona Comisiones Obreras after the rise in repression and the fall in the level of industrial protest in 1968. The first concerned the role of the organization—if it should become more secretive or remain on the surface, whether it was a mainly labour organization or a more political movement. Underlying these definitions lay a wider ideological division about which was the correct path towards socialism. The bitter polemic was the result of isolation from the real concerns of the mass of organized workers. If the sudden crack-down of the authorities had not yet done so, the ideological quarrels among the Left helped to drive the non-political militant out of the organization.

Indeed, between 1967 and 1968, the Comisiones Obreras in Barcelona were converted, as one militant put it, into a 'den of intrigue'.[100] There could hardly be said to be an apparatus over which to fight for control. The manœuvres were about the right to use the name of Comisiones in propaganda and calls for mobilization. It was a name still to be conjured with. Despite their recent set-backs, the groups of the labour opposition still believed Comisiones to be the new constituency of the labour movement. But the accusations about undemocratic practices that both sides threw at each other hardly made sense, since there was no organized base in the factories which could be represented. 'Who is representative?' demanded an FOC engineering worker in an earlier meeting to discuss the dispute. 'A leader capable of mobilizing all the workers in his factory or area? A comisión able to get the workers out on strike at will? If

[98] Díaz, p. 215.
[99] Chicharro interview.
[100] Angel Abad in Centre de. Treball i Documentació, op. cit. 93.

so, nobody is representative in Barcelona, except three men in the dyers' and bleachers' industry and only over very specific economic issues.'[101]

The revolutionary groups, however, were in turmoil. Two events inflamed the atmosphere on the Left: the collapse, on the one hand, of a broadly based student movement that had attempted, as the first Comisiones Obreras had done with the workers, to unite students of different tendencies around a programme of demands related to conditions in the universities; and, on the other, the infectious example of the May 1968 events in France. The May Day demonstrations in the main cities of Spain were marked by a new phenomenon: the irruption on to the streets of commando groups stoning banks and overturning cars. In contrast, there was a noticeable drop in the number of workers on the demonstration.[102] The student section of the FOC was flooded by new tendencies; increasingly, the small group of workers in the organization found itself challenged by more impatient counsels. At the heart of these internal divisions lay not just the revolutionary impatience of the students but frustration: at the apparent failure of the tactic of penetrating the institutions of the regime; and at the absence within the workers' section of the FOC of any clear alternative to the Communists.[103] By July 1968, the hard-liners in the FOC had won out. A new strategy was voted in that pulled the organization away from agitating around labour demands to building area organizations or 'kinds of soviets . . . the future structures of workers' power'.[104] The gap between the new revolutionary strategy and the shop-floor work of its militants hastened the division within the FOC and soon most of its workers resigned. Bereft of a working-class base, FOC abandoned Comisiones Obreras. At the end of 1969, rent by new divisions, the organization itself disintegrated.

By the end of the decade, the Comisiones Obreras in Catalonia was largely under the sway of Communist militants.[105] The

---

[101] From the minutes of an Engineering Coordinadora meeting on 15 July 1967, published in Díaz, p. 156.

[102] *Treball*, May 1968.   [103] Sanz Oller, pp. 172–3.

[104] FOC, *Tactica-plan del sector obrero*, quoted in Díaz, pp. 192–9; *Comisiones Obreras Informan*, 2 Apr. 1969.

[105] As well as the revolutionary groups, the workerist union USO had pulled its activists out of the organization in 1968 on the grounds that it had become a party machine rather then a labour movement: Reyes Mate, *Una interpretación histórica de la USO* (Madrid, 1977), 71–2.

organization would later gather into its fold new political and union tendencies, while the acrid divisions of the 1967–9 period would give way in the early seventies to greater unity. Nevertheless, members of the labour opposition proved unable to work together to build a rank-and-file organization, that 'single union movement' without which, according to one of the first documents of Comisiones Obreras, the working class would be divided in the approaching democratic society.

The test of the new organization was not so much whether it could bring together the organizations of the Left, whose numerical strength was very weak, but whether it could attract wider sections of the working class. The first Comisiones Obreras had succeeded in winning support for its programme among the more organized workers, whose driving force was the pursuit of better wages and conditions. The success of Comisiones militants in the 1966 elections was due to their close connection with this new movement born of the economic boom, and to their ability to relate to the needs of the workers who constituted its base. Two factors made the incorporation of this base into Comisiones Obreras difficult; the first was the fragmentation of collective bargaining, and the second the combined effects from 1967 of police harassment and economic recession. Neither of these were insuperable barriers, however. It was still possible for Comisiones activists to organize around labour issues on the shop-floor and among union delegates and shop stewards.

Yet the Communists and above all the revolutionary Left attempted to give the new movement a more political dimension. Under their leadership Comisiones Obreras launched frequent street demonstrations, organized youth committees, and campaigned around urban issues, while the Communists sought to lead the national movement. They did so not only because they believed the dictatorship was about to collapse, but also because they misjudged the nature of the labour movement. A typical leaflet of Comisiones Obreras, one distributed in preparation for the demonstration of 27 October 1967, had called on workers to hold mass meetings and march from their firms to the OSE headquarters. In the event, few actions had taken place in the factories that day. None the less, *Treball* reported that the Day of Action had shown that the conditions for the General Strike and the National Strike were 'incessantly maturing'. Again, the May Day demonstration of 1968, in which the Communist paper had noted a marked absence of workers from the big factories, called forth the following comment from *Treball* , 'The Day of Action appears to confirm that the dictatorship is entering its death agony.'[106]

The actions of the Left cannot be judged merely on the basis of its propaganda, which could hardly be described as an accurate reflection of reality. Yet, apart from the shop-floor work of individual militants, there is little evidence of any serious attempt on the part of Comisiones between 1967 and 1969 to gear its organization and agitation to the problems of the wider labour movement. There was no concerted effort, either to work within the industrial committees of the OSE or to strengthen the organization of Comisiones Obreras. It was symptomatic of the subordination of labour agitation that the industrial bulletins of Comisiones appeared late and infrequently, in contrast to the profusion of party leaflets. No full-time organizers were appointed to look after propaganda or agitation.[107] Moreover, the political tasks that militants were asked to take on inevitably led to a dilution of their industrial work. They were expected to don different hats. As an ex-FOC worker said, 'What was happening in the factories was one thing, the discussions in the party were another, and what we had to do in the Comisiones Obreras was a third thing.'[108] A notable exception was the industrial work carried out in the dyers and bleachers industry, described thus by one of the militants:

. . . paradoxically there were only three or four of us who did all the organizing. We would 'multiply ourselves'. We used to go to the factory gates at 6 a.m. and at the end of the workday we would be at other factory gates to link up with other people and give out propaganda. We had meetings specifically of workers in the industry, quite separate from the joint meetings [of Comisiones Obreras]. Although we had nobody responsible for finances . . . we had working groups led by the three or four leaders already mentioned.[109]

---

[106] For the leaflet see Díaz, pp. 209–12. The two issues of *Treball* are Nov. 1967 and May 1968.

[107] J. L. López Bulla in Centre de Treball i Documentació, op. cit. 94. The first issue of the engineering workers' *coordinadora* appeared in June 1968, that of the building workers in November, and that of the textile workers as late as May 1969. Few of these reached beyond five issues.   [108] Díaz, p. 131.

[109] Lluis Moscoso, in Díaz, p. 104.

In the short period from 1967 to 1969, therefore, when repression and wage freeze drove a wedge between the labour opposition and the labour movement, Comisiones Obreras was redefined according to the conflicting priorities of the underground parties. The new organization was charged with various political roles that corresponded only in part with the aspirations, as expressed through strikes and bargaining platforms, of those workers who had supported it in the elections of 1966. Nevertheless, it was the militants of the labour opposition above all who had built Comisiones Obreras into an organized movement. It was they who sustained this movement through a period of brutal repression, suffering victimization, torture, and imprisonment. More than any other reason, it was the offensive of the authorities and the employers between 1967 and 1969 that provoked the crisis within Comisiones Obreras. The disputes which divided the labour opposition arose fundamentally out of the contradiction between the 1966 model of Comisiones Obreras as a representative movement and the progressively isolated and clandestine conditions in which it was forced to operate. The extraordinary resurgence of militancy from 1969 onwards among ever-increasing numbers of workers would give Comisiones Obreras, now under Communist hegemony, new opportunities to connect with the wider working class.

4

Local Patterns of Protest

> We are an open and indiscreet window on industry and labour in Barcelona and its province.
>
> (Extract from a secret police report, 1967
> (CG archives no. 1378))

In the short period of six years, between 1970 and 1976, a mass movement emerged in Greater Barcelona embracing hundreds of thousands of workers and reaching into all industries and urban centres of the area. The common thread binding this movement together was the collective struggle to improve conditions at work and in the community. However, no simple picture can be drawn of its composition and its character. This was no monolith of combative workers united by a single purpose, as the clandestine press tended to suggest. On the contrary, it is truer to say that there were several labour movements, separated by occupation and by geography, each with their own patterns of activity and their own subcultures. Such differences can be found elsewhere. In Francoist Spain they were intensified by two processes: on one hand, police repression had the effect of atomizing the organization of protest, and on the other, the speed and extent of social change gave little time for the consolidation of a common working-class culture across the boundaries of place and industry.

The divisions separating one labour movement from another were marked out firstly by the confines of towns. Despite the extraordinary urban growth that had taken place since the fifties, the towns surrounding Barcelona retained a somewhat provincial structure. They were not too large to prevent militants creating informal networks of communication that extended beyond the limits of each workplace and industry. Union activists of different trades were able to share experiences and develop collective strategies which infused the local movement with a common identity. In the metropolis, on the contrary, the magnitude of urban growth and the resulting dislocation of communities hindered the convergence of different agitations. Moreover, outside the narrow circles of the labour opposition, it was difficult for militants from different areas to make contact with each other except on an individual basis. Even party members knew little of what was happening elsewhere. Their main source of information was their own press, but since clandestine papers and leaflets were more concerned with agitation than analysis they were more likely to derive a distorted picture of the struggle in other areas; indeed, knowing the reality of their own environment, they must have wondered about the accuracy of reports in the underground press.

Another obstacle to the spread of common labour traditions was the disparate interests of workers of different industries. While informal links were established between militants of all trades in the smaller conurbations, these contacts were not extended beyond the town limits, nor generally within the metropolis. The pattern of collective bargaining strengthened the boundaries separating one labour movement from another. Within each unit of bargaining (and the extreme segmentation of the OSE should be recalled), it was possible for militants to evolve common ideas, to make contact with other union delegates, and to argue for union and political demands. But the extent of these contacts depended on the level of nego-tiations—whether they were plant-based, local, or provincial—as well as on the degree to which the delegate system had been penetrated by militants. The presence of union activists was stronger in the local committees of the OSE, while on a provincial level only a rudimentary co-ordination was possible in all but one or two industries. Thus the structure of collective bargaining, and the repressive control of the State, combined to reinforce the parochial nature of the labour movement, whether it was on a local level or within a particular trade.

In this chapter, the different forms of labour protest in Terrassa, Sabadell, Baix Llobregat, and Barcelona will be compared. These conurbations not only were the largest industrial and urban centres in Catalonia but also contained the most important labour movements in the region.[1] A 'close-up' of

---

[1] The fifth-largest centre in the province, Mataró, is not examined in this chapter because in many respects it shared a similar pattern of development to Sabadell, both with regard to its structure and its local labour movement.

each area will illuminate the complex dynamics of labour dissent. We will examine the role played by local conditions in shaping the character of the working-class movement, concentrating in each case on those features that were most influential. In the next chapter, in which the narrative is renewed, the same theme will be viewed from a different perspective, that of the differences between the labour movements of the main industries.

One palpable sign of the diversity of the new labour movement was its different rhythm of growth in each area. During the fifties, those of Sabadell and Baix Llobregat had been confined to small pockets of activists, while in Terrassa the labour movement was strong enough to take to the streets in open confrontation with the authorities. Indeed, the Terrassa movement became a paradigm for Communist militants in Catalonia.[2] After 1970, however, it was overshadowed by the spectacular rise of the Baix Llobregat labour movement, which launched three local general strikes in the space of two years between 1974 and 1975. For its part, Sabadell was a relatively quiet town until the early seventies. On the eve of democracy in 1976, two general strikes in the town wiped out any lingering reputation for passivity with which local workers had once been labelled. Barcelona, though it was the hub of the labour movement in Catalonia, witnessed no concerted working-class protest of the kind that had brought the city to a halt in 1951.

These different patterns of growth had complex origins. Terrassa and Sabadell, for example, shared a residue of labour traditions dating back several decades. It was argued in Chapter 2 that the social and economic transformation of Greater Barcelona swept away the culture of the pre-Civil-War labour movement. In the case of these two old textile towns, both of which had claimed the title of the Catalan Manchester, old traditions died hard. Of course, the latter were no longer expressed in terms of institutions or ideological debates. But it is possible to detect in the forms that labour dissent took a certain continuity with the past. This continuity was underpinned by two factors: the persistence into the sixties of long-established relations of production, and the measured growth of the two towns from the forties onwards.

[2] *Treball*, in its July 1968 issue, called it 'the example and guide for the whole of the Catalan working-class movement'.

The economic activity of both Terrassa and Sabadell had been dominated for over a century by the woollen trade. Though the industry continued to expand throughout the forties and fifties, the vast majority of firms in the sixties in Terrassa, for example, had been founded at least two decades previously.[3] Neither town underwent the violent upheaval in the social and urban landscape that marked the experience of other areas of the industrial belt. Because their industries were already established, Terrassa and Sabadell witnessed a steady flow of immigrants from the early forties onwards. During the first decade of the dictatorship, for instance, both towns received some 13,000 immigrants apiece, while only 3,000 settled in Baix Llobregat during the same period.[4] Hence in Terrassa and Sabadell the rapid expansion of the sixties was built on long-standing urban and industrial foundations. For the same reason, labour relations were influenced by old patterns of behaviour, though the balance of forces between workers and employers had been drastically altered by the imposition of the dictatorship. Here, the similarity between Terrassa and Sabadell ends. We need to look now at the differences that separated them.

TERRASSA: THE CULTURE OF THE POPULAR STRIKE

Terrassa had always witnessed a more acute class confrontation than Sabadell. Since the beginning of the century, the town had been in the hands of a powerful right-wing bourgeoisie, who had ruled the woollen industry with a rod of iron. An idea of their political leanings may be gathered from an anecdote of 1936. On the eve of the Civil War, a secret military mission had toured Catalonia to raise financial support for the uprising. Over a dozen leading local employers had contributed to the fund, and were shot for their pains shortly afterwards by the left-wing militia. The same mission had met with a very different reception in neighbouring Sabadell, where the local employers' organization had advised its members to have nothing to do with the military envoys.[5]

[3] Ll. Barbé i Durán (ed.) *Dinámica y perspectiva del Vallés* (Sabadell, 1970), iii. 37–8. [4] Calvet i Puig (1981).
[5] Pagés interview.

The labour movement of Terrassa in the early thirties had been dominated by the insurrectionary wing of the Anarchist movement, the FAI. During the abortive revolt by miners of the Alt Llobregat region in 1932, the town hall had been assaulted and occupied for a short while by local Anarchists. In the revolutionary aftermath of the 1936 military uprising, 226 people had been assassinated in Terrassa in contrast to 83 in Sabadell.[6] The collectivization of local factories had been immediate and widespread. Among Catalan government circles during the Civil War, Terrassa had gained the reputation of being a rebellious town.[7]

For their part, even two decades after the Civil War, the Terrassa employers were still marked by an authoritarian brand of conservativism. At a time when a new vein of progressive Catholicism was running through sections of employers elsewhere, the liberal wing of the Terrassa bourgeoisie was notoriously weak. Problems of industrial relations were given short shrift. For example, whereas the Sabadell employers negotiated the period in the summer during which the factories would be closed with OSE representatives, their counterparts in Terrassa imposed it without question.[8] Some sections of the local bourgeoisie were even prepared to resort to violence to curb the radical Catholic movement that arose in the sixties. Supporters of a left-wing priest were beaten up during a church ceremony by an assorted group of employers, Falangists, and officers. Another priest was assaulted by the personnel manager of a local firm brandishing a knife.[9]

After the violent repression of the labour movement in the forties, the radical tradition of Terrassa could be seen again in the street riots, the clashes with the police at factory gates, and the occupations of the OSE headquarters during the fifties and especially the sixties. A decade after the Communist Party's decision to abandon guerrilla warfare, some local activists who had left the CNT to join the Communists were discovered by the leadership in 1958 to have planned to smuggle arms across the

[6] Castells, v, 21. 38.

[7] X. Marcet, 'La Guerra Civil a Terrassa', *Terme*, Nov. 1986, p. 31. For more details about Terrassa during the Civil War see this special issue of *Terme*.

[8] Interview with Ramón Escudé, 9 Dec. 1985.

[9] Ricart Oller, pp. 84–5.

border. As late as 1968, Comisiones militants, encouraged by the Far Left, were contemplating forming a terrorist bomb squad.[10]

There were more important reasons than tradition, however, for the greater aggravation of the class struggle in Terrassa during the dictatorship. The demand for textile products in the post-Civil-War period, and especially after the outbreak of the Korean War, meant that Terrassa's (and Sabadell's) industry continued to expand before the new era of swift industrialization began elsewhere in the belt surrounding Barcelona. The formative years of the local labour movement lay in this period, before the introduction of collective bargaining and the emergence of Comisiones Obreras. As was stressed in Chapter 1, the struggle to defend living standards in the mid fifties depended as much on mobilizing protest to force the authorities to raise basic wages or keep down prices as on negotiations with individual employers. The style of Terrassa militants was characterized by more public and collective gestures of dissent.

There was another reason for this open mode of agitation. From the late forties, the local labour movement was dominated by the Communists, whose strategy throughout the fifties was the preparation of a Popular National Strike. Taking protest on to the streets was seen as a means of mobilizing a supposedly disgruntled population. The success of the 1951 General Strike encouraged the view that generalized actions could be sparked off by the example of a small group of militants. The open defiance of the authorities was seen as preparing the conditions for the coming Great Strike. Indeed, the Terrassa workers' leaders were made in a heroic mould. Consisting largely of immigrants who had experienced fierce struggles on the rural estates and in the mines of the South, they led some of the first mass demonstrations that took place in Catalonia in the post-Civil-War period. The repression with which these demonstrations were met, and the solidarity struggles that were generated as a result, lent a radical tone to labour dissent in Terrassa.

The more political character of the local labour movement persisted in the very different circumstances of the sixties. The continued climate of confrontation was reflected in a stream of

[10] Cipriano García and Baños interviews.

letters from the Mayor of Terrassa to the Civil Governor begging for more Armed Police. One such letter, dated 16 January 1969, complained,

> Once again, I have to reiterate the delicate situation that our town faces because of the continuous and unpunished activity of people interested only in social agitation who, it seems, have turned Terrassa into their headquarters . . . Since my last report, the situation has got worse. In fact the only thing that has not changed is the lack of repressive forces; for a long time now, Terrassa has been unable to maintain law and order . . . The initiative has always been in the hands of these activists. [11]

Such was the prestige of Communist Party leaders of the previous decade that their strategy was not significantly modified in the new conditions of the sixties by the younger generation of Communists in the town. Moreover, because the PSUC dominated the labour movement (there were over a thousand members in the town by the mid sixties, according to the calculation of an informed Party leader from elsewhere in the province[12]), the Comisiones Obreras of Terrassa were impregnated with the political culture of the local Communists. Indeed, the new movement seems to have been treated to some extent as a recruiting-ground for the Party. The predominance of the Communists and their style of open defiance held back more moderate and union-oriented groups of workers, such as the Catholics of the JOC and HOAC, from working within Comisiones or taking part in any united-front activity.[13]

The high profile of the Terrassa labour movement made it especially vulnerable to police repression. It also rested on a narrow base, even if numerically it was one of the strongest movements in Catalonia. This was not only because it was difficult to organize among the small factories of the town but also because, even in the sixties, industrial agitation over collective bargaining was relatively less important in Terrassa than in Barcelona or Baix Llobregat. Thus the Terrassa labour movement relied less on extending its network of contacts throughout the factories of the town than on the exemplary leadership of the most militant plants, the largest and best-organized of which was the electrical firm AEG. For all the

[11] CG archives no. 1320.   [12] López Bulla interview.
[13] Interviews with Francisco Gordillo, 2 Dec. 1985, and Ramón Puiggrós, 17 Mar. 1983.

solidarity that existed within the town among sections of the middle class, the bitter defeat of the AEG strike of 1970, which resulted in the dismissal of 71 militants, was a severe blow to the whole labour movement (see Chapter 5). It broke a pattern of struggle that had begun 20 years previously when the AEG workers had walked out of their plant to bring out other workers on the general strike of 1951. By the early seventies, the initiative had passed on to the labour movements of other areas.[14]

SABADELL: FROM CONSENSUS TO REVOLT

The character of the Terrassa labour movement stands out more clearly when contrasted to that of Sabadell. In many respects, the Sabadell movement was its antithesis. This is remarkable considering the fact that, by the seventies, the two towns were separated by a mere two-mile stretch of waste land. Both were dominated by the woollen industry and had a similar population level. Yet they were divided by a long-standing rivalry that had its roots in economic competition but which took a social and cultural shape also. The writer Josep Pla encapsulated the difference by comparing Terrassa to a French textile city in which 'there are only bourgeoisie and workers' and Sabadell to a small English textile town in which 'everyone is part of the people, up to the largest employers'.[15] Even the architecture of the two towns expressed their different class structure, Terrassa's grand and florid buildings contrasting with the dour squat urban complexion of its rival.

Sabadell was indeed a different town. For one, its social gradients shelved more gently. The population census of 1970 listed over twice as many employers in Sabadell as in Terrassa, some 5,683 in the first and 2,439 in the second. Sabadell was dotted with small textile workshops employing handfuls of

[14] Between 1971 and 1975, there was little labour protest in Terrassa relative to other industrial centres of the region. A chronological account of events in the town, based on newspaper reports, lists only 5 stoppages in that period: V. Villatoro i Lamolla *et al.*, *Terrassa 1964–1977* (Terrassa, 1981). During the wave of strikes in protest at the 1973 incident at the site of the power-station in San Adriá, according to police reports, only two firms in Terrassa stopped work in contrast to the 30 plants in Baix Llobregat where protest actions were registered: CG archives no. 1563. [15] J. Pla, *Cataluña* (Barcelona, 1961), 255.

workers. Relatively less fragmented, Terrassa's industry was dominated by the presence of a few big factories; the electrical plant AEG employed 3,000 workers and the largest textile firm some 1,200 workers, whereas the two biggest companies in Sabadell had only 1,400 between them.[16] The subtler, mediated social structure of Sabadell may help to explain the more muted class antagonism that had long been a feature of its history. Because the woollen industry was less monopolized by big concerns, the skilled textile worker or the commercial agent was more easily able to rise to the status of a small employer. Several of the leading bosses of the fifties began their careers as textile workers.[17] In times of economic recession, the small employer had been almost as afflicted as his workers.

An indication of this political moderation can be found in the figures already quoted of those assassinated in the reprisals against the army uprising of July 1936. Moreover, during the Civil War, almost a majority of the small and medium employers had remained in Sabadell working as managers of their firms, which had been placed under the control of workers' committees.[18] After the Falangist-inspired paroxysm of revenge in the first years of the dictatorship, the more paternalist rule of the big Sabadell bosses had reappeared. It was personified in the figure of the textile employer, Josep María Marcet, who held the office of Mayor for 20 years from 1940. A gesture typical of Marcet was his decree obliging local employers to take on 250 workers whose jobs had been lost when their factory was burnt down.[19] Among the engineering employers of Sabadell were

[16] In the mid sixties, almost half of Sabadell's 949 textile firms employed less than five workers, compared to 37% of Terrassa's 671 plants. Conversely, only 5.6% of Sabadell's firms had more than 100 employees, in contrast to Terrassa where 7.8% of textile companies employed over 100 workers. The same was true of the engineering industry of both towns. In 1970 Sabadell had 525 plants with 8,500 workers, compared to Terrassa's 273 firms containing just over 7,000 workers: author's calculations from COCIS, *Memoria*, 1968; R. Duocastella, *Estudio socioeconómico y de planificación de servicios sociales: Terrassa* (Barcelona, 1967), 68; and Consejo Económico Sindical del Vallés Occidental, op. cit.; J. Costajussa Oliver, *Sabadell 1972* (Sabadell, 1973). A. Balcells (1974) suggests that the greater concentration of Terrassa's wool industry may explain the higher level of militancy among its work-force between 1930 and 1936.

[17] Ferras, p. 61.

[18] Castells, 21. 48. In contrast, some Terrassa employers had moved away from their town in the early thirties out of fear of reprisals.

[19] Marcet, pp. 82–3.

several progressive Catholics, influenced by the shift that had taken place in the Church since the late fifties. The directors of the four largest metallurgical firms were members of the liberal Catholic Association of Employers, *Asociación Católica de Dirigentes* (ACD), whose founder, the managing director of the local electrical firm Asea-Ces, had run the Sabadell technical college throughout the Civil War.[20] The ACD was in close contact with workers of the JOC even while some of the latter were taking part in the first local branch of Comisiones Obreras.[21] Though the main concern of ACD members was to counter the influence of the Communists within the new movement, they were less given to victimizing militants in their own firms. A secret police report of 1969, for example, described the personnel policy of the most important factory in the town, Unidad Hermética, as 'soft and over-tolerant . . . It is known that Comisiones militants in the firm have continued to receive their wages even while they have been under arrest.'[22]

The labour movement of Sabadell also was steeped in a tradition of moderation. In the early thirties, the local trade unions had split from the Catalan CNT, when it had been taken over by the radical FAI organization, to form their own *Federació Local de Sindicats* or Local Federation of Trade Unions. At the outbreak of the Civil War, the Sabadell Federation had had 20,000 members compared to the 5,000 of the Terrassa CNT, which had been torn apart by the divisions within the Anarchist movement. Faced, in 1936, with the choice of rejoining the CNT or affiliating to the UGT, the Sabadell Federation had voted overwhelmingly to belong to the more moderate Socialist Union.[23]

During the first two decades of the dictatorship, there were few reports of labour unrest in Sabadell. No evidence exists of any significant support for the most widespread action of the fifties in the province, the General Strike of 1951. Marcet claimed that in his 20 years as Mayor, Sabadell lost not one hour in industrial dispute. His boast was an exaggeration but it highlights the relative quiescence of the local work-force in that period.

[20] Trives and Pagés interviews.
[21] Alvaro García interview, AAS archives.
[22] JSPB report, 27 Sept. 1969, CG archives no. 1387.
[23] A. Balcells (1974), 204–5; Castells, 21. 17.

Marcet argued that it was the result of two factors: his own much-vaunted concern for the welfare of workers, and the collaboration of former unionists of the UGT and the CNT.[24]

There was some truth in his assertion. In the atomized relations of production of the textile industry, the paternalism of many employers such as himself served as a powerful instrument of social control. Moreover, the officials of the OSE, among whom were the ex-union collaborationists sponsored by Marcet, were able to negotiate favourable wage settlements for Sabadell workers. The first local contract in the Spanish wool industry was signed in Sabadell in 1960 by Marcet's protégé, Ramón Navarro, while the town-wide engineering agreement negotiated in 1962 by the Left Falangist, Diego Pérez, awarded higher basic rates of pay than any other agreement of its kind in Spain.[25] The local OSE was thus able to win some support among Sabadell workers, helping to dampen militancy. Such was the strength of support enjoyed by officials of the local textile union, for example, that it was not till the early seventies that Comisiones militants began to make headway among its delegates.

The climate of consensus that seemed to hang over industrial relations in Sabadell began to disperse in the mid sixties. This was in part the result of the crisis that hit the Sabadell textile industry from the early years of the decade. The hundreds of wool factories that abounded in the town had flourished in the fifties behind Spain's protectionist barrier. The partial opening up of foreign trade, the switch in the world market to synthetic fibres, and a sudden rise in costs led to a severe restructuring of the wool industry of Sabadell. Within little over half a decade, one in five local textile workers had lost their jobs (the number of engineering workers, in contrast, more than doubled).[26] By 1975, according to the President of the employers' organization, over half of the wool-producing companies of Sabadell had disappeared.[27]

The crisis eroded not just the traditional relations of production in the town but also its class structure. Many small

---

[24] Marcet, p. 124.

[25] OS, *Cuadro comparativo de salarios resultantes de diversos convenios de la industria siderometalúrgica* (1963), CG archives no. 1243; COCIS, *Memoria*, 1962 and 1963.   [26] COCIS, *Memoria*, 1961–74.

[27] *Sabadell*, 18 Feb. 1976.

workshop owners were driven back into the working class or into jobs such as commercial agents. Middle-class families who had set up small textile factories, at a time when it had seemed a worthwhile investment, began to abandon the industry for more profitable ventures such as property speculation. Indeed, from the sixties, the social fabric of Sabadell began to disintegrate. The paternalistic sense of community began to give way to starker class divisions.[28]

The death of Marcet in 1963 symbolized the beginning of the end of an epoch. Shortly before he died, his workers had staged their first strike. From his office on the first floor, Marcet had asked them for an explanation, to which one had replied, using the familiar and in the circumstances pejorative *tú*, 'Come down and we'll tell you.' Stung by their attitude, Marcet shut down the plant. The dispute went on for four days, at the end of which he was forced to reopen his factory and pay the workers for the time they had been locked out. Afterwards, in a long discussion with one of his ex-UGT collaborators, Marcet is supposed to have burst into tears. 'Why has this got to happen to me?', he is reported as saying. 'Haven't I treated my workers well?'[29] Upon Marcet's death, the tradition of giving each of his workers a Christmas hamper was discontinued by his son. In fact, by the mid sixties, the practice seems to have been ended by most Sabadell employers.[30] It was a small token of the rise of more abrasive industrial relations. Between 1963 and 1976 stretched a new period during which the social consensus that had underpinned class relations in the town broke down. It is significant that while Marcet's death was mourned by one of the largest gatherings seen in Sabadell, his next successor but one, Mayor Josep Burull, would be hounded from his office in 1976 by an angry populace.

The erosion of paternalism in Sabadell did not go unnoticed by the authorities. The secret police, in a 1971 report on the textile firm Estruch, noted how in recent years the company had failed to buy off militancy among its workers.

This is a typically paternalist firm, given the ultra-Catholic nature of the two brothers who run it. The company has always been one of the most

[28] For a brief discussion of this point, see J. Gómez, 'Apuntes para una historia de los últimos años sabadellenses', *Can Oriach*, Mar. 1970.

[29] Castells, 27. 69.   [30] Trives interview.

generous in the amount of bonuses it has paid, in the housing facilities it offers its workers, in the help it extends over problems and difficult family situations, in scholarships and many other gestures . . . Nevertheless, its workers reject this paternalism and measure their demands according to their contribution to the firm, which has been declared a Model Company by the Ministry of Labour. In short, the management has shown kindness in its personnel relations but has not been able to win over the work-force, who have been poisoned by a tiny group of people . . .[31]

The same change was observed by the head of the Provincial OSE in 1972 in a report to the Civil Governor on another Sabadell textile firm, Castelló.

. . . The meticulous industrial organization in this factory, on top of the range of social benefits which the company offers its workers . . . are worthy of mention. Until 1971, there was a good social climate in this firm with the result that no dispute had ever broken out. From that year onwards, coinciding with the arrival of subversive elements on the shop-floor, the number of disputes has not ceased to rise, and now the firm has one of the worst records for industrial conflict.[32]

That this was a general process in Sabadell was admitted by the head of the local OSE, Ramón Castro, in a newspaper interview in 1975. Lamenting the erosion of traditions of moderation, 'that high degree of responsibility of people here . . . which is the result of an old union tradition typical of the area', he admitted, 'In the last few years, there has been a change in the dynamic of unionism in Sabadell that has given rise to new demands and attitudes . . .'[33]

Two of these reports attributed the breakdown of paternalist relations to the agitation of the labour opposition. This sort of interpretation, of course, was typical of the demonology of the regime, which ascribed all social unrest to the nefarious influence of Communists. But the authorities were not wrong in seeing the hand of the opposition in the changing climate of the factories. Unlike its equivalent in Terrassa, the labour opposition in Sabadell had been inconspicuous until the mid sixties. The local Communist party had remained a highly clandestine organization, split between a group of immigrant workers in the

---

[31] JSPB report, 19 Feb. 1971, CG archives no. 1418.
[32] Report dated 15 Nov. 1972, CG archives no. 1425.
[33] *Sabadell*, 23 May 1975.

outlying districts of the town, and a much smaller pocket of members in the centre. It had only been in June 1959 that the two groups were able to reach agreement to act together, and only some nine years later that they fused.[34] In contrast to Terrassa, many of the leaders of the new labour movement in Sabadell came from the Catholic workers' movement, which had played a more active role than local Communists in the few outbursts of protest before 1966.

It was only towards the end of the sixties that militants began to spread their network of supporters beyond the half-dozen engineering plants and the two or three textile firms where they had some base. In this new movement, the Communists, reinforced by a younger generation of activists, had a leading role. In this sense, the authorities were right to highlight the part that 'subversives' were playing in the growing industrial unrest in Sabadell. The catalyst of the new labour protest was the workers of the massive building-sites on the outskirts of the town—in particular, the new university being built a few miles to the south-west and the massive estate of Ciutat Badía to the south. Frequently, the building workers took to the streets of Sabadell to register their protest; their flying pickets could be seen moving from one site to another in the town gathering support. During more generalized protest, such as the struggle over the provincial agreement in 1973, the construction workers marched from the outlying sites into the centre of Sabadell, taking in factories and building-sites on the way. Their more public actions un-doubtedly helped to generate a new climate of protest in Sabadell.

The role of the predominantly immigrant building workers in the labour movement of Sabadell points to another clue as to its different rhythm of growth. While Terrassa received an influx of southern immigrants from the forties onwards, the tide of Andalusian immigration into Sabadell got under way only in the sixties.[35] The former town, therefore, experienced the impact of

[34] Castells, 28. 16. For a history of the Sabadell Party see PSUC, *40 anys de lluita*.

[35] By 1960, almost 30% of Terrassa's population were Andalusian in origin compared to only 19% of that of Sabadell. Conversely, 19% of Sabadell's inhabitants in the same year were immigrants from inland Catalonia, in contrast to only 5.7% of Terrassa's population. Duocastella, graphs 1–12, and Calvet (1982), pp. 57–62.

southern immigration earlier than Sabadell, which remained a predominantly Catalan town until the sixties. Militants from the South began to play an important role in the Terrassa labour movement from as early as the end of the forties. While most immigrants had had no experience of collective organization, an important group in Terrassa had brought with them the traditions of the more direct and violent class struggle that had taken place in a few areas of the South. The Sabadell labour movement was infused until the sixties with a tradition of negotiation and moderation more typical of Catalan traditions, whether in the countryside or in the towns. The growth of a new militancy in the seventies in Sabadell may therefore be linked in part to the later incorporation of immigrants from the South into its labour movement.

What is certain is that from 1974 Sabadell witnessed a wave of industrial and urban struggles which, for their impact on the local community, had no parallel elsewhere except in Baix Llobregat. Labour and social protest converged in two general strikes in 1976 that represented the culmination of two related processes: the decomposition of the old class relations, and the rise of a new militancy led by immigrant workers. Of course, these struggles took place within a wider context of political change, but their rhythm and the form they took were peculiar to the history of Sabadell.

BAIX LLOBREGAT: THE MAKING OF A NEW COMMUNITY

So far we have looked at the labour movement in two areas with old industrial roots and strong union traditions. Baix Llobregat, on the other hand, was a relatively new urban zone. Situated along the narrow valley of the Llobregat river, it had consisted at the beginning of the fifties of a string of small market towns separated by rich agricultural land. Industrial nuclei had existed at its southern end, while towns further north like Olesa and Martorell possessed small textile factories. The transformation of the valley into one of the most important industrial areas of Catalonia was accomplished in a matter of 20 years. It was determined not by a local bourgeoisie but by multinational and

Barcelona capital seeking cheaper land and more space. Its dynamic was the industrial and residential overspill of the capital.

The southern half of Baix Llobregat became the earliest recipient of this industrial and speculative investment. Later, factories and housing estates began to creep up the valley until the physiognomy of the whole area had changed. In the space of these 20 years, between 1950 and 1970, the population grew from 96,000 to 351,000 inhabitants. By the seventies, the valley was filled with industrial towns, emitting plumes of smoke and displaying rows of tenement blocks, while between each conurbation stretched a few miles of fruit orchards and market gardens. The greatest concentration of industry lay in the area around Cornellá, which was now a continuous sprawl of factories and housing estates joined indiscriminately to south-west Barcelona (see Map 3).

The most important feature of the Baix Llobregat labour movement was that it grew in step with the industrial development of the area. Unlike Terrassa and Sabadell, the influence of old traditions was negligible. Only the engineering factory of Siemens, which had been founded in 1910, represented some continuity with the past. The old textile industry, on the other hand, hardly plays a part in this history. The parallel growth of industry and the labour movement in the area can be traced in the spread of militancy from the earliest industrial centres, in particular from the Siemens plant, whose strike of 1962 set a new pattern of labour protest, to the more recently industrialized areas in north Baix Llobregat.[36] The development of the local labour movement in the post-Civil-War period thus began in the sixties and was located in a more modern industrial structure than either Terrassa or Sabadell.

Indeed, industry in Baix Llobregat was highly diversified and capital-intensive, as indicated by Table 3 comparing the distribution of jobs in 1970 in the three areas so far under discussion.[37] The vast majority of engineering and chemical

---

[36] For a descriptive account of the Siemens strike and the later struggles of the Baix Llobregat labour movement, see I. Riera and J. Botella, *El Baix Llobregat: 15 años de luchas obreras* (Barcelona, 1976).

[37] The table is based on the author's calculations from Caja de Ahorros de Sabadell, *Dinámica y perspectiva del Vallés 1969* (Sabadell, 1970), and Consejo Económico Social del Bajo Llobregat, *Informe*, May 1971. It should be remembered also that much of the engineering industry in the latter two towns was connected with the textile industry.

MAP 3   *Baix Llobregat*

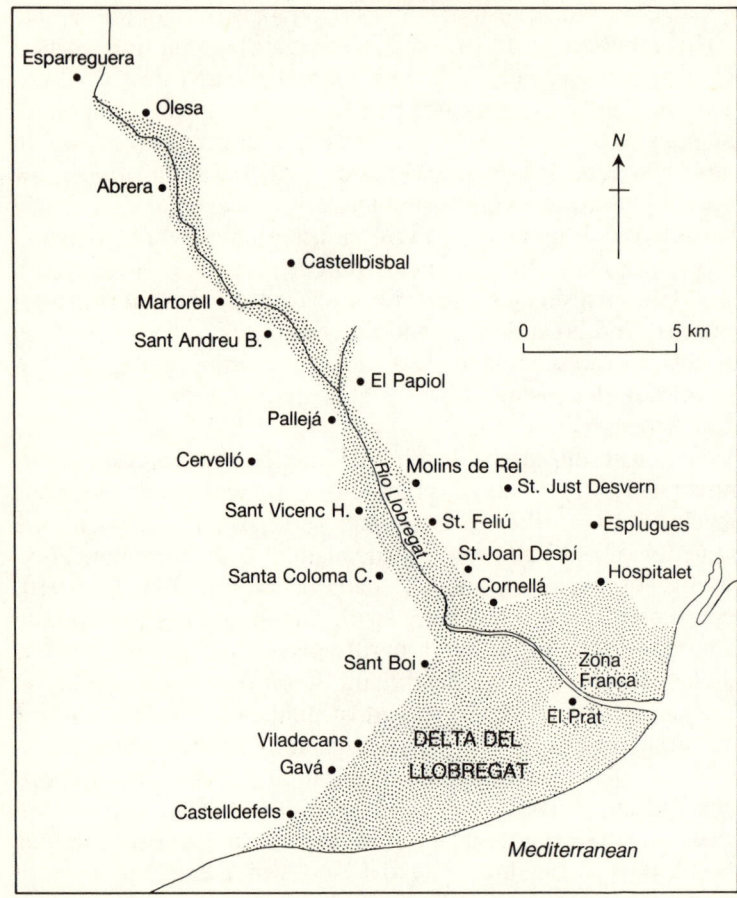

TABLE 3   *Distribution of Employment by percentage of Active Population in Three Towns in 1970*

	Engineering	Chemicals	Textiles
Baix Llobregat	48	15	7
Terrassa	19.7	0.79	66
Sabadell	25	0.80	62

Source: see n. 37 of this chapter.

plants in Baix Llobregat were multinationals; of the larger factories in the area only three were based on Spanish capital. The dynamism of local industry can be judged by the fact that between 1968 and 1976, Baix Llobregat registered a higher percentage of investment in new industry than any other area in Catalonia.[38]

The labour movement that emerged in Baix Llobregat was thus based on a more skilled working class than that of Terrassa or Sabadell.[39] Its hard core of leaders consisted of skilled immigrant workers from the main engineering factories in the Cornellá area. A report of the secret police in 1966 on the leadership of Comisiones Obreras in the area lists 17 militants, of whom 15 were engineering workers. Six of them worked in Siemens and the others in just four firms. Of the 17, only three were Catalan, and only four lived outside the area.[40] The working class of Baix Llobregat was also younger and composed predominantly of immigrants. In Cornellá, for example, there were almost twice as many people born outside Catalonia as indigenous inhabitants; in Terrassa and Sabadell, the reverse was true.[41] The majority of immigrants had settled in the area relatively recently, bringing with them higher expectations of social improvement than those who had fled hunger or rural oppression in the forties. The labour movement thus drew its support from a socially mobile working class with few traditions in common. It was moulded by the immediate social and political environment.

The single most important influence on the shape of the Baix Llobregat labour movement was collective bargaining. This was so not only because the movement developed in the sixties when bargaining was first introduced but also because of the structure of industry in the area. In Terrassa and Sabadell, plant agreements were confined to a handful of firms; if the centres of agitation were the local engineering and wool industry agreements, there

[38] Lleonart *et al.*, p. 89.

[39] There are insufficient data, however, with which to compare skill levels in the three areas, because the census of industrial workers in Baix Llobregat covered those workers resident rather than those who worked in the area. Since many local people worked elsewhere, the available figures do not reflect the reality in the factories. We have instead to rely on the profile of industry in the area. [40] JSPB report 1966, CG archives no. 1243.

[41] Comín and García-Nieto, p. 72, and A. de Unzueta Y Yuste, *Estructura económica de España* (Barcelona, 1980), 98–101.

were also contracts, such as that affecting the dyers and
bleachers, which were negotiated elsewhere. The Baix Llobregat
labour movement was more directly involved in the practice of
bargaining. The vast majority of medium-to-large firms in the
area negotiated their own collective agreements. In the recurrent
process of agitation and bargaining over plant agreements,
militants cut their teeth, developing new skills and qualities of
shop-floor leadership.

By 1967, the leaders of the engineering workers had managed
to negotiate a local agreement, embracing companies with plant
agreements and those smaller firms without, that became the
nerve-centre of agitation in the area. This was a remarkable
achievement for which there are no parallels elsewhere in the
labour movement in Catalonia and it requires some explanation.
It was argued in Chapter 3 that plant bargaining was both a
strength and a weakness in the labour movement, for while it
helped to create well-organized work-forces it also hindered the
co-ordination of industrial struggle. The division between plant
and area agreements was most acute in Barcelona but it also
adversely affected the labour movement of Sabadell and
Terrassa, where the workers of the few large firms with plant
negotiations paid scant attention to the local agreement. The Baix
Llobregat engineering contract, on the contrary, was negotiated
exclusively by militant shop stewards from firms that had their
own particular mechanism of bargaining.[42] Its immediate
relevance to workers in the larger companies was marginal. It
was true that they had negotiated clauses in their own
agreements whereby they could incorporate any improvements
won in the local contract. Wages and conditions, however, were
almost invariably better in plant bargains. The importance of the
area agreement was that it provided a focus of agitation that
could unite the engineering workers of Baix Llobregat. A political
motive, therefore, as well as a long-term economic strategy, lay
behind the support of militants for the area agreement. It says
much for their leadership that they were able to convince their
rank and file to come out on strike over negotiations that had no
immediate bearing on their own conditions.

As a result, there was a greater ferment of union activity in Baix

---

[42] Interview with José Cano, 23 Oct. 1985.

Llobregat than in either Terrassa of Sabadell. Labour agitation not only reached into the dozens of factories where negotiating mechanisms existed, thereby generating a continuous process of debate between militants and rank and file, but also extended to scores of smaller firms which were covered by the local agreement. The labour movement grew in depth and in breadth. The centre of this web of union life was the OSE headquarters in Cornellá and its various sub-branches in the surrounding municipalities.[43] As militants penetrated the local industrial committees of the unions they were able increasingly to control the bureaucratic machinery of the OSE. As part-time officials, they were in touch with delegates from numerous small firms who would not normally go to meetings of Comisiones Obreras.[44] Through these contacts, they were able to spread the demands of the labour movement to new layers of workers. But they also gained an invaluable insight into conditions in industry. With their finger on the pulse of the local working class, the Baix Llobregat militants developed a style of agitation more in tune with the social reality of the area than their counterparts in Terrassa.

This is not to say that labour protest in Baix Llobregat was confined to constitutional channels of action. For all their increasing grip on the delegate machinery of the local State Union, militants of Comisiones Obreras continued to hold clandestine meetings in which political and union policies were discussed. Nor were public forms of protest avoided. On the contrary, of the four areas under discussion, the Baix Llobregat labour movement of the seventies was perhaps the most conspicuous. How far this was the result of a more lenient policy on the part of the local authorities is difficult to judge. It is

---

[43] For the purposes of collective bargaining and union administration, southern Baix Llobregat was designated as the *comarca* of Cornellá and it was in this town that the area headquarters were located. For this reason, Cornellá became a reference-point for industrial struggles in the whole area, from Gavá and El Prat in the south to Martorell in the north. It is significant that the OSE was proposing in 1973 to split the *comarca* into three in order to weaken the organized labour movement. Delegación Comarcal de Cornellá, *Informe confidencial sobre el Bajo Llobregat*, 20 Jan. 1973, CG archives no. 1425.

[44] An example of the effort made by militants to get in touch with local workers was the twice-weekly counselling service established by the President of the San Feliú engineering union, a Communist militant. Riera and Botella, pp. 50–1; Cano interview.

probably true that in Terrassa and Barcelona the forces of law and order responded with a greater degree of violence and prohibition. Terrassa had become a target for the heavy hand of the police ever since the labour movement had taken to the streets with such determination in the fifties. Barcelona, on the other hand, was a more politically sensitive area than the suburbs; a march of striking workers along the fashionable Paseo de Gracia in the centre of the city was a very different thing to a demonstration in the outer suburbs.

One clue as to why the authorities were less implacable in their pursuit of militants in Baix Llobregat can be found in a police report of December 1972, written at the height of a wave of labour protest in the area. The Social and Political Brigade had shadowed a secret meeting of the co-ordinating committee of the Baix Llobregat Comisiones Obreras, consisting of 35 local workers' leaders. Yet the secret police decided not to move in on the meeting. Their report stated, 'The police authorities judged that, in order to avoid worse trouble in this time of crisis, it was not wise to arrest these individuals.'[45] What restrained the police in Baix Llobregat in the early seventies was the fear of generating solidarity strikes. When, in a desperate move to forestall a one-day stoppage in the area in 1974, the authorities arrested 24 local militants, they succeeded merely in ensuring that the action became a general strike that lasted for three days (see Chapter 6). The incident was another testimony to the strong links that bound the leaders of Comisiones Obreras to the local working class.

It was distinctive of the style of Baix Llobregat militants to seek the support of the broadest sections of the local community. Minority actions were frowned upon and popular forms of protest were usually pursued. It became a tradition for workers on strike to spread through the town of Cornellá in small groups dressed in their work overalls. While the militants of Terrassa sought to take over the Rambla, the tree-lined avenue that runs through the urban centre, with a mass of demonstrators until they were driven away by police charges, their counterparts in Cornellá permeated the streets of their town.

There were other reasons, however, for the more broad-based

45 JSPB report, 5 Dec. 1972, CG archives no. 1418.

culture of the Baix Llobregat movement. Firstly, the area had a more homogeneous social structure than either Sabadell or Terrassa. Its social composition was overwhelmingly working-class; 66 per cent of the population in the municipality of Cornellá were blue-collar workers, compared to 51 per cent in Terrassa and only 31 per cent in Barcelona (see Table 1). Also, as we have seen, two-thirds of the population of Cornellá were non-Catalans, and of these the vast majority were Andalusian. Moreover, because the stimulus of economic and urban growth had come from Barcelona in recent years, there was no indigenous bourgeoisie nor middle class with an established culture such as that of Terrassa or Sabadell. The white-collar workers in industry, the professional middle class, and the petty bourgeoisie were to a great extent caught up in the problems of the working class. This can be seen most clearly in the case of shopkeepers, bartenders, cinema managers, and the like, whose custom depended largely on workers and their families. Increasingly in the early seventies, they could be found backing labour and urban protest by closing down their services on days of general action.

The involvement of other social groups also gave the local labour movement a more popular and peaceable character. Working-class women of the area played a dominant role in campaigns against the local Council. They were active in struggles against redundancies and victimization; during the Laforsa strike of 1975, for example, the wives of the workers on strike donned their husbands' work overalls and guarded the entrance of the church where the workers were holding a sit-in.[46] The presence of many women in the demonstrations of 1974 to 1976, although it did not deter the riot police from indulging in its customary brutality, set a less violent tone to public protest than in Terrassa where the labour movement was more steeped in a male culture. This tendency was reinforced by the participation in public protest of young people from the local sixth-form college and the evening training-school, as well as teachers, residents' associations, and other official organizations in the area. All these groups shared the same social and urban tensions. This link between neighbourhood and labour dissent

---

[46] Riera and Botella, pp. 160–2.

was stronger in Baix Llobregat than in Terrassa and Sabadell partly because its urban problems were more acute. A town like Cornellá had suffered a demographic explosion in the past 20 years that had left severe strains on its meagre resources. The problems of flood damage, inadequate social services, urban renewal, and so on touched at one point or another on the lives of all its inhabitants. It did not require any great ideological leap to link social problems of this kind to the struggle of workers to prevent the closure of local firms or to release a jailed leader. In fact, one of the most important dynamics of collective protest in the area was the spate of redundancies that took place there from 1967 onwards. The struggle for jobs that year in the firms of Matacás and Rockwell Cerdans forged a tradition of solidarity actions that embraced not only the labour movement but the local population.

By 1972, the community of Cornellá and the surrounding municipalities was involved in common social and occupational tensions. The authorities were aware of the danger. It was seen in Chapter 2 how the local OSE warned of the disaffection of the inhabitants. The Civil Governor himself urged that something be done about the severe urban problems affecting the Baix Llobregat residents. In a letter to the Managing Director of the Banco de Crédito Local he pleaded for the speedy concession of a loan for a programme of public works, because Cornellá 'is one of the most militant areas I have under my control as far as labour is concerned'.[47] Yet, despite the efforts of the authorities, the various agitations converged into a common movement of protest over the following four years that posed a grave problem of public order.

The greater social diffusion of the Baix Llobregat labour movement had its roots also in the urban structure of the area. Formally, the area of south Baix Llobregat was contained within the so-called *comarca* of Cornellá, and the town of the same name served as its 'union capital'. It was here that the collective agreements for the whole zone were negotiated. This was then the objective basis for unity between groups of workers of the different towns in the valley. Cornellá became their reference-point not only because the OSE headquarters were located there but also because it contained the most militant work-forces.

[47] 17 Apr. 1972, CG archives no. 1526.

Strikers from other towns often marched to the *comarca* capital to try to win the support of its well-organized workers. Conversely, demonstrations would set out from Cornellá in an attempt to pull out workers from other towns. The forging of a common style of struggle can almost be traced in these marches between the towns of the valley, in the extension of solidarity strikes to all parts of the area, and in the strategic timing and location of demonstrations.

If this smaller area of Cornellá is brought into focus, we can see more clearly the influence of urban morphology on the growth of the labour movement. Unlike Terrassa and Sabadell, Cornellá was not geographically a well-defined area. It was the southernmost tip of the spread of houses, factories, roads, railways, warehouses, and waste land that extended from the centre of the metropolis. There was no clear point, at least to the north towards the city, at which the town began, nor were there any visible boundaries separating it from the surrounding municipalities such as San Joan Despí and Esplugues. Cornellá was unlike Terassa in another respect: a large percentage of its population worked outside the area.[48] It also housed workers from factories elsewhere; in the gigantic housing estate of Ciudad Satélite (Satellite City) lived some 5,000 SEAT workers, who brought to the residents' campaigns some of the experience of labour protest in the huge factory a few miles away. Within this fluid urban framework, there took place a cross-fertilization of ideas and experience that enabled the labour movement not only to create a widespread network of support, but also, during the course of struggles, to carve out its own physical space.

The two nuclei of the labour movement in the town where the Almeda district down from the historic centre towards the river, and the zone stretching up from the centre towards the north of the town including the edge of the San Joan and Esplugues municipalities. About 16,500 workers, roughly a third of the total work-force of south Baix Llobregat, were employed in the 700 or so factories in this area.[49] The Almeda district was dominated by

[48] Some 60% travelled daily outside the municipality: Comín and García-Nieto, p. 60. According to the Consejo Económico Social of Baix Llobregat, over 44,000 passengers journeyed each day to Barcelona: *Ponencia de zona y polígonos industriales* (1970).

[49] OSE (Delegación Comarcal de Cornellá), *Informe confidencial*, 20 Jan. 1973, CG archives no. 1425.

medium-sized engineering and chemical plants, around which stood smaller factories and workshops that supplied them with components such as cylinders, gas and water pipes, air compressors, and so on. The jobs of local workers were closely interwoven and the threat of closure or a reduction in the workforce in any factory also affected many people outside it. This may help to explain, for example, the depth of local solidarity for the struggle of the Laforsa workers during 1975–6 against the closure of their steel-mill. In that small area, there was considerable social intermixing. In the local cafés, shops, and bars, points of view were discussed and ideas exchanged between workers of different firms, bartenders, restaurant owners, shopkeepers, local residents, lorry-drivers and the like.[50]

It is not far-fetched to imagine the militant culture of the larger firms beginning to permeate the area through this daily contact, as well as by the more collective campaigns in support of strikes. The local parish priest noted that, when he first arrived in the district in 1961, there was no sign of class-consciousness among its workers. Instead, '. . . when someone talked about these ideas, his workmates made fun of him or dismissed him as an idealist. A general feeling prevailed that there was nothing you could do about the situation; you had to put up with it and that was that. The most important thing for most workers was to earn money by working a lot of overtime.' By the early seventies, on the other hand, he had observed a considerable change in the atmosphere: '. . . there is now a climate of solidarity among workers in the district. We have discovered that the strength of a united working class is invincible.'[51]

The growth of collective agitation in this small area was reinforced by the frequent mobilization of residents against the local Council. Ever since the river Llobregat had overflowed its banks in 1971 for the second time in nine years, severely damaging houses and streets, the Almeda district had been in the forefront of urban unrest. This was no occupational community, since only about 2 per cent of the workers in the surrounding factories lived in the area.[52] Yet the two parallel movements in Almeda influenced each other because they shared the same physical space and, increasingly in the seventies, a common political cause.

The workers in the Almeda district sought their main support among the factories near the centre of the town. Marches of strikers would make their way up towards the town centre, past the Town Hall, until they reached the OSE headquarters on the José Antonio Avenue, directly opposite which stood the largest factory in the area, Siemens. Behind Siemens lay a large industrial estate in which were gathered some of the most militant plants in Baix Llobregat. A few hundred yards up the avenue stood the massive cheaply-built tenement blocks of Ciudad Satélite, one of the most densely populated districts in Spain. The estate housed well over half of the inhabitants of Cornellá; 95 per cent of its residents were immigrants and many worked in the local factories. Bound together by a common language and social origin, the population of Ciudad Satélite also shared some of the worst housing and urban deficits of any estate in Catalonia.[53]

In the space of some 3 square kilometres, therefore, an explosive mixture of labour and social problems was concentrated. As in Almeda, we can see in the morphology of the area some elements that helped in the forging of a common mode of struggle. The route of many marches of workers on strike, for example, led past the gates of other factories, where they could halt to explain their demands and ask for solidarity. A frequent target of demonstrations was the OSE building on the José Antonio Avenue, not only because it was the nerve-point of labour disputes but because the most militant plant, Siemens, stood opposite. A police report of 1968 observed that the workers of the engineering firm Matacás in the nearby town of San Feliú timed their demonstration outside the Union headquarters to coincide with the end of a shift in Siemens.[54] That the Siemens workers played a crucial role in spreading solidarity action is borne out by the regular reports sent to the Civil Governor by the firm's management. According to their figures, in the four years leading to the first general strike in Baix Llobregat, that is, between July 1970 and June 1974, Siemens workers came out on solidarity strike 29 times and only 5 times over their own wage demands.[55]

[53] Alibés *et al.*, (1973), 89–90.
[54] JSPB report, 18 Apr. 1968, CG archives no. 1387.
[55] CG archives no. 1417 (11).

It was also a common strategy of strikers in Cornellá to use public spaces in order to gain the support of local residents and workers. Sit-ins were frequently staged in three parish churches, strategically situated in the middle of working-class residential districts. Impromptu public meetings were held in front of stations after the day shift had ended. During local feast-days strikers were often conspicuous in the festivities, dressed in their work overalls, giving speeches, handing out leaflets, and raising money for their cause.

The three general strikes in Baix Llobregat between 1974 and 1976 were tangible evidence that in the long-drawn-out process of industrial and urban struggle, organic links were being forged among workers and between them and the local population. The making of this common movement was largely the work of hundreds of militants. But the peculiar configuration of social, urban, and industrial structures in the area helped to nurture its development.

BARCELONA: PARALLEL PROTESTS

The Barcelona labour movement stands in sharp contrast to that of Baix Llobregat. It is difficult to perceive a common core of values, methods, and traditions—new or old—which united the diverse agitations in the capital of the region. The different conflicts in Barcelona may have shared the same basic programme of demands, tailored by militants to suit the needs of each dispute. They may also have been motivated especially from 1974 by the same struggle for basic social and political rights. But one always has the sense that they were parallel movements. Indeed, we must demarcate not just the urban from the labour movement but the labour movement of one industry from another, and the workers of one factory from another in the same industry.

To understand this atomization, the sheer size of the city should be recalled. While the population of Terrassa in 1970 numbered some 139,000 inhabitants, that of Barcelona, excluding the outlying districts of Hospitalet to the south and Badalona to the north, was over one and three-quarter million. Barcelona was more fluid and heterogeneous in its social and occupational definition than any of the other towns that have been considered. Some 31 per cent of the active population were white-collar workers, while only just over a third were industrial workers. In addition to a highly diversified industry, the activity of the city was dominated by the tertiary sector.[56] Labour unrest spread in the early seventies to new layers of white-collar workers in offices, hospitals, and schools in Barcelona, but it would prove difficult to knit their different labour objectives into a common movement, and even more so to unite them with blue-collar workers.

Cleavages existed also between the labour movement in different industries. Militants of the textile industry, engineering factories, chemical plants, and building-sites followed their own pattern of agitation, even if they shared the same general demands. They were separated not only by occupational differences but also by traditions, skill levels, and education, by geographical origin, and to some extent by language. The proportion of Catalan workers in the dyeing and bleaching industry, for example, was much higher than in engineering; virtually every building worker, on the other hand, was an immigrant.

In comparison with Cornellá or Terrassa, industry in Barcelona was highly segregated. The bulk of it was concentrated in two areas, the Zona Franca industrial estate south of the port, and a larger area to the north forming a triangle between Barceloneta, San Adriá, and San Andreu (see Map 2). The Zona Franca area was a relatively new industrial site that had grown spectacularly since the SEAT factory was built there in the early fifties. By 1973, 173 firms providing almost 47,000 jobs were located on the estate, making it one of the largest concentrations of industry in the country.[57] The other industrial zone to the north was more dispersed. From the Poble Nou district (just north of Barceloneta), which contained a string of factories along the seaboard and a knot of dyeing and bleaching plants, it stretched across the river Besós to small industrial estates on both banks, and westwards to San Andreu and Sagrera, where some of the larger

---

[56] The main industries were engineering with 33.9% of the active population, construction with 18.9%, textiles with 10.6%, and chemicals with 10.3%: Ferras, p. 91.

[57] Alibés *et al.*, (1973), 102–4.

engineering plants such as La Maquinista and Enasa (Pegaso) were located.

This concentration of industry, however, did not provide the same opportunities for spreading common agitation as in Cornellá. It has already been argued that the structure of collective bargaining encouraged the growth of sectional labour interests among many workers of the capital. Thus in the engineering industry, the work-force of each large and medium-sized firm pursued its own objectives and deployed its own bargaining pressure. It was only in 1974 that engineering militants began to take the provincial agreement seriously and only in 1976 that the first strikes broke out over its conditions. There was a far greater diversity—in size, skills, and traditions—between plants of the same industry in Barcelona than in the other three areas that have been looked at. To compare just two of the larger firms, La Maquinista was a century-old engineering firm with a strongly pro-Catalan management and a highly skilled work-force, almost half of whom were Catalan-speakers.[58] In contrast, the car factory SEAT was set up in 1950 by the State-holding firm INI and run for some time from Madrid by generals appointed by the government. Its work-force was overwhelmingly immigrant in origin, recruited initially by SEAT foremen from their own villages in the South and made up predominantly of semi-skilled production-line workers.[59]

Another feature that distinguished one firm from another was the different level of repression in each. A few companies such as SEAT and Enasa were organized like military barracks. Some had Civil Guard personnel posted permanently at the entrance to the plant. In order to make unofficial factory organization difficult, the heavy engineering firm Macosa obliged its employees to wear different-coloured overalls to differentiate workers of one section from another.[60] On the other hand, some companies were prepared to engage in dialogue with unofficial

---

[58] S. García, pp. 112–17. Concerned about the nationalist sentiments of the management, the authorities put pressure on the company to annul the appointment, as Director of the Maquinista apprentice school, of a man known for his pro-Catalanist sentiments. JSPB report, Feb.–Mar. 1965, CG archives no. 1387.

[59] Miguélez Lobo (1977); S. Gilaberte Herranz and J. Zamora Terrés, *Le lotte operaie alla SEAT* (Turin, 1977).

[60] Interview with Rafael Gispert, 7 Dec. 1985.

representatives of the shop-floor. The managing director of La Maquinista in 1967 admitted in a speech to a gathering of employers that he had had discussions with members of Comisiones Obreras in his factory.[61] This uneven response among employers in Barcelona helped to create a greater disparity than elsewhere of levels of militant shop-floor organization.

Nor were the well-organized work-forces connected in any vital way with local communities. Although the working-class population of the capital was concentrated in residential ghettos on either side of the city, it was a mobile population, travelling some distance from home to work. Industrial relocation, urban renewal, immigration, and the construction of overspill estates had combined to erode the occupational communities that had existed, to some degree, in the old working-class districts of Barcelona.[62] Yet even where factories and residential estates stood close to each other, the links between the labour and urban movements were tenuous. The old working-class district of Poble Nou, for example, was a shadow of its former self. While it had been the densest working-class district in Barcelona and the centre of Anarchist organization in the twenties and thirties, Poble Nou had suffered an urban and industrial decline that had eroded its cohesion as a community. Much of its industry had moved out or closed down, and the former industrial sites were being occupied by transport companies taking advantage of the convenient location of Poble Nou. Of the dozens of dyeing and bleaching factories that used to dot the area, only 21 were still working in 1975. Other districts suffered a worse fate, virtually disappearing as roads and urban projects cut through their heart. Poble Nou at least retained some of its old traditions, and new local organizations including two residents' associations were established in the early seventies. Yet it was an older, less working-class population than the more militant districts such as the Nueve Barrios to the north-west, where there was little industry.[63]

---

[61] *La Vanguardia*, 27 Dec. 1967.

[62] For the example of La Maquinista see S. García, pp. 118 and 148.

[63] A. Alabart Vilà, 'Els barris de Barcelona i el moviment associatiu vëinal', Ph. D. thesis, (Barcelona University, 1981), 179–81. For further details of Poble Nou, see J. Fabre and J. M. Huertas Clavería, *Tots els barris de Barcelona.* (Barcelona, 1976–7), i. 81–125; de Solá-Morales *et al.*, p. 32.

This is not to say that workers in dispute failed to win the support of local residents. But there was no process of convergence between labour and urban movements of the kind found in Cornellá. The relationship between the two was tenuous and fluid. Workers' leaders of local firms chose sometimes to locate their public campaign of protest in another district, hoping to win greater support for workers. During the bitter dispute in 1976 over the closure of the Poble Nou plant of Motor Ibérica, the wives of the workers staged a sit-in in the parish church of San Andreu rather than in their local church. On the other hand, the striking workers of the textile firm S. F. Vila chose to demonstrate in Poble Nou because they expected to win greater financial support there than in their own district of Verneda.[64] Nor was there any organized support from local workers for the urban struggles in the district. The successful campaign in the seventies against a massive urban renewal plan that would have demolished part of old Poble Nou was led by local organizations and professional associations such as the Institute of Architects; there was no visible participation of local workers.[65]

The point was that militants were caught up in their own process of agitation, which revolved around collective bargaining. A more or less intense union struggle took place in each factory where shop-floor organization was strong, but it was usually confined within the gates of the plant. On the other hand, militant dyers and bleachers, whose collective agreement covered all the local plants in the industry, took their agitation also to the formal meetings of union delegates in the OSE and the unofficial gatherings of militants in the corridors of the building. But it was only in the building trade that industrial disputes took on a more public dimension. There were two reasons for this: firstly, urban projects such as road construction and the building of office and tenement blocks were directly related to the sources of urban protest; secondly, because of the nature of site organization and the structure of collective bargaining in the industry, building workers in dispute depended on the support of workers on other sites.

---

[64] Interview with Josep María Huertas Clavería, 6 Nov. 1985.
[65] Ibid.

For the most part, however, the militant plants of the capital were like citadels within which fierce struggles raged, and from which, occasionally, workers sallied out into the streets in search of support. That they were backed by many sections of the population and by workers in other factories of the capital is evident in the money they collected during the course of bitter disputes. In three years between 1971 and 1974, SEAT workers raised over 4 million pesetas (or some £24,000). But this support was not translated into the sort of solidarity action witnessed in Baix Llobregat. For several months in 1974 and 1975, the SEAT dispute took the centre of the political stage, as the workers of the largest plant in the country brought their conflict on to the streets of Barcelona. Yet the attempt to launch a general strike in solidarity was a failure. Unlike the labour movements elsewhere in the province, that of Barcelona proved unable to bring the different agitations together into even one day of united action.

This chapter has highlighted the differences that separated the labour movement of the four main conurbations of Barcelona province. In each centre a distinct culture emerged that was shaped to a great extent by the different pattern of social, industrial, and urban organization therein. The speed of economic change in the sixties and the prohibitive conditions created by the dictatorship restricted the spread of these new labour traditions across the threshold of towns and industries. Yet from the early seventies, and especially from the end of 1973, some of these boundaries began to be broken down. The new connecting medium between workers of different areas and industries was the common struggle for basic political, social, and economic rights, as the Franco regime descended into a fatal crisis of legitimacy.

5

The Rise of Militancy 1970–1973

> During the anti-Franco struggle, it was easier to dream;
> since nothing was possible. everything was imaginable;
> any plan (even the most revolutionary) was as plausible as
> it was implausible.
>
> (Josep M. Colomer, *La ideologia de l'antifranquisme*, p. 77)

The sixties had been a period of radical social and economic change throughout Spain. In the new decade of the seventies, the tensions created by this transformation rose to the surface, catching the dictatorship off balance. During the era of the 'economic miracle', the regime had tried to put its house in some sort of constitutional order. A series of cosmetic reforms had been carried out designed to make the State appear more in tune with the new society. This bureaucratic face-lift had culminated in the Organic Law of 1967 that confirmed the monarchy as the form of the State in Spain. Two years later, Juan Carlos was proclaimed heir to Franco. Yet by the early seventies, the dictatorship found itself assailed by forces it had brought into being by opting for economic modernization.

The new decade was ushered in by a wave of disputes that swept across the industrial centres of Spain. From the end of 1969, except for a short period during 1971–2, the graph of strikes recorded by the Ministry of Labour never ceased to rise. By 1976, on the eve of democracy, it had reached higher levels than in most countries where strikes were legal. Table 4, based on the Ministry's record of disputes, gives a conservative but revealing estimate of the rising level of industrial conflict in Spain. Labour protest was no longer confined to the traditionally militant sections of the working class. The use of the strike weapon spread to teachers, hospital staff, bank employees, insurance clerks, building workers, young women workers in the food industry, and a host of people who had never stopped work

TABLE 4 *Industrial Conflict in Spain 1968–1976*

Year	Disputes	Workers involved	Working hours lost
1968	351	130,742	1,925,278
1969	491	205,325	4,476,727
1970	1,595	460,902	8,738,916
1971	616	222,846	6,877,543
1972	835	277,806	4,692,925
1973	931	357,523	8,649,265
1974	2,290	685,170	13,989,557
1975	3,156	647,100	14,521,000
1976	40,179	2,519,000	106,560,000

Sources: Ministerio de Trabajo, *Informes sobre conflictos colectivos,* 1968–75 (Madrid); L. Enrique De la Villa and C. Palomeque, *Introducción a la economía del trabajo* (Madrid, 1977), 314.

before. The rise and spread of labour dissent had its parallel in the upsurge of urban protest in the working-class estates of the big cities. Mounting unrest in the universities provoked the government into declaring a three-month State of Emergency in 1969. The early seventies saw the cause of regional autonomy in Catalonia and the Basque Country rapidly transformed into a popular movement supported even by immigrant workers whose cultural roots lay in distant villages of Andalusia or Murcia. Increasingly these movements were drawn together under the common banner of anti-Francoism. It was as if society, in the words of a Spanish historian, arose and stretched itself.[1]

The rise of labour dissent in Spain was part of a broader pattern of militancy that convulsed the industrialized countries of Western Europe. In Britain the number of working days lost in strike action rose from around 3 million a year in the early sixties to almost 12 million annually between 1968 and 1974. France and Italy were shaken by a wave of militancy that culminated in the General Strike of May 1968 and the 'hot autumn' of 1969 respectively. The source of this upsurge of protest lay partly in the expansion and renewed strength of the labour movement in Europe as a result of the boom of the early sixties, coupled with increasing inflationary pressures that were undermining living standards.

[1] Abella, p. 223.

In Spain the situation was exacerbated by the contradictions engendered by rapid economic and social change. The most important of these was the gap between the archaic structures of the Francoist State and the new social forces unleashed by economic growth. Presiding over a modern urban society increasingly integrated into Western Europe, the political system of Spain remained rooted in the Nationalist victory of 1939. Economic growth was transforming the class structure of Spain, generating new values that could not find expression within the political framework of the dictatorship. The expansion of higher education produced new generations of students, thousands of whom rejected the ideology of the regime. The growth of the service industries created a new class of professionals and white-collar workers whose aspirations placed them at odds with an authoritarian political system. On the shoddy estates built to house the labour force for the new industries, working-class families began to organize in protest at the poor conditions of their environment. The national movements also gathered force, fusing old demands for autonomy with new claims for democracy. Unable to stem the tide of protest, the regime increasingly fell back on to its instinctive reflex: to step up repression. But the action of the police and the courts only fanned the flames. Towards the end of the dictatorship, victimization and police brutality became one of the most important causes of popular protest.

Of the social forces that began to destabilize the system in the seventies, none posed a greater challenge than the working-class movement. Not only did it represent a problem of public order, as did the students and increasingly the Basque terrorist organization ETA, but it also threatened to undermine the high rates of profit of the sixties. The growth of the Spanish economy had depended on a mobile and quiescent labour force that could challenge neither low wages nor the low levels of investment in social infrastructure. The industrial relations system of the Francoist State had been designed to keep the working class disorganized by bureaucratic and repressive means. It was also believed that as some of the benefits of economic growth percolated downwards, workers would not seek to organize politically.[2]

[2] R. Carr and J. P. Fusi, *Spain: Dictatorship to Democracy* (London, 1979), 62.

By the seventies, however, it was clear that neither palliative nor repressive measures were keeping workers in check. The 1966 elections had shown that the State Union, the OSE, had failed to secure any real allegiance among the mass of workers. It was being infiltrated by new militants as fast as old ones were being sacked or deprived of their credentials as union representatives. It was also being bypassed frequently, as employers sought to negotiate with more representative spokespeople than the full-time appointed officials. The police offensive against Comisiones Obreras seemed only temporarily to have checked the growth of the labour movement. For each militant sacked or arrested in the seventies, two more would seem to spring up.

The growing pressure of labour militancy can be seen in a series of letters from employers to ministers and top officials of the State begging for help in dealing with industrial disputes. A secret document dated 1971 from the engineering employers' organization in Barcelona to the head of the Provincial OSE claimed that 'A feeling of utter despondency had crept in among employers at the moment. We are being forced to spend most of our time dealing with disputes to the detriment of our most important mission, that of creating wealth.' The letter complained that neither the OSE nor the courts acted with sufficient severity against known militants, and called on the government to step up its repressive measures against subversive organizations. 'More aggressive political and economic measures are absolutely vital in order to guarantee a free hand for management and complete social and economic peace . . .'[3]

There were other influential industrialists, however, who saw the need for a radical reform of the industrial relations system.[4] While the Franco dictatorship had immensely benefited the employing class, it was no longer providing a certain guarantee of continued profits. The industrial reforms from the late fifties had been designed to make labour relations more responsive to the changing needs of the employers. Within the OSE they had

---

[3] Gabinete Técnico Económico Sidero-Metalúrgico, *Extremos de mayor consideración expuestos al Delegado Provincial de Sindicatos por la presentación empresarial del más alto nivel del Sindicato del Metal de Barcelona* (Barcelona, 4 Feb. 1971), ANC archives.

[4] See for example the correspondence between the managing director of La Maquinista and Franco and his ministers in GC archives no. 1486.

been given a wide margin of manoeuvre. But the unwieldy nature of the system—its continued legalistic basis, the dominant role of the State in determining the internal regulations of industry and factory, and the paternalistic elements intrinsic to the Francoist ideology of integration—impeded any rapid response on the part of the employers to the changing conditions of the market. For the time being, however, the veiled calls for reform were drowned by the cries of others, cosseted by years of protectionism, for greater intervention by the State in suppressing militancy. As industrial unrest grew throughout the first five years of the decade, exacerbated by the very measures of repression intended to quell it, a more thoroughgoing reform increasingly appeared as the only option that could ensure the continued generation of profits.

It is significant that the level of strike action began to rise dramatically during the bleakest period suffered by the labour opposition since the fifties. Between 1967 and 1969 thousands of militants were arrested, sacked, or dismissed from their representative posts in the unions. The clandestine meetings of Comisiones were abandoned by all but the most committed activists, the vast majority of whom were members of the underground organizations. Yet it was at the height of this offensive against the opposition, during the State of Emergency of 1969, that the graph of disputes began to rise abruptly. It was true that the labour opposition played a crucial role in organizing protest actions. Nevertheless, it neither determined nor controlled the pattern of strikes. Nor can the partial lifting of the wage freeze imposed in 1968 and the resulting surge of pay-claims to compensate for rising inflation be an adequate explanation of the spread of labour protest. To understand it, we need to look instead at some of the deep-lying changes in the social and psychic structures of the working class brought about by the transformation of Spain.

This chapter will first examine some of the causes of the upsurge in militancy in the early seventies (Sources of Labour Dissent). The attempt by the different groups of the labour opposition to draw this protest together under a common banner will then be studied (Comisiones Obreras and the Labour Opposition). A third section will look at the varieties of agitation in the three main industries of the province; and in this part, the narration of the major strikes of the period between 1970 and 1973 will be related to the problems faced by workers in these industries (Varieties of Labour Agitation). The final section will analyse the continuing efforts of the opposition to channel labour unrest into political protest (Solidarity, Labour Protest, and the General Strike).

SOURCES OF LABOUR DISSENT

Chapter 2 outlined the dramatic rise in living standards experienced, in a matter of a decade, by the urban working class of Spain. The material benefits that economic growth offered workers, if they were prepared to labour long hours in sometimes appalling conditions, were tangible rewards, displayed on television and in the shop-windows. The dark ages of the forties and fifties could be rolled back by individual effort. The modernization of industry and the expansion of the labour market offered new opportunities to acquire skills and move up the occupational ladder. In a matter of six years, between 1964 and 1970, the number of unskilled workers dropped from 28.1 to 19.8 per cent of the total work-force across the nation as a whole. Similarly, the percentage of non-manual workers with urban working-class fathers rose from 10 per cent in 1960 to 22 per cent in 1969.[5] The new expectations were fuelled by increasing contact with the realities of life in other European countries. Images of the higher living standards enjoyed by workers elsewhere were brought back by emigrants or flickered across the screens of cinemas and television sets.

A curious report of the secret police, dated 1965, affords a vivid picture of this process of changing expectations among workers. Marked top secret, the report had landed on the desk of the Civil Governor of the province of Barcelona just after Christmas of that year. In urgent language, the Social and Political Brigade, as Franco's secret police were called, claimed to have discovered a new threat to the stability of the regime. Their plain-clothes men had been listening in to conversations in the bars of

[5] From the FOESSA report, 1970, quoted in John R. Logan, 'Affluence, Class Structure and Working-Class Consciousness in Modern Spain', *American Journal of Sociology*, Sept. 1977, pp. 386–402.

Barcelona between local workers and Spanish emigrants in Europe who were taking their holidays in their native city.

From the comments that have been picked up, it seems that in these conversations, they [the emigrants] talk of grand things, of fabulous wages. Some have brought their own cars, and ridicule the wages in Spain, dazzling their listeners with imaginary grandeurs. All this is stirring up discontent among the local working class who feel inferior as a result. Insults have even been proffered against the regime and the Unions.[6]

The somewhat lurid picture drawn by the over-zealous police was not without truth. For contact with the more prosperous societies north of the Pyrenees was bringing home to Spanish workers a new measure of the remuneration they could claim for their labour—after all, many multinationals now operating in Spain were paying wages far lower than in their plants elsewhere in Europe. It also reinforced latent hostility against the regime for denying the basic right enjoyed by workers elsewhere to organize collectively in defence of their living standards.

Indeed, one of the most important causes of unrest in the early seventies was the frustration of the expectations that had been encouraged by economic and social change. On one hand, the opportunities for social advancement began to shrink, as the expansion of the working class outstripped the possibilities of upward mobility. In the early sixties there had been a rise in the proportion of white-collar workers from working-class families. Yet by 1969, owing to the very increase in the size of the working class, the proportion of children of urban working-class fathers entering non-manual occupations dropped from 33 per cent in 1960 to 27 per cent.[7] Nor was the rise in educational levels matched by an increase in occupational opportunities. In a survey carried out in Barcelona in the early seventies, only 22 per cent of young people from working-class families considered that their studies had enabled them to rise socially. It was even more difficult for young people to move from a manual to a non-manual occupation. Of those questioned in the survey, only 5 per cent had managed to do so.[8]

    [6] JSPB report, 29 Dec. 1965, CG archives no. 1249.
    [7] Logan (1977).
    [8] Pinilla de Las Heras (1979), 263–91. These findings were confirmed in several important surveys carried out in the late seventies, to which we will refer in Chapter 6.

In fact, even more than the material conditions of life, it was the culture of the working class that was transformed during the course of the sixties. The aspirations of a more affluent, skilled, and educated working class accorded ill with the authoritarian and exploitative structures at work and in society. A new self-esteem permeated the values of many workers as their social status advanced. Fresh and more complex perceptions of social relationships were replacing the old certainties of class identity. A survey conducted in Barcelona in 1972 found that over half of the skilled workers questioned considered themselves to be middle-class.[9] Yet far from dampening militancy, this new sense of status aroused a greater assertiveness about social and political rights. In the growing movements for Catalan autonomy and urban reform, and in the labour movement itself, upwardly mobile white-collar and skilled workers played a prominent role.

The most striking process of cultural change took place among the immigrants.[10] While there were many among them of lower-middle-class background who had moved from small provincial towns—clerical workers, tradespeople, bar owners, and the like—the vast majority of immigrant families came from a rural background, and it is their experience that will be discussed in the following pages. On their arrival in Catalonia, the rural immigrants were plunged into an unfamiliar and largely indifferent world where the only guidance was a relative or fellow villager who had settled earlier. As Chapter 2 indicated, the tasks of the newly-arrived immigrants were formidable. They had not only to find accommodation and a job, but to survive within a bewildering new environment—the crowds of strangers, the underground railway, the unfamiliar sound of Catalan in the streets and shops, skirmishes with landlords, red tape, foremen. They came on the whole without skills that could be sold in the labour market. Most had been employed or semi-employed as agricultural labourers on the great estates in the South. Some had owned a smallholding with a clutch of animals.

---

[9] Logan (1977).

[10] The following account is based on a number of sources: Botey Vallés, op. cit.; C. Solé, *La integración sociocultural de los inmigrantes en Cataluña* (Madrid, 1981); Pinilla de las Heras (1979); Castells, op. cit.; Candel (1963 and 1968), and by the same author, *Emigrantes y trabajadores* (Barcelona, 1972) and *Apuntes para una sociología del barrio* (Barcelona, 1972); and author's interviews.

Others had found occasional work building roads, digging in the mines, burning charcoal, or felling trees in the forests. Almost all had experienced a brutal existence that they were determined to cast off. Though they had no knowledge of the ways of the industrial city, they came with an enormous capacity to work and learn the many skills that would enable them to build a new life.

By the early seventies, the vast majority of immigrants to Catalonia (who by 1975 were to number almost half of its population) had arrived and settled, mainly in Barcelona and its industrial belt. By dint of unstinting sacrifice, many had overcome the basic problems of subsistence. The jerry-built shanty towns on the outskirts and in the waste lands of the city were rapidly giving way to cheaply built tenement blocks, whose bright cramped flats could be acquired with a down payment that swallowed all their savings. Many of the rural immigrant workers had found jobs as labourers on the building-sites in and around the city—new office-blocks, high-rise estates, and hotels. But many had then moved on to better-paid jobs in the new engineering and chemical factories that offered them a chance of acquiring some sort of skill, not through any training programme but by their willingness to learn on the job.[11] In the process of moving around the city, buying a flat, and changing jobs, immigrants were exposed to new experiences that rapidly transformed their values. They had to learn the narrow discipline of production-line work; they had to become accustomed to the alienated life on the high-rise estate. To move from a rural community to the monolithic blocks of flats, like those of Bellvitge in Hospitalet, whose balconies hang in fume-laden air over the motorway to the south, meant an upheaval that must have been barely compensated for by the greater material opportunities of urban life. Yet the immigrants, though socially and geographically isolated, increasingly came to see the estate, the city, and Catalonia as their own.

This process of assimilation was not a uniform experience and it can only be traced in the life of each individual. Yet in the early seventies, a new collective consciousness seemed to emerge out

[11] A study of workers in the heavy-engineering firm of La Maquinista showed that most had acquired skills through work experience rather than training: S. García (1983), 138–44.

of the immigrant community, as if the new decade marked the end of a phase of settling in, of a primitive accumulation of basic resources, and the beginning of a new period of assertion. The evidence of this transformation can be found in the sudden upsurge of organized protest on the working-class estates and in the industries, in particular the building trade in which immigrants formed a majority of the labour force. The earlier deference of immigrants was giving way to a fresh confidence in their right to decent living and working conditions and a new sense of collective power to achieve them.[12]

Among the sources of this new consciousness, perhaps the most important was the experience of work. In the large factories, the immigrants were thrown in among Catalan workers, with whom initially they shared little except their common exploitation. The influx of immigrants had provided indigenous workers with the opportunity to ascend the occupational ladder. In the early stages of industrial growth in the mid fifties, the skilled workers, not to speak of the supervisors and technicians, had all tended to be Catalan while the labourers had almost invariably been immigrants. Yet the introduction of new technology had transformed the occupational structure, undermining the traditional skill divisions and creating a new class of semi-skilled workers from both indigenous and immigrant labour to service the production lines in the engineering industry. Towards the end of the sixties, the opportunities for upward mobility for both Catalan and immigrant workers were beginning to shrink.[13] Although the least skilled jobs continued to remain in the hands of immigrants, the dynamic of economic growth eroded the potential divisions between the two groups of workers.

In any case, Barcelona had a long tradition of absorbing immigrants. Each period of economic growth for the last hundred years had brought with it a wave of immigrants from the countryside. Since the late twenties, the vast majority of them had come from the South and neither spoke Catalan nor shared the culture of their new neighbours. The attitude of indigenous

---

[12] For a discussion of the changing perceptions of immigrants, based on a field survey in Barcelona province, see J. R. Logan, 'Rural–Urban Migration and Working-Class Consciousness', *Social Forces*, June 1978, pp. 1159–78.

[13] For partial evidence of this trend see Pinilla de las Heras (1979), 349–59.

workers towards the newcomers had been a relatively receptive one, not least because the immigration had occured at times of economic expansion. The absence of any serious friction between the two communities in recent years was also due to the willingness of immigrant families to settle in their new home and identify with some of its national aspirations. Yet there was a conspicuous residential segregation between the two groups, as indeed there had always been in the past.[14] The most important point of contact was the workplace, and it was collective work and struggle that helped to overcome the divisions between indigenous and immigrant workers. Only this can explain the similarity of behaviour among work-forces in the same industry but of different origin.[15]

It can be argued that the labour movement of Barcelona in the seventies represented the confluence of Catalan traditions of working-class mutualism and organization and the new, rawer militancy of rural immigrant workers. The point is made repeatedly in interviews which formed part of a 1978 survey of immigrants in Catalonia.[16] As a worker from Andalusia said, reminiscing about his first impressions on arriving in Catalonia, 'Here, a man would take the liberty of arguing with the boss, make demands of him. You couldn't do that back there.' And of the traditions of solidarity of Catalan workers, he had this to say, 'Here there's been more of a tradition of unity. A call for support for a lad who's been sacked generates a strength and unity around the campaign to reinstate him. Nothing like that existed back there . . .' On the other hand, in the same survey another immigrant argued, 'The Catalans . . . don't struggle with the same fierceness as the immigrant, because the immigrant is filled with a hatred for the misery he has been through which has crushed him all his life.' Yet factory work was a melting-pot. Referring to industrial conflicts in the seventies, another immigrant stated, 'During shop-floor struggles, nobody is worried any more

[14] Jutglar *et al.*, op. cit.

[15] For example, there was no evident difference between the demands and methods of struggle adopted by the workers of La Maquinista, where there was a balance between immigrant and indigenous workers, and those of the Cispalsa workers next door, the vast majority of whom were immigrants. Interview with Isidor Boix, 18 Feb. 1983.

[16] C. Solé, *Los inmigrantes en la sociedad y en la cultura catalanas* (Barcelona, 1982).

whether you are a Catalan or an immigrant. The important thing is pushing the struggle along and defending the rights of all workers.'[17] Collective action forged a common culture between workers of different backgrounds. It was the nature of work that shaped the style of struggle and not the origin of the workers.

The rise of dissent among immigrants was matched by the growth of militancy among groups of white-collar workers. Economic development transformed class alignments. The extraordinary expansion of the tertiary sector had created a new white-collar proletariat who were led to organize collectively against their employers because their status as members of the middle class was being eroded. In doing so, they began to emulate the demands and methods of militant shop-floor workers.[18]

The best-organized among them were the bank workers. Though they were a relatively privileged group among salaried employees, bank staff in Spain were less well paid on average than their counterparts elsewhere. Yet the profits of Spanish banks were among the highest in Europe. The extravagant new banks of tinted glass and fountains along the Avenida del Generalísimo in Madrid were a token of the central role that finance capital played in the economic growth of Spain. Of the motives for labour protest among bank staff, this unequal distribution of the profits that they had helped to create was an important factor. A survey in 1970 also found considerable dissatisfaction among those whose work was more impersonal and without initiative. It concluded that the causes of dissent among bank workers were fundamentally concerned with monetary questions and very little to do with political or labour issues.[19] The bargaining power of bank staff was reinforced by the relative homogeneity of conditions in the different banks, and by the fact that there was one agreement for all bank workers throughout the country. Moreover, unlike industrial workers, they had the use of a vital means of communication, the telephone. By 1970, militants in Catalonia had created an

[17] Ibid. 131–3, 86, and 143.

[18] For a general discussion of white-collar militancy, see S. Mallet, *The New Working Class* (Nottingham, 1975), and R. Crompton and G. Jones, *White-Collar Proletariat* (London, 1984).

[19] J. F. Tezanos *et al.*, *Las nuevas clases medias* (Madrid, 1973), 182–3 and 207–8.

unofficial committee, called the *Interbancaria*, to co-ordinate agitation over pay and conditions. Their influence was evident in the strikes that took place in 1970 and 1972 in support of a platform of demands similar to that of Comisiones Obreras.[20]

From 1971 onwards, the example of the bank workers began to spread to other sections of white-collar workers, such as office staff in industry, hospital personnel, teachers, telephonists, and journalists. Underfunding had created unbearable strains in the social services and fuelled the growing resentment over low salaries. The new unrest among white-collar workers had a political dimension too. It was part of a broader process of shifting allegiances in which large sections of the middle classes, including the clergy and the professions, had come to identify the dictatorship as an obstacle to social progress. Thus the regime was rapidly losing whatever legitimacy it had once held among those classes that had welcomed the Nationalist troops when they paraded through the streets of Barcelona in February 1939.

While the rise of white-collar militancy created a new constituency for labour agitation, it was among industrial workers that the labour movement drew its main strength. As the decade advanced, its support broadened immeasurably from the base it had won in the sixties among workers of the large engineering and textile factories. Strike action spread like wildfire across the province, from the main urban centres into new towns, and from traditional to modern industries.

The catalyst of labour protest was collective bargaining. It was no coincidence that the year in which the number of strikes shot up, 1969–70, was also a boom period for collective bargaining. By the beginning of the decade over one million workers, that is some 96 per cent of the work-force of the province of Barcelona, were covered by a collective agreement of one sort or another. It is true that the majority of these were bound by provincial or national agreements over which they had no influence whatsoever. Yet collective bargaining was seen as an important means of improving living standards, or defending them against the increasing rate of inflation. In a survey carried out in 1968 by

[20] Interview with Paco Giménez, 4 May 1983; Trabajadores de Banca, *La Lucha de Banca*, leaflet Feb. 1972 (ANC archives). For further details of the bank workers' actions see *Informaciones Obreras*, 1 Feb. 1972, and Carlos Esteban, 'Paco Giménez: lluitar a banca', *Arreu*, 24–30 Jan. 1977.

an institute funded by the OSE, almost three-quarters of workers interviewed believed that it had benefited them more than their employers.[21] Nevertheless, these benefits were monetary ones; for the employers on the contrary, as we saw in Chapter 3, collective bargaining had been a vital means of raising productivity on a plant level, and on a local level of ensuring competitive equality.

What had once been a useful system for the employers, however, became a source of repeated unrest in the seventies. A group of engineering employers from the newly industrialized town of Mollet wrote to the Civil Governor in 1975, requesting that no local bargaining be allowed in their area. 'We are of the opinion that collective agreements on a local level have been a seed-bed of generalized conflict, a clear example of which is the Baix Llobregat area . . . We believe that the best framework is the provincial agreements in which the same results are achieved without the great social trauma of conflict.'[22] The alarm of the regime over the increasingly volatile nature of collective bargaining was reflected in a secret circular from the Ministry of Labour in 1971 to all the provincial headquarters of the OSE.[23] In this remarkable document, the Ministry admitted the growing influence of militants in politicizing industrial disputes. Despairingly, it confessed that 'a labour dispute is always a political problem and a problem of public order even when it seems to have a purely economic nature'. The heads of the local OSE were urged to ban all mass meetings in their headquarters, to suspend all negotiations if any industrial action was staged, and to encourage the press to keep silent about the strikes that were occurring. The circular went on to admit that many employers, under shop-floor pressure, were continuing to evade State wage norms, and it called on OSE officials to put pressure on them not to enter any unofficial pacts with workers. The Ministry, for its part, promised to intensify police harassment of militants and strike pickets.

Clearly, collective bargaining was no longer the effective instrument of social control it had been in the sixties. It was

[21] Instituto de Estudios Sindicales, Sociales y Cooperativas, op. cit.

[22] *Memoria*, 18 Feb. 1975, CG archives no. 1753.

[23] The circular, Ministerio de Trabajo, *Criterios ante una posible situación conflictiva* (Madrid, 6 Dec. 1971), ANC archives, found its way into the hands of the semi-legal opposition and was published in *Ya*, 28 Jan. 1972.

argued in Chapter 3 that it had helped to defuse the political repercussion of labour disputes by creating a channel for the economic demands of the more militant workers. Yet by the early seventies, it was no longer serving as a stable wage mechanism. Official wage norms were being overtaken year after year; in the 1971 round of negotiations, over 28 per cent of agreements went through the ceiling set by the government.[24] The State once again found itself stepping in to impose compulsory awards or *laudos*. The rise in the number of these awards provides a guide to the increasing militancy. By 1974, 42 per cent of workers in the province of Barcelona, mainly those covered by plant and local contracts, were bound by them.[25] After a period in the sixties during which the State had seemed to step back from too overt an intervention in industrial relations, it was now moving in again, using compulsory awards as a means of imposing wage controls, and sending in the riot police when workers protested too loudly. Once more, the modernizing reforms of the regime had served to deepen the contradictions of Spanish society.

The very dynamic of collective bargaining also politicized the demands of workers. It is true that questions of pay continued to dominate shop-floor negotiations throughout the seventies, though more qualitative demands began to spread, as if at last the basic wage was high enough for workers to turn to the problem of their working conditions. However, the key role of the workers' negotiating team in the bargaining process made democratic representation a central question affecting all aspects of shop-floor life. The increasing resort by employers to the dismissal of militants helped to bring the demands for reinstatement and democracy to the fore in the claims of workers.

What is striking about these packages of demands or *plataformas* is their consistency. Against the fragmentation and diversity, the local and the particular that were highlighted in Chapter 4 must be set the similarity of demands which also characterized the new labour movement. This unity was in part the result of a common experience of economic exploitation and State oppression. But it was also inspired by the work of the

---

[24] Ll. Fina, 'Política salarial i lluita de classes sota el franquisme', *Materiales*, no. 7 (1978), pp. 105–30.   [25] Miguélez Lobo (1976).

labour opposition, in particular of Comisiones Obreras. How did the clandestine organizations respond to the new upsurge of militancy? We need to look first at the changing profile of the labour opposition.

COMISIONES OBRERAS AND THE LABOUR OPPOSITION

As we saw in Chapter 3, Comisiones Obreras had suffered a severe setback in 1967 after the court ruling that it was an illegal organization and the police swoop against its leading militants that had followed the ban. The internal crisis had been compounded by the wage freeze of 1968, effectively suspending collective bargaining, the main point of contact between the movement and its rank-and-file supporters. The frenzied polemic about strategy that had ensued among the clandestine organizations neither involved the mass of workers who had voted for Comisiones militants in the 1966 elections, nor indeed touched on their main preoccupations.

The organization that emerged from the crisis was now firmly in the hands of the Communists, its overall strategy guided by the Party.[26] Except for the volatile engineering *coordinadora* (or co-ordinating committee of engineering workers) of Barcelona city, their militants dominated the skeletal apparatus of Comisiones Obreras. The revolutionary Catalan Workers' Front, the FOC, had disintegrated, leaving only fragments of a left-wing opposition to the PSUC. The workerist organization, Unión Sindical Obrera, USO, had dropped out in 1968 on the grounds that the Communists had taken over Comisiones Obreras. With greater sensitivity towards shop-floor problems than most other groups of the Left, USO was now attempting to create its own rank-and-file groups in the few workplaces where it had members.[27]

Even less influential was the old Socialist union, the UGT, which continued to refuse to dirty its hands in the structures of the regime. The UGT's tenth congress in exile, in August 1968,

[26] Secret police evidence is contained in a report entitled *Comisiones Obreras*, Nov. 1971, CG Archives no. 1418.

[27] The Catalan USO's main strength lay among bank workers in Barcelona, and its paper, *Catalunya Obrera*, had appeared in Nov. 1969. For more details of USO in this period see *Avui* Feb. 1976 and USO, *Spagna: sindacato e democrazia* (Rome, 1976), 116–17.

had called for the creation of democratically elected but clandestine committees outside the framework of the OSE, as well as the continued boycott of collective bargaining until these committees had been recognized as the true representatives of the workers. The UGT criticized the policy of Comisiones Obreras for 'recklessly' exposing militants to repression, yet the alternative it offered—small cabals of Socialists who failed to make their presence felt, at least in Catalonia—was scarcely inspiring.[28] The insignificance of the Catalan UGT at the time can be judged by its report to the national bulletin of the Union on the 1970 May Day actions. While large street demonstrations were taking place in Barcelona and its industrial satellites, the Catalan UGT hired a coach for an excursion to the countryside to avoid the 'street disturbances'. On their way back, according to the UGT correspondent, the members sang the Internationale, suitably impressing the coach-driver.[29]

Nor was Communist hegemony in the labour movement under any serious threat from the revolutionary Left, made up in 1970 of a bewildering array of minuscule groups with grand titles. Indeed, within the labour opposition of the early seventies, the PSUC's most active competitor was a product of the University. The *Sindicato Democrático de Estudiantes de la Universidad de Barcelona* (SDEUB), a kind of student equivalent of Comisiones Obreras, had disintegrated in 1968, leaving in its wake a confused mêlée of radical tendencies. The most distinctive voice among them was the Bandera Roja (Red Flag) group, which, by the end of 1970, had a following among students rivalling that of the Communists.

Armed with a centrist and somewhat eclectic ideology, Bandera Roja began to occupy that middle ground between the Communist Party and the Far Left recently vacated by the FOC. Without offering a concrete alternative strategy to the PSUC, the new group criticized the 'reformism' of the Party and the 'sclerosis' of some of its members. By the summer of 1971, Bandera Roja had set up its own rank-and-file workers' organization, the *Coordinadora de Sectores de Comisiones Obreras* (henceforth known as Sectores). As the name suggests, this new group was established as an alternative to the

---

[28] *Boletín de la UGT de España*, Mar. 1970.   [29] Ibid., May 1970.

Communist-dominated movement. Yet it was distinguished only by a different organizational model. To the Communists' view that Comisiones Obreras should be an open movement, co-ordinated by industry, Bandera Roja counterposed its own belief in a more stable and therefore necessarily clandestine form of organization linked by area.[30] Though it failed to become anything more than the rank-and-file group of Bandera Roja, the Comisiones Obreras rival, Sectores, breathed fresh life into sections of the labour movement. Its young militants threw themselves into organizing on the shop-floor and in the neighbourhoods. In Baix Llobregat the new organization succeeded in drawing in dozens of young workers from the local factories. Its dedicated work in this area helped to prepare the ground for the three general strikes which would take place between 1974 and 1976.[31]

Another rank-and-file organization laid claim to the title of Comisiones Obreras, the *Plataformas de Comisiones Obreras*. Set up in 1971, this new organization was promoted by a number of tiny groups that had arisen out of the ashes of the FOC. A rather ill-defined revolutionary workerist tendency, Plataformas spurned participation in collective bargaining and the OSE. Without ever being able to establish a stable base among workers, it managed to attract a fleeting audience of young, mainly immigrant workers, principally in Vallés Oriental.[32] But it was no rival to the expanding Comisiones Obreras under Communist control.

The Communists' domination of Comisiones Obreras placed them in a dilemma. They continued to stress that it was a united and non-party movement of workers, and this was indeed the case at times of mass mobilization.[33] Comisiones Obreras, however, was also an apparatus with printing-presses and a

[30] For more details of Bandera Roja see its papers, *Bandera Roja, Estrella Roja*, and *Prensa Obrera*, and for a critique of its political line see A. Sala and C. Durán (José Antonio Díaz), *Crítica de la izquierda autoritaria en Cataluña 1967–74* (Paris, 1975).

[31] For a picture of the rank-and-file base of Sectores see the independent underground news bulletin *Agencia Popular Informativa (API)* in its edition of 13 Oct. 1972.

[32] See *API*, 28 Oct. 1972, on one of Plataformas's meetings.

[33] See, for example, the speech of José Ruiz (Simón Sánchez Montero) for the Central Committee of the Communist Party in the 8th Congress in 1972, HOAC, op. cit. 117–33.

network of clandestine committees that were run almost entirely by members of the Communist Party. It was they who wrote and printed the bulletins, drew up the programmes, decided on the Days of Action, and met nationally to determine strategy. In the long run, it was difficult for Comisiones Obreras not be seen as the creature of the Communists.

The danger that the labour movement might divide into different tendencies once the dictatorship had been overthrown had been perceived in the earliest definitions of the movement (see Chapter 3). The problem was raised again in a document which was to be discussed in a nation-wide meeting of Comisiones Obreras leaders in a convent in the Pozuelo district of Madrid in June 1972. Prophetically, it warned,

If we do not reach an advanced stage of unity when democracy arrives, if the freedoms we win are purely formal, it is probable that different unions will arise creating a situation like that in some European countries after the Second World War . . . At this moment not all the ideological tendencies are fighting with the same strength or the same methods and the impression may have been created that almost the whole of the working class is right behind the one which is most active. But when democracy has been restored, it will not be like that; the differences that divide labour will surface as distinct union organizations.

To avoid this, the document urged greater efforts to open up the organization to other tendencies, even raising the possibility of changing its name if that were necessary.[34]

In the event, the question was not discussed because the meeting of Comisiones Obreras leaders never took place. The police had been tipped off and, apart from the three delegates from Catalonia who had been held up, the entire general staff of Comisiones Obreras was arrested. Their trial in December 1973 was to be a *cause célèbre*. Meanwhile, the direction of the nation-wide organization passed into the hands of the Catalan leaders, with whom it would remain until 1976. But the proposals of the Pozuelo document remained on ice. It met with the approval of neither the exiled leadership of the Spanish Communist Party nor the full-time organizers of Comisiones Obreras in Catalonia. The latter suspected that it was part of an operation by the PCE

---

[34] *Sobre la unidad del movimiento obrero de masas*, *API*, Feb. 1973. See also Jáuregui and Vega, iii. 77–80

leaders to forge a moderate alliance with Christian Democratic and liberal opponents of the regime, while the PCE leadership feared losing control of Comisiones.[35]

Of course, it was far more important to unite the mass of workers than to bring together the numerically small ranks of the labour opposition, as the Party kept stressing.[36] However, unity on the shop-floor could not be solid unless it was built on the foundations of union work, that is, the everyday, collective defence of conditions of work, the mass meetings to debate action, and so on. The activists of Comisiones Obreras did indeed help to forge this kind of unity among the more militant and organized sections of workers in Catalonia; this was to form the base of the new Union in the coming democracy. But for many workers who came into contact with Comisiones Obreras during the dictatorship, the movement was more of a programme and a set of respected working-class leaders than a union organization.

The problem was partly that the leadership of the Communist Party did not actively encourage the development of a union culture in the factories and offices. In contrast to its coverage of factory disputes in the fifties, the Party press was content to see labour protest through the distorting lens of its political vision. Each mass strike was portrayed as yet another nail in the coffin of the dictator. No special attention was paid to the conditions that gave rise to this protest. If in the press of the Catalan Comisiones Obreras there was evidence of a greater seriousness about union work from the early seventies, the PSUC's and the PCE's strategy continued to be guided by the politics of the General Strike.[37]

Indeed, while individual militants were keenly aware of what was going on in their workplace, their knowledge was not incorporated into the perspectives of the Party. There was little evidence of any rank-and-file impulses flowing to the top of the hierarchy. Communist activists were left to get on with their job of agitation while the Party leadership reserved to itself the task

[35] Jáuregui and Vega, iii. 77–80, and conversation with José Luis López Bulla and Cipriano García, 16 Jan. 1987.

[36] For example, in Sánchez Montero's and Santiago Carrillo's reports to the 8th Congress, pp. 124–6 and 122–3 respectively in HOAC, op. cit.

[37] For examples of the changing approach of the Catalan Comisiones Obreras see the editorial of the second issue of *Lluita Obrera* in June 1972, and the special issue in March 1973.

of defining the correct political strategy according to the circumstances. The relative autonomy of militants was limited to their union work. In an article in 1943, the PCE leader, Santiago Carrillo, then the rising star of the Political Bureau, had called for the decentralization of the Party's organization in view of the clandestine conditions of the anti-Franco struggle. But he had also argued that the Party should remain centralized politically; that is, that the political line should be laid down by the central committee and carried out without question by the members.[38]

In this dichotomy between local autonomy and democratic centralism lay the key to the behaviour of working-class activists of the PSUC. The political discourse of the Party, concerned as it was with the grand strategy of the organization, did not generally relate to the everyday work of militants. They were less likely, then, to challenge the Party line, because it left them free to develop their own practices over matters they knew about intimately. The critical voices in the PCE and PSUC were invariably students and intellectuals who were more concerned with theory. But this decentralization of the work of shop-floor militants discouraged any debate about union strategy. The problem was magnified by the secretive conditions in which they had to operate.

The response of individual militants of the Party to labour problems thus varied widely. At one pole was the close involvement in the minutiae of union life that characterized the Baix Llobregat leaders. In Sabadell, on the other hand, the Communist leaders of Comisiones Obreras tended to refer most matters relating to shop-floor problems, such as shifts, bonuses, and the interpretation of collective agreements, to left-wing labour lawyers. Those militants who held important posts in the local OSE used the place as a centre of agitation, dealing little with the more mundane problems affecting broad layers of workers in the town. Again, while the militants of the Baix Llobregat Comisiones took union training seriously, helping to run local evening classes under Catholic auspices, the Sabadell equivalent was concerned more to recruit Party members than train shop stewards.[39]

---

[38] 'Características del trabajo de los comunistas españoles en el período actual', *Nuestra Bandera*, Apr. 1943.

[39] Fernández interview. The Baix Llobregat training-school was established in

In any case, the political tasks that the Party assigned to Comisiones Obreras could not fail to dilute its shop-floor work. As part of the broad anti-Franco alliance that the Communists hoped to build, the Catalan Comisiones Obreras played an important role in setting up the popular movement for national rights in Catalonia, the *Assemblea de Catalunya*, in November 1971. The Assemblea was the climax of a process of convergence between opposition forces in Catalonia that had begun in the mid sixties. Unlike previous political alliances, it brought together not just the clandestine parties but representatives of social movements such as the residents' associations, cultural groups, and the nationalist and organized labour movements. The programme adopted at its first secret meeting reflected the breadth of its social base, calling for an amnesty for political prisoners and exiles, for democratic freedoms, including the right to strike, and for the restoration of Catalan autonomy.[40] It was the first time since the Civil War that a united front of the opposition had been created with some roots in society. The support for Catalan rights by Comisiones Obreras strengthened the contacts between the labour movement and the middle class. It forestalled the divisive growth of a Catalan labour union along the lines of the nationalist union ELA-STV in the Basque Country. Yet to some extent it diverted Comisiones militants from industrial agitation.

Working-class activists of the PSUC, then, had two different functions, that of the shop-floor organizer dealing with everyday union questions, and the political leader arguing the broad strategy of the Party. The two causes did not always concur. Moreover, for all the strictures about the independence of Comisiones, the almost complete hegemony of the Communists often led to a blurring of distinctions between the Party and the movement. Militants frequently doubled as union organizers and Party officials. The PSUC's labour organizer was also one of the two co-ordinators of the nation-wide organization of Comisiones. Another Communist was full-time organizer in the

---

1967 and set up branches in the various towns of the area. It functioned until 1975, when it was closed down by order of the government: interview with Juan García-Nieto, 15 Mar. 1983. See also *Escola Sindical 1 de Maig* (Baix Llobregat CCOO archives).

[40] J. M. Colomer, *Assemblea de Catalunya* (Barcelona, 1976).

engineering industry of Barcelona for both the Party and the movement. Meetings of Comisiones and the Party were often attended by the same people, making a distinction between the two merely formal. One of the dyers' and bleachers' leaders recalls 'this dual representation . . . Who is talking, the union leader or the Party leader? Because in those days, these things were quite mixed up.'[41] In conditions of illegality, such an overlap may have been expedient or at times unavoidable, but it did not help to establish Comisiones Obreras as an independent union movement.

How then did militants of the labour opposition set out to capitalize on the new wave of labour protest at the beginning of the seventies? It should be noted that the strikes were led largely by shop stewards elected in the 1966 union ballot, many of whom had backed the programme of Comisiones even though they may not have taken an active part in the organization. If the movement had faltered between 1968 and 1969 under the onslaught of arrests and sackings, it was clear from the rapid adoption of its model programme of demands in the early seventies that Comisiones Obreras had not lost the support of the workers who had rallied to its banner in 1966.

The renewal of collective bargaining on a massive scale in 1969, after a year of virtual suspension, gave militants the opportunity to reconnect with this base and to spread their demands to new layers of workers who were striking for the first time. Outside the heightened moments of strike action, it was agitation over plant and local agreements that enabled militants to engage in debate with workers. The first stage of a campaign to negotiate a good agreement was the creation of a *plataforma*. In the well-organized factories, this list of demands was drawn up on the basis of a questionnaire that went round all the workers. It was followed by a series of meetings in different shops, culminating in assemblies of the whole work-force during which its contents were discussed and approved. It says a lot for the growing strength of shop-floor organization in many of the larger plants that these meetings could take place at all. Not many years previously, militants had been forced to hold small, furtive meetings in the toilets, or impromptu assemblies in the factory yard at lunch break or by the gates at the end of a shift.

41 Interview with Agustí Prats, 18 Mar. 1983.

What is surprising about these *plataformas* is their uniformity. Despite the disparities among workplaces and industries, the demands that were taken up by workers in their thousands were almost exactly the same. A sample of 26 *plataformas* in the engineering, textile, chemical, and construction industries, in 1974, for example, shows that the only differences in the claims concerned the amount of the pay rise, and the inclusion of an item or two specific to a factory or industry. At the top of the list usually came the demand for a wage rise. It was followed by claims for a reduction of basic working hours to 40 hours a week spread over 5 days (instead of the 44 to 48 hours which were common at the time), a month's holiday (as opposed to the three-week period normally conceded), and full pay during illness and on retirement. Other demands called for Social Security payments and the State tax on each worker on the payroll to be paid entirely by the company; for one-year rather than two-year agreements; for the right to strike and hold mass meetings; for trade-union rights, amnesty for political prisoners and exiles, and the reinstatement of sacked militants. The most striking feature of these claims was their mix of grievances over pay and working hours with highly charged political demands that could hardly be conceded within the context of the Francoist system. The point is that the platforms served a political as well as agitational purpose. While it was usually the case that the more political demands were tagged on the end of the *plataforma*, by 1974 the demand for democratic representation and reinstatement had become paramount in many struggles, because workers learnt by experience the vital connection between the defence of living standards and the defence of their leaders.

Nevertheless, the *plataformas* had only a partial bearing on the agreements that were finally drawn up. If the most important items on the shopping-list of grievances were pay and hours, many other questions not raised in the campaigns, such as bonuses, productivity measures, work-grading, and the like, were negotiated by militants on the works council. Indeed, the final contracts bore little resemblance to the contents of the *plataformas*. Even though militants were likely to be involved in these matters individually in their role as shop-floor delegates, labour agitation did not always reach deep into the peculiar conditions of each workplace.

There is little evidence, for example, of any serious campaign about equal pay for men and women. Excluding the building trade, women workers made up about a quarter of the industrial work-force of Barcelona. In the factory towns surrounding the metropolis, a high proportion of single women were employed; almost 80 per cent in Cornellá, and 77 per cent in Mataró.[42] Trades filled almost exclusively by women, such as lace-making and knitwear, were traditionally less well paid than those dominated by men. But even in industries, such as wool-weaving and engineering, where women worked alongside men, they were discriminated against in their wages. The different levels of pay between men and women were disguised on the payroll; an unskilled woman, for example, would be classified as a cleaning labourer (*peón de limpieza*) while her male counterpart would appear as a specialized labourer (*peón especializado*), earning up to three times as much as her.

The demand for equal pay for equal work was one that figured prominently in the *plataformas*, yet there is little mention in the clandestine labour press of the particular problems of women workers. Indeed, the organized labour movement was almost exclusively the preserve of men.[43] This was not because women workers were consistently less militant than male workers. It was true that many were employed in sweat-shops where they could not organize, and many were part-time workers whose major concern was child-rearing. But women workers played an important part in agitation in the engineering firms of Barcelona.[44] In the early seventies, several factory disputes were led by women, in particular in the newly-industrialized area of Vallés Oriental. Nevertheless, there seem to have been few attempts by the labour opposition to campaign over the specific problems of pay and conditions of work which they faced. This relative lack of concern to agitate among what was an important section of the working class was not unconnected with the rural context from which many workers proceeded, where women's role was especially subordinate. The male culture of the organized labour movement was thereby reinforced.

[42] S. García, 'El movimiento obrero, de nuevo', in Nous Horitzons, *Nuestra utopía* (Barcelona, 1986), 61; for the second set of figures, Martín Moreno and De Miguel, p. 98.

[43] See *API*, 13 and 28 Oct. 1972, for a comment on the composition of rank-and-file organizations of the labour opposition.

[44] S. García (1986), 61–2.

Another vital problem connected with conditions on the shop-floor was the question of health and safety. Yet it was not one that the labour movement seems to have taken seriously until the mid seventies. Spain had the highest rate of accidents at work in Europe. By the early seventies there were 20 times as many injuries in Spanish workplaces as in the United States. The annual average of mortal accidents rose from 640 in 1960 to 2,418 in 1974. One in five workers suffered an accident every year; in Barcelona and province in 1969 there were on average 16 accidents at work every hour.[45] Low pay, the absence of union protection, and the employers' push for productivity had all combined to worsen conditions at work. The greater risks to body and limb from speed-up, toxic fumes, noise, and new machinery had been exchanged for higher pay. Yet there had been no campaign around this issue by the labour movement. It was only in the seventies that the first struggles over health and safety took place, and these were mainly in the building industry, where conditions were dramatically bad.

Matters such as health and safety, however, were not ignored in labour agitation merely because they were less likely to raise the political consciousness of the workers. The *plataformas* were also intended to unite different sections of the working class across the barriers of skill and trade. Indeed, the disparity in conditions of work and degree of shop-floor organization from one industry to another was so great that only a generic programme of demands could knit together the different agitations. In Chapter 4, the labour movement of the four main industrial centres was contrasted. The following pages will examine the differences that separated the organized workers of the three main industries of the area. Into this analysis will be woven the major events that marked the history of the labour movement between 1970 and 1973.

---

[45] A. Figueruelo, *Cataluña: crónica de una frustración* (Madrid, 1970), 318–21; F. Miguélez Lobo, *El sindicato obrero ante la organización capitalista del trabajo* (Barcelona, 1978), 19; Jordi Estivill *et al.* (1973), 130–3. See also Sartorius and Díaz Cardiel, 22; J. Montesinos *et al.*, *Anuario de relaciones laborales* (Madrid, 1975), 75–9; *Plan nacional de higiene y seguridad del trabajo* (Madrid, 1972); also a report by SEAT workers to the Ministry of Labour in 1972 in CG archives no. 1461.

VARIETIES OF LABOUR AGITATION

The Textile Workers

Of the three industries, textiles were the most diversified. The industry spanned a range of different trades and factories, from sewing-machinists in the metropolis to skilled wool-weavers in Terrassa, from old cotton-mills on the river banks in the interior to brand-new synthetic-fibre plants in the hinterland of Barcelona. The heart of labour militancy in the industry was the larger wool factories of Sabadell and Terrassa, and the dyeing and bleaching factories in the same towns and in north-east Barcelona. Outside these centres of militancy, it was difficult for the mass of textile workers to be mobilized. Indeed, until the advent of democracy, the majority of them would have no contact with the organized labour movement. In many workplaces shop-floor organization was virtually impossible. The rag trade, for example, was made up of hundreds of small workshops dotted about Barcelona in which young women worked up to 70 hours a week sewing labels, buttons, or pieces of cloth.[46] The cotton industry was scattered about inland Catalonia and many of the cotton-spinners lived in 'colonies', blocks of flats by the side of the mill rented out to them under a tied-cottage contract. Neither of these groups of workers, nor many others in the countless trades that made up the industry, could be expected to challenge their bosses.

The textile work-force, moreover, was on average older than that of other industries and employed mainly female labour. The strong traditions of paternalism that persisted in the textile industry were noted in Chapter 4. If the crisis that had hit the sector in the mid sixties loosened these ties of loyalty, it also dampened militancy by increasing fears of unemployment among workers, especially women, who had nowhere else to sell their labour. While textile workers still made up over a quarter of the total labour force of Catalonia in the early sixties, this proportion had dropped to less than a seventh by the mid seventies.[47] As early as 1965, in the midst of the 'economic

---

[46] Interview with María Dolores Rojas, 28 November 1985.

[47] Banca Catalana, *Catalunya: industria i demografia* (Barcelona, 1986); Centre d'Estudís de Planificació (1982).

miracle', the secret police were sounding a note of warning about the growth of unemployment caused by restructuring in the textile industry.[48]

The gulf that separated the militant sections and the unorganized mass of workers in the textile industry would not be bridged until the post-Franco period. But the foundations were laid by the campaign of Comisiones union delegates in the early seventies to unite all the branches of the industry into one bargaining unit. Such a demand of course put at risk the higher pay and better conditions of the more militant groups in favour of the unorganized workers. It was remarkable that these militants were able to win support for the campaign among the best-paid workers in the industry. Indeed, the strength of their leadership in the most militant branch of the textile trade—the dyers and bleachers—needs some explanation.

The *Ramo del Agua* or Water Branch, as it was known, had always been one of the best-organized sections of workers in Catalonia. Some of the outstanding Anarchist leaders of the thirties, such as García Oliver and El Negre, had been shop-floor leaders in the industry. The strongest base of the CNT had been the Poble Nou district, where the majority of the dyeing and bleaching factories of Barcelona were located. It was from a flat in this district that the FAI leaders Buenaventura Durruti and the Ascaso brothers, all dyers in local firms, had set out on 18 July 1936 with their followers to crush the military uprising in Barcelona.[49] In the first two decades of the dictatorship, the *Ramo del Agua* had been a centre of labour and political agitation. But following the Day of Action for National Reconciliation in 1958, a wave of detentions—no less than 90 shop stewards were arrested by the police—had effectively destroyed the leadership of the labour movement in the industry.[50] In the mid sixties, a small group of Communists from factories in Poble Nou had begun to organize among militant union representatives, who were among the delegates to the regular meetings called by the bureaucracy. They met unofficially every Monday in the

[48] JSPB reports, 8 Jan. and 7 Sept. 1965, CG archives no. 1249.

[49] Fabre and Huertas Clavería, i. 87.

[50] Xavier Vinader and Carlos Esteban, 'Ram de l'aigua: una llarga agonia'. *Arreu*, 25–31 Oct. 1976. For another analysis of the labour movement in the industry see Cuadernos Rojos, 'Informe sobre el Textil', *Cuadernos Rojos*, Feb. and June 1973.

corridors of the huge edifice of the OSE in Barcelona, to the evident discomfort of OSE officials, who often felt obliged to call in the police to disperse the crowd. Of the growing numbers of union delegates who were turning up for the informal gatherings, the most active had helped to create the dyers' and bleachers' branch of Comisiones Obreras in 1965.[51]

The militancy of the dyers and bleachers of Barcelona stemmed in part from the defence of their special status within the textile industry. Unlike the vast majority of other trades in textiles, they were a predominantly male and relatively old work-force; only 2 per cent of their total were women. Although they were not among the highest wage-earners in Catalonia, they were the best-paid in the textile industry. A skilled dyer, for example, earned almost three times as much as a skilled wool-weaver. The long tradition of union organization in the trade rested on main-taining this relatively privileged position.[52] Their organizational strength, moreover, was increased by the centralized structure of collective bargaining in the industry and by the geographical concentration of the main dyeing and bleaching factories in a small area.[53]

The new union leadership of Comisiones militants was the catalyst in the renewal of the old militancy. Such was their prestige among the dyers and bleachers by the early seventies that the sectionalist tendencies so encouraged by the ex-CNT officials were giving way to a new concern to unite textile workers of all trades in order to halt the decline of jobs in the industry as a whole. Yet the dyers' and bleachers' more favourable terms of work were sacrificed, as the Comisiones Obreras union would recognize later, to the needs of the less organized textile workers.[54] In any case, the privileged status of the dyers and bleachers was being rapidly eroded by the crisis of

[51] Prats interview.

[52] OSE officials complained in the 1966 round of bargaining that the employers were violating the traditional wage differentials by offering the same rise to both wool workers and dyers and bleachers. For this and the figures above see OSE, *Informe sobre la situación general en el Ramo de Agua*, Mar, 1966, CG archives no. 1243.

[53] Until 1972, the provincial agreement of the *Ramo del Agua* affected only the Barcelona factories. In that year, a new agreement was signed drawing in workers from Sabadell, Terrassa, and Mataró: Escudé interview.

[54] See Federación del Textil de CCOO, *2 Congreso: ponencias, conclusiones y resoluciones* (May 1981), 17.

the *Ramo del Agua*, which had begun to gather in the sixties. Between 1965 and 1975 over 50 firms in Barcelona collapsed, with the loss of 7,000 jobs out of fewer than 25,000.[55] By the late seventies, the industry had been devastated. The old centres of labour agitation were now ghost factories, their gaunt ruins serving as the only reminder of what had once been a flourishing industry.

The engineering workers[56]

The problem of unity was even greater among the engineering workers of Barcelona and the industrial belt. Although the sector embraced a wide range of products, from pins to pig-iron, the majority of workers were employed in the production of metal goods, electrical and electronic components, and vehicles and accessories. The industry, however, was highly fragmented; in 1976, over half of registered firms employed less than five workers, and over 95 per cent less than 50. As in the case of the textile industry, the majority of these workshops and small plants would remain unorganized until the post-Franco period. The militant work-forces were concentrated in the larger firms, of which the most important was SEAT, employing in the early seventies some 28,000 workers. We have seen how the atomized structure of collective bargaining in the industry turned each well-organized plant into an 'island' of militancy with only tenuous contact with other work-forces. Out of about 327,000 metallurgical workers in the province, fewer than a third were covered by plant agreements, while the number of workers governed by local agreements, such as those in Sabadell, was even smaller. Agitation over collective bargaining, which, as has been stressed throughout, was the catalyst of labour protest, was therefore confined in practice to less than half of the total work-force of the province.[57] Furthermore, each unit of bargaining had

---

[55] Vinader and Esteban, op. cit.

[56] Many of the points made in this section were also true of the well-organized chemical factories in the province, and so a separate treatment of the labour movement in that industry has not been considered necessary.

[57] The above figures are taken from CONC, 'Informe sobre el sector del metal', unpublished study (1978); and Servei d'Estudis del la Banca Más Sarda, 'Les industries metal·liques a Catalunya', *Mon Laboral*, 2nd semester 1986, pp. 51–61.

its own rhythm of negotiation and agitation that rarely coincided with another.

Militants of Comisiones Obreras had made sporadic attempts to link the struggles over plant agreements with agitation over the provincial contract. Part of the problem they faced was that the negotiating apparatus for this agreement, and indeed the whole of the provincial engineering union, was in the hands of an ex-CNT 'mafia' who kept themselves in power through their control over hundreds of small engineering plants throughout the province (see Chapter 3). It was only in 1974 that the first concerted effort was made to organize opposition against them among the shop stewards of the smaller plants covered by the agreement; and only in 1976 that the first strikes took place in this sector of the industry. Militants of the big plants, in any case, were too involved in organizing in their own factories to be concerned with the wider sections of the industry. Nor, with the exception of Baix Llobregat, were they able to persuade their rank and file to support an agreement that brought no tangible benefits.

There was also a tendency within the labour opposition to rely on the most militant work-forces to be the spearhead of the movement, creating a breach through which the less well-organized could pass. Commenting on the strike in the electrical appliances firm AEG in Terrassa in early 1970, *Treball*, after calling the AEG workers 'the spearhead of working-class action in Catalonia', wrote, 'Once more, life has demonstrated that . . . by being responsive and organizationally agile, the workers' struggle in one factory can rapidly spread to others, encouraging new layers of the population to join decisively in the movement of solidarity.'[58] Yet the AEG strike ended in disaster, with a toll of 72 dismissals, including the whole of the shop stewards' committee, 10 jail sentences, and a demoralized and divided work-force, who ceased thereafter to be the model of militancy so singled out by the Communist press throughout the sixties. The history of this violent struggle suggests, on the contrary, that the main problem was the isolation of the strikers from the rest of the workers of Terrassa. For the principal reason for the defeat of the AEG strike was, despite *Treball*'s words, that it did not

[58] *Treball*, Mar. 1970.

spread. There were several stoppages in local firms in support of the AEG workers and over $1\frac{1}{2}$ million pesetas (about £9,000) were collected. But the struggle did not connect with the vital interests of metallurgical workers elsewhere in the town, because they had already negotiated their own local agreement. AEG workers, in contrast, had their own plant contract which, because of their greater shop-floor organization, contained levels of pay and working conditions far superior to the latter. Thus the strength of the labour movement in the engineering industry could also turn out to be, at times of heightened repression, its Achilles' heel.[59]

The surge of militancy in the early seventies among the well-organized engineering plants can best be illustrated by the factory occupation of the state-owned car firm SEAT on 18 October 1971. The incidents were doubly significant: not only was SEAT the largest plant in the country, with over 28,000 workers, but it was also the much-publicized model of the regime's industrial relations. Set up in 1949, with the major interest owned by the State-holding company INI but with technology imported from FIAT, the company was organized on military lines; indeed, for many years the managing directors were generals. In 1957, accompanied by a blaze of publicity from the governement, the SEAT 600 car was launched. It rapidly became the symbol of the economic 'miracle' in Spain as the more affluent workers began to be able to afford the down payments necessary to acquire one.

The original SEAT work-force had been recruited largely among immigrants from the South. In a concern to avoid taking on any militants, it was often the foremen who did the recruiting in their own towns or villages.[60] Unlike other large engineering work-forces in Barcelona, the SEAT workers had little tradition of shop-floor organization. The incidents that took place in October 1971 were therefore all the more surprising. Three explanations may be offered for the factory occupation. Firstly, it was the expression of that new confidence among immigrants that was discussed at the beginning of the chapter. The deep

[59] Interview with Josep Arán Trullas, 15 May 1983; Instituto de Estudios Laborales (IEL), 'Boletín Informativo', no. 10 (1971); *La Vanguardia*, 4, 5, 7 and 26 Mar. 1970; *Nuestra Clase*, July 1970; Ricart Oller, op. cit.; and JSPB reports, 26 and 31 Mar., 7 and 25 Apr. 1970, CG archives no. 1418.

[60] Interview with Silvestre Gilaberte, 19 Feb. 1983.

sense of injustice among these workers was exacerbated in SEAT by the appalling conditions of work and the repressive, military style of management. The sheer number of workers concentrated in one plant also created the potential for strong factory organization, despite the apparatus of control, with its network of secret police and informers, that had been set up by the management. Finally, the source of the new co-ordinated action of SEAT workers was the leadership of Comisiones militants, who were among the 6,000 workers the company had recently taken on as part of a process of expansion.

The occupation was the climax of a campaign led by Comisiones Obreras to secure the reinstatement of several dozen SEAT militants sacked in an earlier dispute over compulsory overtime. The dismissed workers had taken their case to the Labour Tribunal, which had found in favour of all but one. SEAT, however, fell back on the notorious Clause 103 of the Labour Laws, enabling firms to compensate rather than reinstate workers whose dismissal had been ruled unlawful. In the run-up to negotiations over the 1972 company agreement, SEAT workers had adopted the reinstatement of their sacked colleagues as the main plank of their list of demands. This was the beginning of a long struggle that would end only in 1977 with the triumphant return of those militants victimized by the company throughout a decade.

On 18 October, some of the sacked militants were smuggled into the factory behind a diversionary picket at the gates.[61] Impromptu meetings were held in different plants and the stoppage began to spread. The underground paper of the SEAT Comisión takes up the narrative:

It is not easy at first to get workers to leave the machines and go to the other plants. After a lot of discussion and not without hesitation, over half of Plant One come out; the others will follow later. They enter Plant Two, the workers gather round, then Plant Three, from there to Four, and then on to Seven. Already, several thousand workers have joined the march . . . Soon most of the office staff have joined in; it has been difficult, there have been moments of tension and hostility between

---

[61] The following account is based on: Gilaberte and Zamora, 246–65; *Asamblea Obrera*, 20 Oct. 1971; *Tele-Exprés*, 30 Oct. 1971; *Informaciones Obreras*, 10 Nov. 1971; Gilaberte interview, and JSPB reports in CG archives nos. 1461 and 1962.

white- and blue-collar workers but finally the former join the march and are received with applause.[62]

By now, some 8,000 workers had joined the stoppage. The march left the production plants and moved across the huge factory yard towards the management block. There it was halted by massed ranks of riot police called in hastily by SEAT. A police helicopter flew overhead. The strikers then held a meeting in the open air. *Asamblea Obrera* continues: 'It was difficult at first. Then some powerful speeches were made explaining very clearly the aims and methods of our struggle. The most striking thing was how quiet everyone was as they made an effort to understand what each speaker was saying.' The *plataforma* of demands, at the head of which stood the reinstatement of the victimized workers, was read out and voted in, and a delegation elected to take it to the management. SEAT refused to negotiate. Mounted police were deployed near the mass meeting and the strikers retreated to Plant One. Over the police radio came an order from the Civil Governor to clear the factory.

The assault began late that afternoon. The riot police entered Plant One firing CS gas. Behind them, mounted police forced their way in, and charged their horses down the aisle between the machines. They were met with a hail of tools and pieces of metal as the workers seized anything to hand. Soon the smoke was so dense the strikers were forced to run out of the building towards the next plant. In the open space between the two plants, the police launched a cavalry charge at the fleeing workers. A volley of shots from the armed police rang out. One of the workers, a young Jehovah's Witness called Antonio Ruiz Villalba, was shot in the stomach, another received a bullet through his cheek, and a third had his scalp torn off. The battle continued in Plant Four. Gradually the workers were split into groups. Some were able to make their way out of the factory, including all the sacked militants. Others were arrested and beaten up on the spot. Only after 13 hours were the police able to regain control of the plant.

Over the next few days, Barcelona witnessed large-scale demonstrations in support of the SEAT workers. On the 29th, several thousand workers answered the call of the Catalan

---

[62] *Asamblea Obrera*, 20 Oct. 1971.

Comisiones Obreras and downed tools for a short while in protest at the violence. On 1 November, Antonio Ruiz died in hospital, twelve days after he had been shot. The next day the SEAT workers returned to work after the management lifted the lock-out it had imposed immediately following the occupation. However, agitation in the factory continued in support of reinstatement and the programme of demands; a new strike broke out and once again the police were called in, arresting 74 workers. Finally, the government intervened to impose an arbitrary award.

The management of SEAT, and the government itself, had suffered a double blow. Not only had they failed to keep order in the plant without the support of the police, but for the first time they had been unable to secure a collective agreement in the most important State-owned business in the country. The dispute had cost at least 2,000 million pesetas and the company was embroiled in numerous court cases over dismissal. The internal repercussions were swift. The headquarters of SEAT were transferred from Madrid to Barcelona and a new civilian Managing Director was appointed—the first non-military head in the company's history. From Franco's paragon of productive order, SEAT was transformed into a model of militancy for the opposition. The Communist press hailed the occupation as a decisive step towards the General Strike. In triumphant language, the clandestine papers suggested that workers were moving towards direct confrontation with the dictatorship.[63]

It was true that the October struggle in SEAT radicalized somewhat the climate of public opinion. It also provided a model of struggle for many militants outside the plant. But there was no organic link, as there had been none in the case of the AEG dispute, with the immediate interests of workers elsewhere. Some of the reasons for these divisions have already been suggested: bargaining in the industry was fragmented, the big factories were cut off from one another, and their work-forces were used to going it alone. It was not possible to postpone a

---

[63] See, for example, *Treball*, Nov. 1971 (supplement), and I. Bruguera (Isidor Boix, the then full-time organizer of the PSUC and Comisiones Obreras for the engineering industry in Barcelona), *En el camino de la huelga general política* (1971) (ANC archives); also the concluding paragraph of *Asamblea Obrera*, 20 Oct. 1971.

dispute in order to make it coincide with others. Moreover, Comisiones Obreras in Barcelona was unable to co-ordinate the actions even of its factory committees. Rent by divisions between the Communists and various revolutionary Left groups, the engineering workers' committee had virtually ceased to function. The disagreement only served to reinforce the sectionalism among the work-forces in the industry. Indeed, the well-organized engineering plants of Barcelona, such as SEAT, were like fortresses within which discrete forms of struggle and organization developed but did not spread beyond their gates. Unlike the dyers and bleachers, their work-forces were not united by a common process of bargaining nor were their leaders able or even concerned to co-ordinate their actions. On the other hand, events such as the factory occupation of SEAT showed that the militant workers of the engineering industry in Barcelona had taken on board demands that could not easily be accommodated within the authoritarian framework of Francoism.

The building workers

The rise of militancy at the turn of the decade was most dramatically illustrated in the case of the building workers. Before 1970, fewer than 20 disputes a year were officially recorded for the whole industry. In 1970 alone, in contrast, there were as many as 487 conflicts. Thereafter until the return of democracy the construction industry was second only to engineering in degree of industrial unrest.[64] Yet the conditions that gave rise to labour protest among building workers and the forms of organization that they adopted were very different from those of other industrial workers.

From the early sixties the construction industry in Spain and in Catalonia in particular had experienced an extraordinary boom. Whole tourist villages and hotel complexes mushroomed along the coast to the north and south of Barcelona. In the city, great new office-blocks sprang up, and on the outskirts and in the surrounding towns vast tenement buildings arose to accommodate the influx of immigrants. The decision by the urban authorities to switch from the railways to road transport

---

[64] Ministerio de Trabajo, *Informes,* 1970–6.

changed the landscape of the towns and the countryside, as new motorways cut through old residential areas and weaved their way into the interior.

Most of this urban expansion was entrusted to private capital, though private and public concerns were closely interlocked. Without union protection and in the absence of any form of State control, building workers were especially vulnerable to the dictates of the speculative interests that ran the construction industry. Numerous 'cowboy' employers set up in the business, taking on transient gangs of workmen without paying any social insurance. Knowing only the harsh conditions of labour in the countryside, the immigrants who built the new roads, offices, and estates were unlikely to challenge the organization of work on the sites. Their immediate need was to accumulate enough money to afford a decent place for their families to live in, and a level of education for their children such as they had not enjoyed. Their deference at work was reinforced by the precarious nature of the job. Many building workers were hired on a casual basis. Before 1973, they were liable to be dismissed at any time during a period of 120 days with only a week's notice and without any compensation whatsoever.[65] Nor were they entitled, as casual labourers, to any compensation for injuries sustained on the job.

Furthermore, since almost 50 per cent of building workers were unskilled, they were especially vulnerable to the pressure of new waves of immigrants seeking work of any kind. The building industry was the first and only work that many a newly-arrived immigrant could obtain. But it was also a bridge to other more valued jobs such as labouring in the engineering factories, where there were proper work contracts and where it was possible to acquire a skill. Indeed, construction provided a kind of primitive training for the benefit of industry as a whole through which immigrants from the countryside learnt the rhythms of industrial work.

There were additional obstacles to the collective defence of conditions of work on the building-sites. The job was by nature

---

[65] In 1973, the period was reduced to 15 days under pressure of the new militancy among building workers. Equipo de Análisis Laborales, *Los trabajadores de la construcción frente a la crisis* (Barcelona, 1977), 39–40. For a view of the attitude of the legal press to the problem of the 'lump', see *Tele-Exprés*, 24 July 1971.

temporary, unless it was on one of the massive sites on which building workers were employed for several years, such as that of the new University near Sabadell. Most of the sites were too small, and the jobs too dispersed, to allow much organization. There could be several subcontractors on one site employing teams of labourers under different contracts. As for the work regulations and the provincial agreement that bound the industry in the area as a whole, they were not easily enforceable when there were not enough factory inspectors. Nor did the construction union, which also covered the glass and ceramics industry, provide much opportunity for militants to agitate for better conditions. Only building workers on fixed contracts were allowed to stand as union representatives, and in any case the high rate of turnover in the industry impeded the development of a stable delegate organization.[66] Apart from the 'lump', there were two kinds of contracts under which building workers could be employed: the site contract (*fijo de obra*), that lasted as long as the particular worker was required on the building project, and the company contract (*fijo de plantilla*), under which the worker was employed on a regular basis. Of the non-casual workers, the former covered the overwhelming majority.

The result was that the conditions of work on the building-sites were appalling. Pay was based on piece-work so that workers were encouraged to cut corners, thereby putting themselves at greater risk. Many immigrants were unfamiliar with the machinery and materials that they were expected to handle. They had brought with them from the countryside no standards of safety at work. Nor were the numerous contractors and subcontractors bothered about ensuring that there were adequate facilities as well as health and safety measures on the works. On the huge site of the new University, for example, the employers had provided no canteen, toilets, washing facilities, or changing-rooms.[67] It is not surprising then that the rate of accidents in the construction industry was higher than in any other sector. In 1973, 25 per cent of all accidents at work in Spain occurred on the building-sites; one building worker was either crippled or killed every day.[68] In the absence of union

[66] Interview with Juan Ignacio Valdivieso, 11 Nov. 1985.
[67] Equipo de Análisis Laborales, op. cit. 99.
[68] A. González Alonso, 'Situación del sector de la construcción', *Cuadernos para el Diálogo*, Sept. 1974.

organization on the sites, building workers had had little option but to use the Labour Tribunals individually to attempt to settle their grievances. Their case highlights the important role which labour legislation played in the lives of workers during the dictatorship. Of the 11,518 whose cases had been brought before the Tribunals by the OSE lawyers in 1969, almost 4,000 were building workers.[69]

In 1970 the first large-scale collective protest in the building industry swept through the country. The actions began in Seville in June. A demonstration of building workers in Granada in July was fired on by the riot police and three workers were shot dead. The strikes spread to Madrid and Barcelona. In November, 50,000 building workers in the province of Barcelona downed tools for a day in support of their platform of demands for the provincial agreement.[70] The unrest in the industry continued in the following year. Another building worker was shot dead by police in Madrid during a demonstration over the local agreement. Fierce struggles broke out on several sites in Barcelona, and also on that of the half-completed University near Sabadell. Sabadell itself witnessed a widespread strike over the provincial agreement. All these actions were put down ruthlessly. In addition to the brutality exercised by the police, the building contractors responded with mass dismissals, especially of casual labourers without the protection of the law. Against such repression, and against all the odds, the sudden outburst of anger and self-confidence among building workers needs some explanation.

It was, on one hand, the clearest expression of that shift among many immigrant workers from deference to militancy which has already been noted. Of course, this transformation of attitudes did not happen overnight, nor did it take place in a vacuum. It was no coincidence that the strikes were centred in cities where the labour movement was strongest. The example set by militant engineering workers during the 1969 round of collective

---

[69] OS, *Memoria de actividad sindical* (Barcelona, 1969). A. González Alonso calculates that the OSE dealt with some 20,000 cases brought to them by building workers in a short period of five years between 1964 and 1968: *La construcción* (Madrid, 1977), 29.

[70] The demand for amnesty for the five members of ETA on trial for their life in Burgos was also one of the demands of the strike; see later in this chapter for a discussion of this issue.

bargaining was not lost on many building workers. The sudden rise in the cost of living in 1970—the general index of prices rose by almost 6 per cent in contrast to the 3 per cent rise in the previous year—gave an added urgency to the negotiations over the 1970 agreement covering building workers, who were among the lowest-paid in the country. Lastly, a new leadership had emerged on the larger sites in the province built around experienced industrial militants, many of them Communists, who had been sacked from their factory jobs, Unable to find work in the engineering or chemical plants because of the blacklist operated by employers, they had gone into the building trade, where the business of hiring labour was less controlled.

Their influence can be seen in the agitation over the provincial construction agreement of 1972. Despite the difficulty of penetrating the delegate structure of the building workers' union, some militants were able to get themselves elected as union representatives in the partial union elections of 1971. At a meeting of 1,000 delegates in the OSE headquarters on 3 November, a militant package of demands put forward by activists of Comisiones Obreras was voted in unanimously. The provincial head of the Union was dismayed. He is supposed to have said at the meeting that 'in all the nineteen years during which he had been president, everything had always been very quiet, without any problems in the meetings. But recently, the assembly [of union delegates] and its leaders had turned against him.' His only response was to order that such meetings should take place from then on only twice a year.[71]

The rash of disputes that took place in the industry from 1970 was marked by the emergence of new methods of struggle peculiarly suited to the building trade. It has already been mentioned that organizing workers on one site was particularly difficult because of the high turnover of the work-force and the temporary nature of the job. Site branches of Comisiones Obreras disappeared once the work was completed, if they lasted that long. Moreover, unlike the engineers, building workers in Barcelona province were covered by a single agreement, and this put a premium on co-ordinating strike action among more than one site. If the dispute centred on conditions on a particular site,

---

[71] From a leaflet of the Comisión Obrera de la Construcción, Vidrio y Cerámica, Dec. 1972, ANC archives.

on the other hand, the solidarity of other local building workers was essential, because the work-force was not usually large enough to carry the dispute successfully.

Hence the 'flying picket' emerged as the main organizational weapon of the construction workers. There were two kinds: one was a march of strikers that would visit other sites in the same area to try to pull out their workers. It was the building workers' equivalent of shop-floor organization in the factories. The other was a smaller delegation sent to win support from shop stewards' committees, students, churchmen, and influential professional bodies such as the Architects' Association and the Law Society.[72] At the height of a widespread dispute, such as a strike over the provincial agreement, the flying picket would turn into the 'snake' or *culebra* that wound its way from site to site gathering increasing numbers of workers along its path. During the big strike of 1973 in Sabadell, for example, the flying pickets started out from the University site, moved to the works of the massive estate of Ciutat Badía a mile or so away, proceeded towards the town to the Gran Vía, the main road that cuts through Sabadell, and followed through the urban centre to another residential estate in the process of being built, Can Deu, by which time the picket had become a march of several thousand.[73]

The strikes of building workers were, therefore, a more open form of protest than those in most other industries, not only because they took to the streets to make their case known but also because many sites were situated in the centre of residential or business districts. Their flying pickets became a familiar sight in the mid seventies, and helped to popularize the demands of the labour movement. This similarity in the methods of struggle employed by the construction workers in the different urban centres of the province derived from the shared conditions of work and site organization. Carpenters, bricklayers, hod-carriers and the like were nomadic workers familiar with building sites of all kinds.

One dispute in the construction industry, in particular, marked a new phase in the gathering movement of solidarity in Barcelona

---

[72] Both kinds of pickets, for example, were used with some success in the ACSA strike in the spring of 1973: *API*, 20 Mar. 1973; *Informaciones Obreras*, 12 March 1973; and the ACSA workers' own bulletin, *Unidad Obrera*, nos. 1–3 (n.d.).　　　　　[73] Valdivieso interview.

and the industrial belt. The violent strike in the spring of 1973 on the site of a new power-station in San Adriá del Besós in north-east Barcelona embodied all the labour problems typical of the building industry at the time.[74] The power-station was being built by five specialist firms subcontracted by the electricity company FECSA. Many of the 2,000 workers on the site had been hired on a casual basis. They were handed a contract but it was left blank so that the subcontractors could fire them as soon as they were no longer needed. The grievance over job insecurity was compounded by the inadequacy of conditions on the site. There were few facilities such as showers or changing-rooms. Workers were on a 10-hour shift, there were no holidays or sick-pay, nor was any transport to the remote site provided by the firms.

In mid March 1973, a Comisión Obrera was established on the site made up of about a hundred militants working for the different subcontractors. A programme of demands that they drew up as part of a campaign over working conditions was approved at the end of the month by a mass meeting of several hundred workers and then signed by the majority of the work-force on the site. A 24-hour stoppage was held on 2 April when the subcontractors refused to receive the committee elected by the mass meeting to negotiate the list of demands. In reply, the companies suspended the work-force for five days on account of its 'grave acts of indiscipline'. The following day, on finding the gates shut, the workers decided to occupy the site. The police on duty at the entrance called for reinforcements. Summoned hastily to the site, the riot police charged at the strikers, forcing them to retreat behind a railway line which ran alongside the site. The workers seized stones to defend themselves. In the fracas that followed one of their number, a young worker called Manuel Fernández Márquez, was shot dead by the police, and a second received a bullet through his shoulder. According to an eye-witness account,

the strikers regrouped and set off on a march towards the neighbouring town of San Adriá, bringing workers out from all the sites and factories

[74] This account is based on the following sources: IEL, 'Conversaciones sindicales' (internal document, Barcelona, 1974); Guardia Civil report, 6 Apr. 1973, and JSPB report, 3 Apr. 1973, CG archives no. 1563; *Lluita Obrera*, 1 Mar. 1978; *API*, Dossier no. 5, Apr. 1973; Jáuregui and Vega, iii. 125–30.

on the way . . . Meanwhile large contingents of police arrived and surrounded the demonstrators, forcing them to retreat towards the river by repeated charges. The march was dispersed and the police started firing again. Some demonstrators were arrested. Many were forced to wade across the river.[75]

The brutality of the police at the site of the San Adriá power-station caused a wave of revulsion among many sections of the population. As the news of the killing came through there was immediate and widespread protest. The underground organizer of Comisiones Obreras in Barcelona heard the news over his car radio and there and then composed a leaflet that was printed in the evening and distributed the next morning in the main engineering factories of the city. Over the next few days, the streets of San Adriá and the nearby town of Badalona were virtually occupied by police jeeps and squadrons of mounted police. The Catalan Comisiones Obreras called for a Day of Action on 11 April and there were stoppages in dozens of factories, banks, schools, and building-sites.

The most important action took place in the twin towns of Cerdanyola and Ripollet that straddle the main road to Sabadell.[76] In the early morning of 6 April, workers coming off the night shift in two Cerdanyola firms went round other plants to persuade the day-shift workers to come out on strike in protest at the killing. By mid-morning a column of several thousand workers was heading towards an engineering plant on the outskirts of the town when it was attacked by the riot police. The demonstrators were forced down into the valley and were chased by the police through the fields near the river. Many injuries were reported. By the early afternoon, many shops, bars, offices, and factories had closed down in protest. The next night the offices of the local OSE were damaged by fire.

Across the valley in Ripollet, three days after the action, the 200 workers of an engineering factory, Sintermetal, were notified that they had been sacked for taking part in an illegal strike. As in Cerdanyola, the response of other workers and many sections of the local population was to shut down business. The Civil Governor intervened to rescind the dismissal notices of Sintermetal. In May, however, ignoring his instruction, the

---

[75] *API*, Dossier no. 5.
[76] This account is taken largely from *API*, Dossier no. 5.

company announced the sacking of a number of militants for their role in the April action. A new wave of protest began. The growing unrest in both towns was fanned by the presence of large contingents of police. On 22 May, a Day of Action was held, and three days later, in response to the call of the local Comisiones Obreras, the two towns were virtually paralysed by a general strike.

Even though it was largely spontaneous and uncoordinated, the surge of protest over the events at the San Adriá power-station was the most widespread action of solidarity that had taken place in Catalonia since the Civil War. It showed that if there was any bond uniting workers of different industries, trades, and occupations, it was the common experience of repression. The strikes in Cerdanyola and Ripollet were the first in a series of localized general actions that would sweep through the towns surrounding Barcelona between 1974 and 1976. Although they often began as labour disputes, their main dynamic was protest against the victimization of local working-class leaders. The relation between these movements of solidarity and the labour protest of workers of different industries that has been discussed in this chapter needs to be examined before the narrative thread is picked up again in Chapter 6.

SOLIDARITY, LABOUR PROTEST, AND THE GENERAL STRIKE

So far, this chapter has highlighted the disparities that separated the conditions and methods of struggle of workers in the main industries of Barcelona and its surrounding industrial belt. The sources of unrest as well as the forms of agitation that militants adopted varied from industry to industry and even within each industrial sector. Separated by different traditions, bargaining mechanisms, and organizational needs, militant workers in the textile trades, engineering and chemical factories, and building-sites adopted their own forms of struggle. If to these differences are added the dissimilar work stresses of bank employees, hospital staff, teachers, telephonists, and other white-collar workers who began to join the ranks of the labour movement in the early seventies, the problem of unity among the working class becomes all the more pronounced.

The labour opposition, dominated by the Communists, aimed not only to draw the different labour agitations together but to weld the movements of workers, students, residents' associations, and the movement for Catalan autonomy into a common force against the dictatorship. The model *plataforma* drawn up by Comisiones Obreras was an important focus of organization among broad layers of workers, even though it did not penetrate into the particular conditions of each industry and workplace. But it did not serve to co-ordinate the actions of organized workers. To try to harness together the different protests, Comisiones Obreras organized Days of Action, when workers were called on to down tools and demonstrate. These *Jornadas* had been the subject of bitter polemic among militants in the late sixties because of the high toll of arrests during demonstrations. Their results in the early seventies were also meagre (although the number of workers who responded was incomparably greater).[77] Echoing criticism from revolutionary groups, the Communist weekly *Treball* was prompted to write, '. . . the decision of the small circles of the clandestine vanguard to hold a Day of Action on a fixed date does not reflect objective possibilities. Rather it reveals the real difficulties that militants face in trying to generate struggles, in extending them to other sectors, in co-ordinating them . . .' The paper went on to admit that there was a gap between the immediate demands of specific disputes and the generic programme of Comisiones Obreras.[78]

Even more problematic were the calls for Days of Action over political questions. The most important outcry against the dictatorship had taken place at the end of 1970 in protest against the trial in Burgos of 16 members of the Basque terrorist organization ETA. Of all the popular actions against the regime, the nation-wide protest in November and December of that year, which aimed at forcing Franco to commute the death sentence

[77] In the midst of widespread unrest in early 1972, for example, the Catalan Comisiones Obreras called for a Day of Struggle on 8 March around a programme of demands common to the disputes that were taking place in different industries. The only significant response came from Mataró, where 17 firms came out on strike. *Treball*, 22 Mar. 1972.

[78] *Treball*, 22 Mar. 1972. For criticism of the Days of Action from the Left see *Estrella Roja*, Oct. 1970.

imposed on six of the accused, was considered by the opposition to be the clearest proof of the readiness of workers to take part in political strikes. The bulletin of the provincial committee of the PSUC, *Unidad*, exclaimed, 'SOMETHING HAS CHANGED IN SPAIN THESE LAST FEW WEEKS and it is no longer possible to go backwards. Now every economic demand raises in the minds of workers VERY CLEAR POLITICAL DEMANDS: LIBERTY, DEMOCRACY, THE END OF THE FRANCO DICTATORSHIP.'[79]

However, if the conflicting evidence is examined about the number of strikers that took part in the main action against the Burgos trial, the Amnesty Day of Action on 3 November launched by the nation-wide Comisiones Obreras, it is evident that the response among workers in Catalonia was not as massive nor indeed as political as the opposition claimed. While the figures given by the mass media were deliberately deflated—the main daily in Catalonia, *La Vanguardia*, reported only 32 stoppages on that day, involving 6,000 workers—caution should be exercised over the calculations of the opposition press. Among the tens of thousands of workers that the underground papers claimed had joined the strike in Catalonia, no less than 50,000 were building workers.[80] Yet the construction workers' strike was principally in support of demands for their provincial agreement, which was being negotiated at the time. One of their leaders admitted later,

. . . attempts to mobilize over demands which went beyond purely economic, labour issues met with great difficulties in that period. For example the industry which . . . gave the action of the 3rd November 1970 its special character was construction but it was at the time negotiating its collective agreement. In the other industries there was only a token participation in the strike, a few minutes' stoppage here and there.[81]

The response among workers in Catalonia to the call for solidarity with the ETA militants was of course unprecedented. There was nothing to compare it with among the political Days of Action of the late fifties and sixties. But it did not prove the

---

[79] *Unidad*, 16 Jan. 1971 (capital letters in the original). See also *Mundo Obrero*, 22 Jan. 1971, and *Treball*, Jan. 1971.

[80] *Treball* and *Estrella Roja*, Nov. 1971; *La Vanguardia*, 4 Nov. 1970.

[81] J. M. Rodríguez Rovira, in Centre de Treball i Documentació, op. cit. 109.

emergence of a new more political movement among workers, as the undergound press enthusiastically argued.

The SEAT occupation of the following year, and the wave of solidarity actions over the San Adriá killing in the spring of 1973, fuelled the faith shared by most of the opposition that workers were moving towards direct confrontation with the State. For the Communists, the events seemed to confirm their vision that the regime would be swept aside by mass strikes backed by widespread protest actions on the part of broad layers of the population. Even before the general stoppage in Cerdanyola and Ripollet, *Treball* had asserted, 'We have already entered into the phase of the General Political Strike and the National Strike, actions which, together with the Pact for Liberty . . . make up the political revolution which will overthrow the dictatorship.'[82] In the aftermath of the strike movement in the spring of 1973, the Catalan Comisiones Obreras declared, 'In view of the sheer size of the protest, the extent of popular and working-class participation, and the forms of struggle adopted, we consider the Cerdanyola and Ripollet strike the most important action so far. It is a presage of the General Strike: the factories paralysed, the masses in the streets, the shops closed.'[83] The Secretary-General of the PSUC, Gregorio López Raimundo, held up the actions as a model of the National Strike. It was proof, he argued, that in the right situation and with the correct leadership, workers were ready to join strikes for political objectives. The Cerdanyola strike, he asserted, was the path towards the overthrow of the dictatorship.[84]

The persistent concern shown by most of the Left to define the 'correct' theory of the General Strike may appear somewhat of a fetish. In a sense, the Communists and the revolutionary groups were victims of their own propaganda. Since the Civil War, the Communist press had found evidence of the imminent collapse of the regime in each small crisis of the dictatorship. Equally, every large-scale mobilization was proof, in the eyes of the left-wing papers, that the working class was prepared to topple the Francoist State. Despite the failure of the calls for nation-wide strikes in 1958 and 1959, there remained a faith in the

[82] Feb. 1973.
[83] *API*, 4 May 1973.
[84] *Treball*, 8 May 1973.

revolutionary spontaneity of the 'masses' that was underpinned by an unspoken and almost mythical reference-point—the boycott of the trams and the General Strike of 1951.[85] Yet the economic context and the working class itself had been transformed since then. Moreover, the fact that the clandestine organizations could hardly be said to have led the 1951 action did not prevent the Left from arguing that the missing ingredient in the present situation was correct leadership.[86]

It is true that the notion of how the General Strike and the National Strike might occur had been considerably modified since the fiascos of the Days of Action in the late fifties. The third General Meeting of Comisiones Obreras in July 1968 had redefined the General Strike as the 'extension and generalization of a series of partial struggles which begin in a factory, industry, or area, and spread like an oil stain across the whole country'.[87] The idea that it could occur as a result of a call to action by the opposition had therefore long been discarded. The crucial question that militants posed was how to channel the growing labour protest towards more political forms of action. The most clear-headed response could be found among leaders of the Catalan Comisiones Obreras. In a declaration in March 1973, the executive of the CONC made a veiled criticism of the 'triumphalism' prevalent among many Communists and others on the Left. What was important, they argued, was to understand that there were different levels of consciousness among workers. Traditions and experiences of struggle varied widely. Only by searching for unity at a rank-and-file level, in their opinion, could these divisions be overcome. The declaration ended with a call for a more serious examination of the struggles that were taking place.[88]

In this and the previous chapter, it has been argued that the workers of Greater Barcelona were indeed separated by different traditions and experiences. It has also been suggested that the efforts of the labour opposition to draw together the diverse

---

[85] J. M. Colomer, *La ideologia de l'antifranquisme* (Barcelona, 1985), 71.

[86] See for example the leading article in *Treball*, 15 Jan. 1972, 'En el camí de la Vaga General'.

[87] The Communiqué is quoted in full in M. Calamai, *Storia del movimiento operaio spagnolo dal 1960 al 1975* (Bari, 1975), 248–53.

[88] The text is in *Lluita Obrera*, Mar. 1973. For a criticism of the politics of the General Strike see also *Estrella Roja*, 20 June 1973.

interests of these workers were only partially successful. The model *plataforma* of Comisiones Obreras became a common aspiration among the better-organized workers in factories, offices, and building-sites, whether in Terrassa or Baix Llobregat. But it did not result in the making of a common tradition of union organization of the shop-floor. Nor, at the other extreme, did this programmatic unity mean that the organized workers shared a similar level of political consciousness. The labour movement was in reality a number of parallel movements that converged around a general programme, and took common action only in very specific circumstances.

What the solidarity strikes in Cerdanyola and Ripollet suggested was that, at least on a local level, a mass movement of political protest could arise only when workers identified closely with the victims of police brutality and the employers' sanctions. Unlike the Burgos strike, the action in the two towns in Vallés Occidental took the form of local solidarity. This was to be the main characteristic of the mass strikes that would take place in Baix Llobregat and Sabadell between 1974 and 1976. There was indeed an important connection between economic and political struggles, but it was not the case that labour protest could easily be harnessed to the struggle to overthrow the regime. Nevertheless, for the next three years, the mirage of an 'oil stain' of struggles spreading across Spain would haunt the minds of militants.

6
Popular Agitation and Political Change 1974–1976

We have seen fear
Become law for all
And we have seen blood,
Creating yet more blood,
Become law in this 'world'.
No! I say, No!
Let's all say No!
We don't belong to this 'world'.

(Extract of song by Raimón, Ahir (Diguem No!))

During the last years of the Francoist regime, the contradiction between society and State deepened. The assassination of Franco's right-hand man, the President Admiral Carrero Blanco, by an ETA squad at the end of 1973, had made the idea that the regime might continue beyond the dictator's death less credible. The two years that spanned the death of Carrero Blanco and that of Franco himself in November 1975 were filled with political intrigue. Dozens of semi-legal and clandestine fronts sprang up throughout Spain. In an attempt to set up an alternative to the regime, the Communists formed the Junta Democrática in July 1974 with small groups of Socialists and Carlists and some individual politicians. They were followed a year later by the Plataforma de Convergencia Democrática, founded by the Socialists with an assortment of democratic parties. With the exception of the Communists, none of these parties had any organized base to speak of.

The 1974–5 government of Carlos Arias Navarro, having hinted that it would be prepared to introduce a measure of reform, resorted to even greater violence against the growing movements of social protest. In August 1975, barely three months before his own death, Franco signed the death-warrants that sent five young members of ETA and the terrorist organization FRAP to the firing-squad. By the end of 1975, it had become clear that the choice facing Spain was either a complete break with the old regime, as the opposition advocated, or its reform. Which direction would be taken did not rest entirely in the hands of politicians of either side. Rather it depended on how much deeper the process of social and political unrest in Spain would go. The opposition was hoping to use the protest movements as a battering-ram to knock over a regime whose social foundations they believed had crumbled away. But they did not control the unrest, nor could they easily channel it in the direction they wanted.

There were two processes at work, therefore; on one hand, the spread of protest movements rooted in specific economic and social grievances, and on the other, the struggle for political power between the opposition, which claimed to represent these forces, a growing number of people within and on the fringes of the establishment who believed in reforming the system, and the die-hard Francoists, whose power was underpinned by the military and the State bureaucracy. The story of the political contest between these interests has been told in some detail in recent books about the period.[1] What has been less emphasized is the pressure from below that rendered such a contest necessary and made possible its democratic outcome. The negotiations that took place in 1976 had as their backcloth an exuberance of popular activity that greatly influenced their result.

PROTEST IN CATALONIA

Of the movements of protest in Spain between 1974 and 1976, none commanded as much popular support as those of Catalonia. It could be said that in the seventies Barcelona became the capital of the opposition to the dictatorship. It was here that the clandestine headquarters of Comisiones Obreras had been transferred after the arrest, in Madrid in 1972, of the co-ordinating committee of the nation-wide organization. This was

[1] See for example, P. Preston, *The Triumph of Democracy in Spain* (London, 1986); Carr and Fusi, op. cit;. Jáuregui and Vega, op. cit;. D. Gilmour, *The Transformation of Spain* (London, 1985).

not so much because the Catalan leaders had by chance escaped the police net as because of a recognition of the greater strength of Comisiones Obreras in Barcelona than anywhere else in Spain at the time. It was in Catalonia also that the only broad political front with grass-roots support had been created: the Assemblea de Catalunya, founded in 1971. Militants of Comisiones Obreras, who played a leading role in the formation of the Assemblea, ensured that it adopted the defence of working-class interests as one of the main planks of its programme. The Assemblea helped to forge close links between workers and other sections of the population. An ex-shop-steward in Vallés Oriental recollects, 'The Assemblea got many people—shopkeepers, small industrialists, and the like—to support us, sometimes giving us money, sometimes hiding us in their houses if the police were searching for us.'[2]

At the same time, militants worked hard to win support among immigrant workers for nationalist aspirations. That immigrants came to identify with Catalan autonomy would be evident, among other things, in their participation in the massive demonstrations on the national day of Catalonia in 1976 and 1977. Indeed, the strength of support among immigrants for Catalan nationalist aspirations needs some explanation in view of the fact that few could speak the local language and that their roots lay in another culture. It could be attributed in the first place to the greater opportunities that Catalan society offered for self-advancement. The survey of attitudes among immigrants in Catalonia, referred to in Chapter 5, revealed a strong sense of appreciation towards the host community for having provided jobs and homes, despite the terrible hardship to which immigrants were subjected for years after their arrival. But their identification with Catalan autonomy was as much a rejection of the centralized dictatorship as an adoption of a Catalan identity. It can be argued that immigrants supported nationalist aspirations because they saw them as a means of achieving greater control over their own lives. Identification with Catalonia, however, was not the same as integration into its society. As long as urban ghettos and discriminatory policies by the local establishment continued, as they were to do even after the achievement of

---

[2] Interview with Ana Bosch, 5 March 1983.

autonomy, the existence of two different communities would remain a feature of Catalan society. It was not just an economic or social problem, though this was the most important barrier; the deepest responses of the older immigrants were shaped in another culture. As one of the interviewees in the survey succinctly put it, 'I consider myself Catalan, although I am Andalusian. It is here that I have developed the ability to sell my labour, that I have learnt the little culture that I possess, that I have created my home. This is my land, that is how I think of it, although my inner self is full of other tendencies.'[3]

The Assemblea became widely known in Catalonia only in October 1973, when 113 of its members were detained after a police swoop on a church in Barcelona. The much-publicized arrests did a lot to spread its popularity. Yet the support for the Assemblea among workers would always remain diffuse, because it was a political movement without links with their immediate grievances. The working-class orientation of its programme was the work of political militants of Comisiones Obreras and not the result of active support from the shop-floor. Moreover, the involvement of Comisiones Obreras in a broadly based nationalist body embracing different classes lent a tone of moderation to the labour movement in Catalonia that contrasted with the more militant expressions of protest in the late sixties, such as the street riots in Terrassa.

The Assemblea was the most political expression of a new vigour in civic life in Catalonia in the mid seventies. The declining legitimacy of the regime and the failure of its apparatus to deal with acute social problems led to an explosion of alternative grass-roots initiatives. The most dynamic of these were the residents' associations. Given legal status in 1964, the *Asociaciones de Vecinos* did not grow to any extent until the next decade. Before then, the residents of the slums and working-class estates had relied largely on individual solutions to problems of all kinds, resorting to family networks and *enchufes*, or contacts with influence in the local apparatus of the State. The older districts of the city had seen the decline of community life after the Civil War with the enforced closure of the popular

---

[3] Solé (1982), 116. The question of the integration of immigrants into Catalan society has been the subject of much discussion and polemic. For a broad survey of the arguments, see Josep M. Colomer (1984).

social clubs, like the *ateneos*, and the rise in the sixties of new patterns of individual consumption, the most conspicuous symbols of which were the televison set and the SEAT 600. All that was left of the old collective traditions was the religious festivals and the annual local feast-days. However, new forms of association had begun to arise in the early sixties around Catholic organizations, such as the youth clubs, and recreational bodies. Parish churches, run by priests who felt keenly the social injustices that surrounded them, became the centre of community life in many urban neighbourhoods.

The residents' associations began to mushroom in the early seventies. By 1974, 90 had been formed in Barcelona, and four years later some 70,000 people in the city were members of one association or another, though the influence of the movement extended even more widely. The genesis of the residents' associations varied from district to district. It was usual for the associations to be set up as a result of a specific grievance. There were many causes for dissatisfaction on the working-class estates—lack of proper sewerage, street lighting, or paving; poor-quality housing; inadequate health, educational, or recreational facilities; cuts in social services; flooding; and schemes of urban renewal that smashed through old neighbourhoods. No means existed, other than organized collective protest, to force the local authorities to respond to these problems. The town councils were in the hands of the State Party, the Falange. Their mayors were appointed from above and dispensed patronage in the manner of the old *caciques* or local bosses of the Spanish countryside. The Mayor of Sabadell, for example, built an unconstitutional network of district 'mayors', individuals whom he selected personally for each district of the town, and who were accountable only to him.[4] Many of the town halls were staffed by people linked to real-estate interests, who were able to change land classifications at will. The strength of the new urban movement must be understood in the light of these two elements: the depth of social grievances and the absence of the democratic means of rectifying them.

Nevertheless, the growth of urban protest was not an entirely spontaneous process. The residents' associations were often set

[4] *Can Oriach*, Jan. 1972.

up and led by members of the Communist Party or of Bandera Roja. Both organizations had devoted much energy to the creation of clandestine committees known as the *Comisiones de Barrio* to organize protest in the residential areas. The advantage of the residents' association was that it was a legal forum in which people could air their grievances openly, while the Comisiones attracted only the politically committed. By the early seventies, political activists had turned their attention towards organizing the residents' associations. The strong political tone adopted by the new urban movement—the prominence of demands for amnesty and democracy, for example—was in no small measure due to their central role in the new associations, rather than to any spontaneous politicization of the residents.[5]

Yet the activists' influence and the dynamic of urban protest itself combined to shape a new consciousness among working-class families of their right to decent living conditions and of their capacity to achieve them through collective protest. The campaigns conducted by the residents' associations forged a new sense of community on many an estate in Barcelona and the surrounding towns. The actions were particularly defiant in the new working-class districts, where residents staged rent strikes, blocked main roads, occupied churches, organized delegations to seek support among influential people, and campaigned against the local structures of power. The experience of such agitation brought to the fore notions of municipal accountability, solidarity, and democratic government. By 1976, some of the town councils themselves were under siege.

In contrast to the male-dominated labour movement, women played a vital role in the urban protest. They led the most powerful group of residents' associations—those in the Nueve Barrios district on the northernmost edge of the city, once an area of vineyards and now crammed with high-rise estates housing thousands of immigrant families. The woman who was president of the association recalls, 'During mass demonstrations, the younger women would go in the front of marches, while the grandmothers kept watch for the police armed with tin whistles.'[6]

[5] Alabart Vilà, p. 233.
[6] Interview with María-Angeles Rivas, 22 Nov. 1985.

The matriarchal nature of much urban protest was not only the result of the division of labour that kept a majority of women at home and the men at work on long shifts. It was also the consequence of a gulf which separated labour from urban agitation. The Communists, in particular, organized their industrial work not by areas but according to the structure of industry. This separation was especially marked in Barcelona, where there was little coherence between work and residence. The urban movement was seen by the Communists not so much as a social struggle, through which women might achieve emancipation, but as part of the fight for political democracy. While Bandera Roja organized around concrete local issues, the Communists' campaigns focused on more general demands such as amnesty and a halt to the rise in the cost of living. It was also generally accepted that the mainly male shop-floor leaders could afford neither the time nor the added risk of victimization to play a prominent role in the residents' associations. The prevalence of women in actions of protest against the local authorities thus gave the urban movement its special character, at once peaceful and concrete as the grievances from which it arose. Because women had been doubly oppressed in the countryside, the active involvement of female immigrants in collective protest marked a transformation of values far greater than that experienced by the men.

The urban movement of the seventies had a political resonance way beyond the specific grievances which lay behind each struggle. The campaigns were widely publicized by some of the mass media. In contrast to news about labour disputes that were subject to the censorship of the Civil Governor, the press was relatively free to report on local events of all kinds. Journalists were able to publish articles critical of the urban deficits in the suburbs of the city and sympathetic to the cause of popular protest. The residents' associations also drew on the support of influential sections of society such as professional organizations and churchmen. Their campaigns against massive projects of urban renewal relied on the expertise of town planners, architects, lawyers, and civil engineers sympathetic to the cause.[7]

---

[7] For example, the Plan de la Ribera in Poble Nou. See M. de Solá-Morales *et al.,* op. cit.

The *laissez-faire* model of urban development that had shaped the city for over two decades was beginning to be challenged.

REPRESSION AND REPRESENTATION

Support for urban protest was part of a broader movement for social and political reform involving many sections of Catalan society. At the centre of this web of democratic opinion was the labour movement. Each fierce shop-floor struggle that spilled out into the streets set an example of dissent for other aggrieved groups to follow. It also generated a multitude of activities in solidarity with victimized workers. Campaigns to raise money and organize petitions for jailed or sacked militants helped to make public opinion more sensitive to the demands of workers. These initiatives were led by a network of solidarity committees which had sprung from an unusual source. The flood of arrests that had followed the proclamation in 1969 of a State of Emergency had prompted the Archbishop of Barcelona to form a secret solidarity committee for jailed militants. He had appointed a laywoman to run the committee from within the Archbishop's palace itself. From her office, the new organizer set up a string of local committees that worked alongside the support groups of the underground parties to raise money for detained workers, to campaign for their release, to follow their movements between different gaols, and to look after their families. Over the five years of their existence, the solidarity committees raised some 13 million pesetas (about £87,000).[8]

An even more important role in the labour movement was played by left-wing lawyers. Their offices became at times the organizational headquarters of strikes, while the court cases themselves often turned into mass demonstrations. To understand the vital part that the legal defence of workers played in the history of the movement, it is necessary to look briefly at the function of labour legislation in the Francoist system of industrial relations. During the Civil War itself, the regime had begun to draw up an elaborate set of laws designed to regulate industrial relations in the new totalitarian State. Though this legislation was

[8] Interview with Remei Ramírez, 6 May 1983.

subsequently modified over the years, its fundamental purpose was always to prevent the collective defence of working-class interests. Yet it was also a paternalist charter in that workers, as individuals (or 'producers' in the jargon of the regime), were protected from arbitrary dismissal and brought under the wing of the State on all matters relating to their working lives. In place of a free system of industrial relations, the dictatorship installed a centralized bureaucracy made up of government departments and the State Union. The function of arbitration was taken over by the Ministry of Labour, which handed out compulsory awards and dealt with matters relating to redundancies, bonuses, and new working methods. An even more important role was reserved for the Labour Courts, which ruled on individual disputes over dismissals, wages, social security, sanctions, overtime, holidays, accidents, and so on.

The elaborate system of legislation that governed shop-floor life turned industrial relations into a legal maze. Every industry and workplace was covered by a complex set of regulations, in the light of which each dispute had to be interpreted. Workers were encouraged to respond individually to their work problems by turning either to the array of legal advisers of their local union or to private lawyers specializing in labour legislation. No other way of rectifying grievances was offered by a system in which collective organization was banned. As a result, the law acquired a mystique of its own.[9]

Militants had never fought shy of the courts. In the fifties, they had conducted numerous legal battles over matters such as increased production speeds and the management's failure to observe the national Work Regulations. In the first half of the following decade, the incidence of cases in the Labour Courts had tended to drop as grievances were brought into negotiations over collective agreements. From the late sixties onwards, however, the number of cases shot up in line with the explosion of disputes. The legal struggle to defend workers stretched also to the Tribunals of Public Order (TOP), set up in 1963, that tried the growing number of militants detained in the wake of the police offensive against Comisiones Obreras. The defence of

---

[9] The magistrates, however, were professional lawyers who did not always favour the interests of the powerful. See E. Barón, 'Los obreros ante la magistratura', *Cuadernos para el Diálogo*, Feb. 1973, p. 60.

victims of police repression was entrusted to left-wing lawyers who specialized both in legislation relating to the Labour Courts and laws on public order offences dealt with in the TOP.

The practice of the lawyers Albert Fina and Montserrat Avilés became the centre in Barcelona for the legal representation of militants. Between 1960 and 1975, as many as 100,000 workers passed through their offices. But they were not always there only to prepare court cases. Militants came for advice over collective bargaining, though legally only the OSE could deal with such matters. Many a list of demands was drawn up with the help of the labour lawyers. The practice was also used as a meeting-place for workers on strike. The action that led to the occupation of SEAT in October 1971 began there. Montserrat Avilés remembers,

> It began as a simple legal consultation. Some SEAT workers came here one morning to ask if the firm had the right to oblige workers to do night shift. We answered that they probably did, and that there was little chance of winning a case against the company in the courts. It was from that moment that the workers realized that they had to resort to illegal methods to fight for their demand.[10]

In many respects, indeed, the left-wing labour lawyers became the substitute for legally recognized unions. They offered the only place where workers could meet with some degree of legal protection to discuss grievances and organize agitation.

Progressive lawyers and solidarity committees were kept busy between 1974 and 1976, as the employers lashed out against militants in a last attempt to curb unrest in the factories by time-honoured methods. Stoppages were met with lock-outs, and many shop stewards who stood up to management were suspended, sacked or dismissed from their union posts. An analysis of the number of workers victimized in Catalonia, during the hot season of collective bargaining at the beginning of the year, revealed that in the first two months of 1974 almost 1,000 workers were sacked and over 3,000 temporarily suspended without pay.[11] This ferocious victimization often wiped out

---

[10] Interview with Montserrat Avilés, 1 Feb. 1983. See also A. Fina, *Des del nostre despatx* (Barcelona, 1978), 49–50.

[11] J. Maravall, *Dictatorship and Political Dissent* (London, 1978), 41. The figures are based on reports in the legal press and are therefore likely to be an underestimate.

years of campaigning by militants to win control of works councils. The employers' resort to selective repression was on occasion blatantly intended to get rid of any focus of agitation over forthcoming negotiations. Companies could resort to the infamous Article 103 of the Law of Labour Procedure whereby they could opt to compensate rather than reinstate workers judged by the Labour Courts to have been improperly dismissed.[12] The frustration which this 'escape clause' created among workers was reflected in a bitter comment of the Hispano Olivetti clandestine shop-floor bulletin, *Unión y Lucha*, 'When we win a sentence in favour of workers by mass pressure, the company is able to flout the verdict, and there is nothing the magistrates can do about it.'[13] Militants thus 'compensated' or not, as the case may be, found themselves moving from job to job, sacked in each case when the blacklist operated by employers came through.

Victimization may have temporarily weakened shop-floor organization but it also brought workplace class struggle into the open. The campaign against Article 103 by SEAT militants in 1974, for example, found a sympathetic echo in the legal press. Each new wave of dismissals and the subsequent court hearings were accompanied by solidarity campaigns and demonstrations. The street outside the Labour Courts became the frequent scene of disturbances during court cases over dismissal. The magistrates were obliged to suspend court hearings over the SEAT case four times because of the commotion outside.[14] By 1976, numerous companies were being picketed daily by unemployed militants whom they had sacked years previously. Above all, the increased harassment of shop-floor leaders in the seventies gave a concrete meaning to the more political demands of the labour opposition that had been appended for years at the end of the shopping-list of *plataformas*. For work-forces deprived of tough and seasoned negotiators, the demands for the reinstatement of sacked militants and for democratic shop-floor representation acquired a new force.

[12] See, for example, the case of the Cerdanyola motor firm Condiesel; *Mundo*, 9 Nov. 1974; *Informaciones Obreras*, 28 Oct. 1974; and the SEAT case of 1974; IEL, 'Documentos informativos', Dec. 1974; *Asamblea Obrera*, Sept. 1974.

[13] Quoted in *API*, 26 June 1973.

[14] IEL, 'Documentos', Dec. 1974.

One dispute in particular illustrated the shift among the best-organized groups of workers from wage-claims to demands that in effect challenged the authoritarian structures of the regime. Between November 1974 and the following January, the giant SEAT car works was embroiled in a turbulent conflict that centred upon the right of workers to elect their own delegates.[15] Ever since the occupation of 1971, there had been an almost continuous ferment of unrest in the SEAT plant. In the autumn of 1974, a new campaign over the forthcoming negotiations for the 1975 collective agreement was launched by the factory Comisión Obrera. One of the main demands of the platform was the resignation of the works council, which had fallen into the hands of management collaborators after the sanctions and sackings of 1971. At the beginning of November, SEAT effectively halted the process of bargaining by applying to the government for a 39-day lay-off, alleging a drop in orders (under the terms of the so-called *Expediente de Crisis*, the State made up the basic but not real wages during approved lay-offs). The stoppages in protest at the wage cut which this implied were greeted by an unexpectedly harsh response; SEAT suspended the whole work-force for ten days.

Over the next three months, the centre of Barcelona was the scene of unheard-of mass agitation and violence, firstly during the period of the suspension and then after a new lock-out in January. The demands of the SEAT workers included the cancellation of the lay-offs and the renegotiation of the 1975 agreement that had been settled by a compulsory government award. But their most important grievance remained the lack of democracy in the factory. An open letter from the SEAT strikers stated, 'Our central demand is for the firm to recognize our own authentic representatives, elected freely and democratically in mass meetings, and to negotiate with them all outstanding problems . . .'[16] Frequently during the weeks of agitation that followed, thousands of SEAT strikers, backed by other workers

[15] The following account is based on a number of sources: Gilaberte and Zamora, op cit.; *API*. 5–14 Dec. 1974 and 18 Jan. 1975; *Mundo,* 23 Nov. 1974; *Cuadernos para el Diálogo*, Dec. 1974; *Asamblea Obrera*, 25 Nov. 1974; Faustino Miguélez Lobo, *SEAT: la empresa modelo del régimen* (Barcelona, 1977); and interviews with Silvestre Gilaberte and Isidor Boix. For a similar dispute in Hispano Olivetti, see *La Vanguardia Española* and *Tele-Exprés*, 19 Mar. 1975.   [16] Quoted in *API*, 18 Jan. 1975.

and university students, filled the Vía Layetana where the OSE had its headquarters, and after police charges spread throughout the centre of the city—along the Gran Vía, up the fashionable Paseo de Gracia, the Champs-Élysées of Barcelona, down the Ramblas, a crowded avenue that runs from the main square of the city to the port. Tear-gas, smoke-bombs, and the sound of the stamping boots of charging police filled the air in the smart business and tourist centre of the Catalan capital. The confrontations spread to the suburbs, especially those where SEAT workers lived. In Hospitalet, rubber bullets were greeted by stones. The working-class estate of Bellvitge, where several thousand SEAT employees had their homes, became a no-go area for the police.

In an unprecedented move, the Managing Director of SEAT, Javier Clúa, who had been appointed as the first civilian to head the company after the calamitous occupation of 1971, held secret meetings with Comisiones Obreras leaders to try to solve the dispute. It was a recognition that only the labour opposition could halt the actions, The meetings were organized by Socías Humbert, the head of the Provincial OSE, who had already made contact with the underground labour opposition. One of those present at the negotiations recalls, 'Socías Humbert had already held secret talks with leaders of the Catalan Comisiones Obreras. He had even raised the possibility of similar talks . . . between Fernández Sordo [Minister of Labour at the time] and the national leadership of Comisiones but Fernández Sordo was against it.' During the discussions, a telephone call was made to Paris to the exiled Communist Secretary-General, Santiago Carrillo, who was based there, in the course of which the SEAT Director is alleged to have claimed that, although he wished personally to recognize the unofficial representatives of the workers, his hands were tied and he had received strict orders from the Civil Governor not to meet any deputation of SEAT strikers. Carrillo, according to the same source, was against the idea of such talks. 'Carrillo was frightened by the possible consequences of all this; frightened in the sense that Comisiones might become integrated, that the OSE might regain control of the situation . . .'[17]

Twice in the course of the conflict, attempts were made to

[17] Boix interview, and *API*, 18 Jan. 1975.

transform the action and the street disturbances into a general strike. The SEAT workers' bulletin *Asamblea Obrera*, distributed in large numbers on 12 November, called for a general strike in Barcelona and the surrounding region. The call met with virtually no response. Later, taking advantage of a renewed wave of labour unrest, the Catalan Comisiones Obreras called for a Day of Struggle on 15 January in preparation for a general strike. Again there was little response among workers, and the action was not helped by the fact that the SEAT workers called off their strike on the same day. Although some concessions were won, the long and violent strike in SEAT had been a costly one. Five hundred workers had been sacked and dozens arrested. Nor had their demands for the recognition of their own representatives been heeded.

The failure of the SEAT strike to spread led to recriminations within Comisiones Obreras and the PSUC. The SEAT militants were accused of overestimating the willingness of other workers to come out in solidarity with their strike. On the other hand, a small section of the Party most closely connected with the strike argued that the Communists had been too timid and a general strike had not developed largely because of a failure of leadership.[18] The problem, however, did not lie so much in the supposed reluctance of other workers to support the SEAT workers, nor even less in the caution of the leadership, though both reluctance and caution may have been real. It was argued in Chapters 3 and 4 that the lack of solidarity action in Barcelona lay in the absence of both traditions and mechanisms that linked the immediate interests of one group of workers with another. The fragmentation of collective bargaining, the sectionalist traditions that this had given rise to, the isolation of factories from residential areas, and the geographical mobility and dispersal of their work-forces combined to make generalized solidarity strikes difficult, even at times of heightened mobilization.

In contrast, the two general stoppages that took place in Baix Llobregat in 1974, at the height of the SEAT dispute, showed that in other circumstances it was possible for a whole area to come out on a mass strike. Not only did they vindicate the policy of working within the State Union but they seemed to point a way

---

[18] For a defence of each position, see 'Informe de la Permanente de la CONC' in *Lluita Obrera*, Feb. 1975, and Gilaberte and Zamora, pp. 359–62.

out of the dilemma facing the labour opposition of how to transform industrial disputes into political struggles. In the uncertain climate caused by the death of Carrero Blanco, the aborted promises of the new President, Arias Navarro, and the spring revolution in Portugal, the Baix Llobregat strikes appeared to incarnate the process of popular agitation on which the opposition pinned its hopes for a radical break with the dictatorship.

GENERAL STRIKE IN BAIX LLOBREGAT

For the previous two years, the whole area encompassing the southern part of Baix Llobregat had been in a ferment of industrial agitation. In 1972 alone, according to the Communist paper *Treball*, no fewer than a million hours of production had been lost in stoppages in the *comarca*.[19] The major cause of unrest in the engineering factories that dominated the zone was the negotiation over plant contracts and the closely related local agreement. In 1973, the engineering employers and the workers' representatives had failed to concur over the terms of the new area contract and the government had imposed a compulsory award. In the following year, faced by a renewed campaign by militant shop stewards, the employers refused to renegotiate the local agreement and attempted to impose the provincial contract, which contained levels of pay and conditions far lower than the former. The resulting unrest coincided with two strikes in the area, one in the glass factory Elsa in Cornellá and the other in the chemical multinational Solvay further up the valley in Martorell. It was the confluence of these disputes that created the conditions for the events of July 1974. The three-day general strike that took place blended a collective impulse of solidarity with more traditional shop-floor grievances.[20]

The Elsa plant was strategically situated in the middle of Cornellá, its tall chimney towering above the surrounding

[19] 6 Feb. 1973.
[20] The main sources of the following account are: *Lluita Obrera*, Oct. 1974; *Prensa Obrera*, July 1974; *Cuadernos para el Diálogo*, Aug. 1974; *Treball*, 18 June 1974; *Mundo*, 13 and 20 July 1974; *Tele-Exprés*, 15 June 1974; Riera and Botella, pp. 105–28; and interviews with José Cano, Carlos Navales (14 Jan. 1983), José Botella (4 July 1983), Esteban Cerdán, and Emilio García (21 Mar. 1983).

factories. A stone's throw away stretched the best-organized factory in the area, the light-engineering firm Siemens. The dispute in Elsa had several causes: low wages; poor conditions, in particular the stifling heat from furnaces used for glass-making; and the demand by the management that in exchange for a higher wage, the 900 or so employees should work on three Sundays a month, as part of their six-day working week. A strike at the end of May 1974 led to the dismissal of almost the entire work-force. Drawing on a style of struggle that had become a tradition in the area, the Elsa workers brought their grievances on to the streets of Cornellá. Through street collections, sit-ins in the parish churches, and delegations to schools, local dignitaries, and associations of all kinds, they made their dispute known to all the inhabitants of the town. Dressed in work overalls, their roaming pickets became a familiar sight in the markets and squares of the area throughout the early summer of 1974. The press, under the more liberal reign of the new Minister of Information, Pío Cabanillas Gallas, gave much publicity to the strike; some articles were unusually sympathetic towards the workers' cause.[21]

The Elsa dispute coincided with agitation in the local engineering factories over collective bargaining. The continued refusal of the local employers to renegotiate the area agreement prompted the general assembly of engineering union delegates to call for a two-hour stoppage in the industry on 3 July. The date was timed to coincide with a court hearing over the Elsa sackings, and the strike call explicitly linked the disputes in the glass factory and in the chemical firm Solvay up the Llobregat valley, whose workers had also been dismissed, with the grievances of the local engineering workers. On the day of the stoppage, a mass meeting in the headquarters of the OSE in Cornellá, attended by hundreds of workers from the whole region of Baix Llobregat, called for a general strike the next day.

On the 4th of July, after factory-floor meetings, one work-force after another downed tools and marched out of their plants. Separate demonstrations wound their way through the two industrial estates of Cornellá, pulling out workers from the smaller factories, and then proceeded along the valley towards the industrial towns of Baix Llobregat. By the middle of the day,

---

[21] For example *Tele-Exprés*, 15 June 1974, and *La Vanguardia*, 6 July 1974.

some 24,000 out of the 30,000 metallurgical workers in the area, and about 6,000 from other industries, had joined the action. The general strike continued on Friday the 5th, then on Saturday. The centres of the towns were filled with demonstrators. Bars, shops, and services of all kinds closed down in support. The whole area of Baix Llobregat seemed to have come to a halt. From their base in the OSE headquarters in Cornellá, the engineering branch delegates refused to countenance any negotiations over the local agreement unless the Elsa and Solvay workers were reinstated. On Monday, a compromise was reached. The employers agreed to start up discussions over a new area contract, to reinstate all the dismissed workers except for two who were to be found jobs in other plants, and to refrain from making any sanctions against workers for taking part in the action. Throughout the dispute, moreover, the authorities had avoided making any arrests.

In the repressive context of the dictatorship, the general strike of July 1974 in Baix Llobregat was an unprecedented event. Almost all other strikes hailed by the opposition press as victories had left a trail of arrests and dismissals. Unlike the SEAT conflict, it has been backed not only by local workers from all industries, but also by many sections of the community. In contrast to the spontaneous actions in Cerdanyola and Ripollet a year previously, the strike had been led and controlled by militant shop stewards. Indeed, the most notable characteristic of the July general strike was that it was organized from within the 'lion's den', the local headquarters of the State Union. What had once been a mechanism for controlling the working class was being used now to rebuild it.

It was argued in Chapter 4 that the Baix Llobregat labour movement derived its strength in part from the peculiarly cohesive industrial structure of the area. It was also suggested that the social homogeneity of its population and the proximity of factories and residential areas played a part in forging links among workers and the community. At this juncture, it is only necessary to stress the importance of the union work carried out by militants in building the new local labour movement.

The success of the general strike rested on three pillars. Firstly, the local Comisiones Obreras, in which dozens of shop-floor leaders participated, provided some of the main initiatives leading to the action. The campaign to link the Elsa and Solvay dispute to that of the engineering agreement, for example, was launched by Comisiones militants. Secondly, the focus on the local structure of the OSE as the centre of agitation helped to draw into the struggle hundreds of union delegates and shop stewards who would not have dared join the clandestine Comisiones Obreras but who were prepared to defend working-class interests. Of course, it was easier to take over the OSE of an outlying area or *comarca* than the provincial headquarters in Barcelona. Moreover, the local hierarchy were noted for their more progressive views about industrial relations.[22] Finally, the success of the general strike was due in no small measure to the tradition of factory meetings in the main plants of the area, a right that had been imposed on local employers after years of struggle. The key to the involvement of thousands of workers in the action was the shop-floor debates that had taken place in the weeks leading up to the strike.

There was one important limitation to the general strike of Baix Llobregat, however. Throughout Chapter 4, it was emphasized that the labour movements of Catalonia emerged out of local tensions and traditions. Not only were the actions of July 1974 almost entirely confined to Baix Llobregat, which may not be surprising given that the strike arose out of local problems, but militants made little effort to seek support elsewhere, for example through the OSE branches of other areas. The July 1974 issue of the bulletin of the Catalan Comisiones Obreras, *Lluita Obrera*, criticized the '. . . lacked of activity displayed by the strikers and workers of Baix Llobregat as far as winning the support of class comrades in other *comarcas* is concerned'.

Nevertheless, within the local labour movement, the July general strike in Baix Llobregat consolidated the leadership of Comisiones militants. The growth of militant organization was only partly a linear process, the result of a steady accretion of support around the sort of union work carried out by militants that was described in Chapter 4. The dynamic of events such as the three-day general strike, on the other hand, did more to

---

[22] The reformist Head of the Provincial OSE in the seventies, José María Socías Humbert, had begun his career as a lawyer in the Cornellá branch. Also, pressure from branch delegates had led to the successive replacement of three local Heads judged to have been too authoritarian. *Treball*, 6 Feb. 1973.

change the perspectives of the workers who took part than years of patient work on the part of activists in the union or the factory. It threw up new shop-floor leaders who had not been involved before in any action and radicalized more moderate shop stewards.

The new balance of militancy within the local OSE was not slow to reveal itself. At the end of November, a meeting of 500 engineering branch delegates in the Cornellá headquarters voted to call a one-day stoppage on 5 December in protest both at recent victimizations and at the rise in the cost of living. It was the sort of political call to action that Comisiones Obreras had unsuccessfully made over the previous years and it might well have been confined to short stoppages in the best-organized factories in the area had it not been for a ponderous attempt by the police to pre-empt the strike by detaining 25 local shop-floor leaders.[23] The arrests helped to turn the stoppage into a new general strike that lasted for three days. Over 23,000 workers and large sections of the population joined the protest. Again, the local authorities found themselves overwhelmed by the strength of popular reaction, and in the days following the strike the detained militants, all allegedly members of the Communist Party and therefore liable to serious charges of sedition, were released without bail pending court hearings.[24]

The two general strikes in Baix Llobregat showed that the State Union had virtually lost control of its local branch. The December strike was called by unanimous decision of the official representatives of the engineering workers of the area. Yet it was also an illegal action. The law may have been ambiguous about the legality of labour stoppages, but it certainly did not countenance general strikes for political motives.[25] The OSE was

[23] Many more militants were due to be detained by the police, but a sympathetic local magistrate was supposed to have tipped them off and they went into hiding, though they continued to go to their workplace where it was less easy for the police to make arrests. Cerdán interview.

[24] According to Civil Guard figures, which gave details of the numbers involved in each factory on strike, a total of 23,349 workers took part in the strike: Civil Guard report, 5 Dec. 1974, in CG archives no. 1598. For details of the December general strike see Riera and Botella, pp. 129–42, *API*, 5–14 Dec. *Correo Catalán*, 6 Dec., *Treball*, 10 Dec., and *Luchas Obreras*, 13 Dec. 1974.

[25] For a summary of legislation over collective disputes under Francoism see L. E. de la Villa and C. Palomeque, *Introducción a la economía del trabajo* (Madrid, 1977–8), ii, 281–91.

always meant to suppress class struggle. It was now being used to launch mass strikes. The problem was not confined to Baix Llobregat. Everywhere in the region, the bureaucrats and elected right-wing officials could feel shop-floor militants breathing down their necks.

THE UNION ELECTIONS OF 1975

The approach of the union elections of spring 1975 was therefore greeted with extreme trepidation by the bureaucracy and the authorities alike. The officials of the OSE redoubled their efforts to present a progressive image on one hand, and to hinder the candidature of the opposition on the other. Barcelona was the stronghold of a reformist operation within the apparatus of the Francoist Movement led by the Civil Governor, Rodolfo Martín Villa, and his protégé, the head of the State Union in the Barcelona province, José María Socías Humbert. The latter was campaigning for a programme of reforms, portentously named 'the New Frontier of Unionism', that took up some of the demands of the opposition, including the right to strike and full wages upon retirement or illness.[26] It was not a burst of mere rhetoric in response to the menace of Comisiones Obreras. Under Socías's leadership, the Union had adopted a more professional style of intervention in industrial relations, albeit within the authoritarian framework of the law. Die-hard Falangist officials were being replaced by followers of Socías.[27] Indeed, the secret police had complained to Martín Villa's predecessor about the new line of neutrality followed by full-time union officials in labour disputes. It was to lead to Socías's dismissal in the autumn of 1975.[28]

The threat of losing their positions also jolted the ex-anarcho-syndicalist officials within the OSE into outbidding each other in radical talk. The President of the Textile Unions in Sabadell

[26] See the official paper of the OSE, *Acción Sindicalista*, June 1975.

[27] Interview with Carlos Fanlo, 11 Nov. 1987.

[28] JSPB, *Nota Informativa sobre ausencia de intervención sindical en algunas alteraciones laborales*, 4 Oct. 1973, CG archives no. 1418. See also the correspondence regarding this between Pelayo Ros and Socías Humbert, 23 Oct. and 7 Nov., CG archives nos. 1418 and 1425. R. Martín Villa, *Al servicio del estado* (Barcelona, 1984), 20–1.

asserted in an interview, 'A trade union that is the result of an imposed peace . . . creates mistrust.' Another top local unionist, revealing more than he may have intended to about the role of officials such as himself, complained, 'The workers don't trust us because they think we're self-seekers, out to climb the ladder of official posts and make money out of fiddles.'[29] Many officials also indulged in the customary practice of trying to block militant candidates by impugning them, or through gerrymandering and delaying tactics.[30]

As part of the effort to counter the activists, the Falangist mayors of the province of Barcelona were summoned to the headquarters of the Francoist Movement to prepare a secret campaign with the employers and union officials in each town to get right-wing candidates elected. Their reports on what was happening on the ground were not optimistic. The Mayor of Cornellá admitted that conflicts had reach boiling-point in the area and the local employers were alarmed. His counterpart in the newly industrialized town of Rubí, near Sabadell, complained that 'the Campaign of Subversion. is intelligent, brazen, and scientific . . . I have always done what I have wanted in the town . . . but now I don't know if that's the case any more.'[31] The response of some employers to the threat of a militant take-over of the works council was more forthright: they sacked the Comisiones candidates. Across the country 60 candidates lost their jobs.[32]

The fear of the authorities, employers, and union officials alike lest the delegate structures of the OSE should fall into the hands of the labour opposition was well founded. The spring election was the first full ballot since 1966, when, from a far weaker position, Comisiones Obreras candidates and fellow-travellers had given the State Union a nasty shock. Moreover, the political climate had altered dramatically. By the spring of 1975, the

[29] *Can Oriach*, Oct.–Dec. 1974.

[30] See, for example, the Madueño affair, in *Cuadernos para el Diálogo*, Sept. 1975; also *Treball*, 13 and 27 May 1975.

[31] Jefatura Provincial del Movimiento de Barcelona report, 6 May 1975, CG archives no. 1598.

[32] *Mundo*, 28 June 1975. The secret police reported that 14 members of Comisiones Obreras who were about to stand in the shop-floor elections in the Barcelona plants of the large motor firm, Motor Ibérica, were dismissed under various pretexts. JSPB report, 1975, CG archives no. 1598.

clamour for political change was coming from all sides of Spanish society. The turmoil was particularly severe in the Basque Country, where the three-month state of emergency declared by the government in response to ETA's successful terrorist operations provoked an irrepressible surge of protest. The old dictator's health was ailing and at last the end of the regime, so often predicted over the previous 30 years or so by the opposition, seemed to be approaching. The elections were therefore doubly significant. The paper of the PSUC, *Treball*, was confident that 'from these elections will emerge the men and women who will lead, as part of the democratic break with the regime, the constitution of the united union of workers . . . These elections mark the final assault on the Vertical Syndicates and the construction of the class union.'[33]

There was no questioning the new strength of Comisiones Obreras. In Catalonia, the movement commanded widespread support for its programme of demands. Its network of militants stretched throughout the main industries in Barcelona and province, linked by clandestine industrial comisiones or *coordinadoras*. Yet it should be remembered that Comisiones Obreras was a largely unstructured movement, made up of a hard core of activists of whom most were Communists, and a wide periphery of sympathizers with very differing levels of commitment. This base could be found firstly among thousands of workers in factories where there was a comisión, or committee, and secondly among branch delegates in unions where Comisiones militants were active. The vast majority of these sympathizers looked to Comisiones Obreras for leadership but were not ready to risk arrest by attending clandestine meetings. Nor were many prepared to become part of its organization, because they perceived it as a Communist front.

In an effort to draw this wide periphery into a united anti-OSE campaign, Comisiones Obreras launched an electoral slate entitled the *Candidaturas Unitarias y Democráticas* (henceforth known as CUD) around a programme based on its well-known demands. In the run-up to the elections in the spring, the CUD rallied to its banner a broad range of workers in addition to the followers and sympathizers of Comisiones. It also attracted the

---

[33] 1 April 1975.

support of almost all the groups of the labour opposition in Catalonia, including those that had previously boycotted the elections. The bitter divisions among the different organizations of the Left had given way to increasing collaboration, as a result less of converging policies than of the impulse towards unity that flowed from the rank and file of the labour movement. An influential section of Bandera Roja had split off to join the PSUC at the end of 1974, reinforcing the hegemony of the Communists in the opposition in Catalonia. Only the UGT maintained its abstention from the elections, but it could hardly be said to carry weight among workers.[34] Indeed, it could be argued that the electoral campaign of 1975 represented the highest point of unity in the labour movement both during the dictatorship and after.

The new electoral alliance posed an overwhelming challenge to the right-wing lists, made up of an assortment of Falangists, pro-management groups, and the networks led by ex-CNT populist officials (see Chapter 3). In the space between the two stood independent lists made up of apolitical workers who had had and wished to have no contact with Comisiones Obreras. These 'independents' were to figure prominently in the first union elections of the coming democracy. In the mean time, for all the efforts of the bureaucracy and the authorities, the CUD looked poised to wrest control of the rank-and-file structures of the State Union.

The elections were held in a climate of great expectation. As the results for the works councils came through it became clear not only that there had been a record level of participation, with a poll of 90 per cent, but that the CUD candidates had won a crushing victory in all the main factories of the province. It should be remembered that the lists were divided into four categories, technicians, administrative staff, skilled, and unskilled, and the results were therefore comparatively weighted against the shop-floor where support for anti-OSE candidates was strongest. A survey covering all branches of industry and the services, carried out by the progressive Catholic paper *Mundo*,

---

[34] Even where the Catalan UGT claims to have had the strongest shop-floor organization in 1975, that is at Hispano Olivetti, in which there were said to be 30 to 35 members, the participation of workers in the ballot was in the order of 95%, according to figures published in *Mundo*, 28 June 1975. Information on the UGT from interviews with Gil Pachón (22 Apr. 1983) and José Luis Rodríguez (2 May 1983).

revealed that out of the 30 most important firms in Barcelona the democratic candidates had gained control in all but three. Out of over a thousand delegates, the right-wing and independent lists had managed to get only 189 of their candidates elected.[35]

A report sent to the Civil Governor by the secret police gave a curious but none the less revealing breakdown of the results in the province as a whole (see Table 5).[36] A brief explanation of the rather quaint nomenclature of the police is needed here. The so-called 'Reds' were all those successful candidates who opposed, or whom the police suspected of opposing, the regime. Of these, the 'Bad' were reckoned to be members and sympathizers of the clandestine organizations, with a 'criminal' record, or at least a personal file in the vaults of the police headquarters. The 'Neutral' delegates among the 'Reds' were those with no known political affiliation but who were suspected of anti-regime sentiments. The 'Good Reds' were likely to be people, such as Catholic activists, who opposed the dictatorship but shunned the Marxist opposition. The 'Non-Reds, of the CUD camp, on the other hand, were those new union representatives who

TABLE 5   *Police Evaluation of 1975 Union Elections in Barcelona Province, in percentages (rounded)*

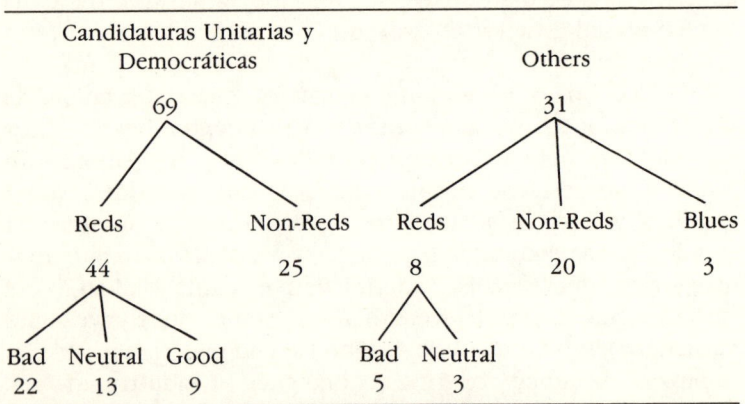

Source: author's calculations from unsigned chart, CG archives no. 1598.

[35] 28 June 1975.
[36] The report is unsigned, but as it is accompanied by a file from the secret police containing a detailed record of the votes in all of the major factories it is almost certain to be the work of the Social and Political Brigade; CG archives no. 1598.

supported its electoral programme but who were not considered opponents of the regime. Of the minority of candidates grouped under 'Others', the 'Reds' were opposition candidates outside the CUD, the 'Non-Reds' consisted of right-wing union slates, independents, and those sponsored by the ex-CNT clan, and the 'Blues' were Falangists. According to this analysis, therefore, almost half of the new crop of union representatives were apolitical, while 49 per cent of those elected on the CUD lists had had no known involvement with Comisiones Obreras nor indeed had expressed any opposition to the regime.

However suspect the police's classifications may have been, they did point to two phenomena that would be an important feature of the new trade-union movement of the late seventies: on one hand, the relatively high proportion of shop stewards who considered themselves independent of any union or party tendency and were therefore unlikely to be militant in any form, and on the other, the emergence of a new generation of shop-floor leaders who had had little experience of agitation. These new delegates would indeed preside over the coming transformation of union life, but there would be many among them who would choose to join more moderate or non-Communist options rather than Comisiones Obreras in the future configuration of union forces.

In the second phase of the elections for all posts above the works councils that followed in the autumn of 1975, the CUD candidates swept the board in the local branches of the main unions. Moreover, in sectors where few CUD candidates had stood for election because Comisiones Obreras did not have a strong base, such as among teachers and journalists, in the health service, and in the water, gas, and electricity union, the official slates were defeated by candidates supporting democratic demands inspired by Comisiones.[37] But this success was not repeated on the higher echelons of the OSE hierarchy, where a complicated system of indirect election ensured once again that control remained in the hands of the bureaucracy. There had never been such a divorce between the top officials and the rank and file. Now nearing the end of its existence, the OSE had become even more of an anachronism. Apart from a cowed

[37] *Treball*, 14 Oct. 1975. For details of the second round of elections see *API*, 15 Nov. 1975.

bureaucracy increasingly retreating into their bunker, the organization, at least in the main industrial centres, rested on many thousands of union delegates committed to its elimination.

The elections of 1975 represented the culmination of the strategy of entrism which the Communists had made their own. Those groups of the labour opposition in Catalonia such as the UGT and the official CNT that had refused to take part in the activities of the State Union remained confined to the sidelines. The Communists' more pragmatic policy of combining agitation in the legal structures of the State Union with the unofficial organization of Comisiones Obreras proved to be a highly successful one. Even a much smaller group of the labour opposition such as USO was able to build an impressive network of militants through its involvement in the official framework of the OSE.[38] Work in the State Union not only gave militants some legal cover for labour activities but, more importantly, put them in touch with masses of workers for whom the official machinery of bargaining, arbitration, and litigation, for all its limitations, was of vital importance. In a sense, Comisiones Obreras was the other side of the coin of infiltration. The first broad-based Comisión, that of the engineering workers in Madrid in 1964, had arisen from within the OSE in response to a need for greater co-ordination and accountability in collective bargaining than that offered by the State Union. But the shapes the new organization took—from a semi-legal or unofficial movement to clandestine committees—varied according to the different levels of agitation or the different historical moments. Comisiones Obreras proved to be a highly flexible instrument, responding not to any ideological model but to the needs of the collective defence of workers' interests in a dictatorship.

Yet the success of the labour opposition and its allies in the elections of 1975 tipped the balance between legal and clandestine union work in favour of the former. The centres of agitation, more than ever before, were the union branches and the mass meetings on the factory floor organized by the recently elected shop stewards' committees. The clandestine networks of Comisiones Obreras, on the other hand, could no longer play such a useful role, because in many areas it was possible to

[38] For evidence of USO's work see its Catalan cyclostyled periodical *Catalunya Obrera*.

organize and co-ordinate within the OSE itself.[39] The new balance of forces in the State Union led a section of the Comisiones Obreras in Barcelona and Baix Llobregat to argue that since the ground floor of the OSE had been taken over, the whole structure should be used to build the new Union of the coming democracy.[40] This strategy was not dissimilar to that of the Portuguese Communists following the revolution of spring 1974, when they sought to transform the State Union in Portugal, the *Intersindical*, into the single Union of Portuguese workers.

The creation of a single democratic Union of all Spanish workers had long been the declared aspiration of most sections of the labour opposition. The divisions between Socialists and Anarchists which had fatally weakened the union movement of the twenties and thirties weighed heavily in the minds of politically conscious militants. For thousands of workers who had engaged in labour protest, moreover, unity was not an abstract concept. In the absence of free unions, it was a *sine qua non* of the defence of their collective interests. The official policy of the two main organizations who followed an entrist strategy, the Spanish Communist Party and USO, was that the OSE should be destroyed from within as part of the process of the democratic break with the dictatorship. Both argued that the coming Union of the new State would emerge from a hypothetical congress of democratically elected workers' delegates, after the disappearance of the regime.[41] The new policy, on the other hand, meant launching this congress under the auspices of the OSE itself, in the belief that it would accelerate the disintegration of the whole apparatus of the dictatorship. Indeed, it coincided with the similarly unsuccessful project of the astute head of the Barcelona Unions, Socías Humbert, to hold a new congress in order to carry through reforms that might give the OSE a role in the approaching democracy.

The proposal of the small minority of Comisiones leaders was regarded by the Communist hierarchy as a heresy and its main proponent was expelled from the Party.[42] What seemed to worry

[39] For a discussion of this problem see *Lluita Obrera*, 12 July 1975.
[40] I. Boix and M. Pujades, *Conversaciones sindicales con dirigentes obreros* (Barcelona, 1975).
[41] For USO's position see *Catalunya Obrera*, Especial Congrés 1975.
[42] Boix interview. For the polemic see the virulent article in *Treball*, 5 Jan. 1976, and the cautious defence of the proposal in *Mundo*, 31 Jan. 1976.

the Communist leadership most was that this ultra-entrist line entailed the liquidation of Comisiones Obreras, their control of which would be a trump card in any negotiations about the shape of the future democracy. But there was a more important reason for doubting its viability. Throughout most of Spain, the OSE bureaucracy still dominated the apparatus of the State Union, controlling the process of collective bargaining and wielding a vast system of patronage and welfare. Any attempt to create a new union within the OSE would be violently opposed by the hierarchy, and, even if it did succeed, tainted with the mark of the regime.

It was true that in some of the areas surrounding Barcelona the local labour movement had seized control of the State Union. In Baix Llobregat and Mataró, militants imposed a new legality. Union affairs in both districts were run by unofficial area-wide committees that broke with the divisive structures of the OSE. In the first, the so-called *Intersindical* brought together the elected representatives of all the unions in the area. In the smaller town of Mataró, the *Pleno de Delegados*, made up of the delegates of all the union branches, met every week to co-ordinate action. In a gesture of defiance at the OSE bureaucracy, the Pleno appointed as their technical adviser (or *colaborador*, an official post sanctioned by the State Union) the oft-jailed clandestine leader and future Secretary-General of the Catalan Comisiones Obreras, José Luis López Bulla.[43] In these areas, it seemed, the new Union was indeed being built on the ruins of the OSE.

1976: MASS STRIKE AND POLITICAL REFORM

The prolonged death agony of Franco in November 1975 seemed to symbolize the slow process of the regime's disintegration. His long-awaited end on the 20th came as something of an anticlimax. Most of the opposition had predicted for years that if

[43] According to the weekly Barcelona paper, *Hoja del Lunes*, 26 Jan. 1976, 'The *Intersindical* is the meeting of three or four workers' leaders of all and each of the towns of Baix Llobregat. Workers' leaders here mean . . . the Presidents and Vice-presidents of the UTTs [the OSE branches]. Between all of them in this area there is an almost complete affinity unlike in most of the rest of the country.' Details of Mataró from López Bulla interview and interview with Francesc Lleonart, 29 Mar. 1983.

Franco were not himself overthrown, the political system, built in the very image of the dictator, would not survive beyond his death. The full-time organizer of the Comisiones engineering workers in Barcelona later described the wishful atmosphere among the underground activists: 'Franco died, and everyone waited for something to happen and nothing happened.'[44] Yet Franco's death profoundly altered the political climate. While there was no transformation in the nature of labour protest, the acceleration of strikes and demonstrations and the greater prominence in them of demands for reform were not unconnected with expectations of imminent political change.

The immediate source of industrial unrest was the sharp increase in the cost of living, accompanied by a decree of the new government of Arias Navarro imposing yet another wage ceiling. As usual, the vehicle of labour dissent was the renewal of collective agreements, most of which were due to be renegotiated at the beginning of the year. The numbers of workers who took strike action quadrupled. Over the whole year, some $2\frac{1}{2}$ million workers were involved in stoppages across the country. In the first months of the year, Madrid, Bilbao, Barcelona, Vitoria, and many other cities witnessed demonstrations on a scale that had never been seen before during the life of the regime. In January, the capital was inundated by a wave of strikes that swept through its main industries; the industrial suburb of Getafe was gripped by a general strike and the city itself was brought to a halt by a dispute involving underground workers. The violent suppression of a demonstration in the Basque town of Vitoria led to a general strike in the whole region. In Barcelona, sections of workers such as firemen, municipal workers, and dockers stopped work for the first time. A new 15-day general strike broke out in Baix Llobregat in protest at the victimization of the steel workers of the Laforsa mill.

The response of the government of Arias Navarro to the wave of popular agitation was a familiar one. While attempting to introduce timid measures of reform in the Spanish parliament, it stepped up the repression of protest. Arias's failure to contain the growing agitation helped to swing increasing numbers of people

---

[44] Boix interview.

within the Francoist establishment and among influential business circles behind the idea of a radical reform of the system. The King, who nourished democratic aspirations, contrary to popular belief at the time, dismissed Arias in June. In a carefully thought-out operation, the old die-hard Francoist was replaced by the young Secretary-General of the Movement, Adolfo Suárez, a politician newly converted to the idea of democratic reform. The fusion of the two organizations of the opposition into the *Coordinación Democrática* or *'Platajunta'* in March, and later in the year the talk of a negotiated end to the regime (the Communists eventually abandoning the old ambition of overthrowing the regime by a 'peaceful general strike'), paved the way for dialogue with the new government. Contrary to the age-long predictions of almost all the opposition, the Franco regime was transformed into a parliamentary democracy from within and by institutional means.

Yet the coming of democracy in Spain cannot be understood without reference to the mass pressure for change from below. No amount of 'political engineering' could have persuaded influential sections of the oligarchy and the Francoist establishment to renounce what had been for decades a profitable political system. By 1976, the regime was proving incapable of dealing with a mounting crisis that affected almost all sections of society. The most flagrant problem was one of public order, disrupted by ETA terrorism, mass demonstrations, and right-wing backlash. The State's industrial relations system no longer served the interests of employers. Not only were wages rising faster than productivity, but the job protectionism enshrined in Franco's social legislation severely hindered their efforts to deal with the growing economic crisis.[45] More than any other factor, it was the destabilizing effect of popular agitation and the threat of declining profit margins that pushed the oligarchy to seek finally to bring Spain's polity into line with that of Western democracies.

The extent of these political reforms was also defined, in part, by the nature of this mass pressure. The movements of protest had moderate political aspirations. If popular unrest often took

[45] Between 1964 and 1976, wages had risen three times as fast as productivity: V. Pérez Díaz, *Clase obrera, orden social y conciencia de clase* (Madrid, 1980), 33.

the form of open confrontation with the authorities and the local representatives of the State, the political demands that accompanied it were confined to basic rights taken for granted in other European countries. The limited response to calls for political action by the opposition in late 1975 and early 1976 suggested a perception on the part of many workers that their main grievances had a better chance of being rectified through a dimly foreseeable process of political compromise and reform, than in any mass action that threatened to plunge the country into a new civil war. Had the process of political change been blocked or delayed much longer, it is quite feasible that the movements of protest would have become more radical, giving rise to alternative forms of popular power on a local level.

The General Strike, or, in its more recent formulation, the National Democratic Action, thus remained a mirage. The Communists and the revolutionary Left had clung to the idea that such an action was not only feasible but also a necessary condition for any reform of Spanish society. Throughout the sixties and early seventies, the formula of the General Strike and the Peaceful National Strike had been redefined in the light of successive disappointments. Not even at the height of popular unrest at the beginning of 1976, however, had it been possible to weld together the different agitations into a force that could challenge the system.

The failure of their policy had two fundamental causes. The analysis on which it leant underestimated the consensus, albeit a passive one, that the regime had built among many sections of the population. The most evident sign of this consensus had been the massive endorsement of the dictator's policies in the 1966 constitutional referendum. Though the official campaign leading up to the referendum had hardly been a model of democracy, the result could not be dismissed simply as manipulation by the regime, or fear on the part of the electorate. Behind this tacit acquiescence of masses of Spaniards lay the dramatic rise in living standards that had begun in the late fifties and had continued throughout the sixties and early seventies. The fierce political passions that had gripped Spanish society in the thirties had given way to very different values characterized by the individualism and self-advancement so encouraged by the regime. The enforced silence of the vanquished, the distortions of history propagated by the new order, and the triumphant images of material progress broadcast by the State-controlled mass media had combined to create a largely apolitical society. The new consensus for the regime, enthusiastic or merely grudging, was underpinned by the paternalist role played by the State. While workers were deprived of the right of collective defence, they were offered, in return, job security and legal protection against the arbitrary actions of employers. The State Union itself wielded enormous funds, with which it was able to build a widespread network of patronage. For all its venality and collusion with the regime, the OSE coloured the responses of masses of workers towards industrial relations.

The second reason why the strategy of the Left failed was its tendency to disregard the social and economic transformation that had taken place in the previous 20 years or so. A new complex and stratified working class had emerged, with many different aspirations and levels of consciousness.[46] The high level of strikes in the early seventies was not incompatible with moderate political expectations; moreover, the experience of industrial relations in other European countries suggested that militancy and political moderation could go hand in hand.[47] As we have argued also, the convulsive nature of many disputes was the result of victimization and police brutality, not of any desire to confront the authorities directly. If Spain in the seventies was in the throes of a social and institutional crisis, the demands for reform that had won widespread popular support could be accommodated within the existing social and economic order.

In a few areas of the country, however, there did take place the sort of process envisaged in the Communists' strategy of the National Democratic Action.[48] Throughout this book, it has been

[46] For empirical evidence, see the surveys of workers' attitudes carried out between 1977 and 1981 in V. Pérez Díaz, *Clase obrera, partidos y sindicatos* (Madrid, 1979); by same author, *Clase obrera, orden social* (op. cit.), and 'Los obreros ante el sindicato y la acción colectiva en 1980', *Papeles de Economía Española*, no. 6 (1980); and J. F. Tezanos, *¿Crisis de la conciencia obrera?* (Madrid, 1982).

[47] The classic formulation of this argument was that of J. J. Goldthorpe *et al.*, *The Affluent Worker* (Cambridge, 1968, 1969).

[48] According to the Executive Committee of the PSUC the National Democratic Action of Catalonia was a '. . . broad front of united mass activity . . . in which the working-class general strike was the key element', *Treball*, 13 May 1975.

stressed that there was a wide gap separating the more militant sections of the working class and the mass of unorganized workers. While, by the mid seventies, the struggles of the former had spread the fight for economic gains into previously weak groups, the majority of workers had still had little experience of workplace organization or of strike action. Despite this fact, the General Strike strategy tended to project the activity of the most militant groups on to a national screen, taking the more radical conflicts as a paradigm of what could happen elsewhere; hence the constant exhortations in the clandestine press for workers to follow the 'model' struggles of Baix Llobregat or Terrassa. Yet the mass strikes or general strikes that occurred in these cases arose out of local problems and specific conjunctures and had, as their objective, relatively modest aspirations.[49] One of the most important actions of this kind took place in Sabadell in February 1976. The analysis of the events in Sabadell will help to evaluate the strengths and limitations of the labour movement on the eve of democracy.

ANATOMY OF A LOCAL GENERAL STRIKE

It was suggested in Chapter 4 that the rise of militancy in Sabadell in the early seventies was connected with the breakdown of a traditional class consensus between different layers of its society as a result of two factors: the crisis of the wool industry in the mid sixties, and the influx of immigrant workers who shared none of the traditions of the local working class. The main evidence of this shift in attitude can be found in the startling rise in the number of labour disputes at the beginning of the decade.[50] By the mid seventies, the traditionally peaceable Sabadell had become one of the most restless industrial centres in Catalonia.

A parallel movement of protest over conditions in the working-class suburbs had given rise to a powerful network of

---

[49] 'Mass strikes' here refers to large-scale uncoordinated strike action, while 'general strike' is meant to signify a concerted stoppage over a single or multiple issue.

[50] No separate figures exist for disputes at this local level, yet it is clear from a study of the local paper *Sabadell*, apart from other evidence which has already been included, that the early seventies saw an unprecedented surge of disputes.

residents' associations. In a self-contained town of relatively modest proportions (whose population in 1976 numbered about 180,000) labour and urban dissent were mutually influential. Moreover, the causes of discontent in both cases were immediately at hand in the shape of local employers and the Town Council that they dominated. If this small-town intimacy between different classes had once been a source of integration, it served, in the different circumstances of the seventies, to aggravate class conflict.

By the beginning of 1976, Sabadell was in a ferment of agitation.[51] There were three strands of protest. The first months of the year were the traditional period of conflict over the renewal of collective agreements in the different trades. Teachers, bank employees, and workers in the building, engineering, and wool trades were all campaigning for their own programme of demands. The announcement by the government in mid February of a new wage ceiling exacerbated the climate of dissatisfaction among the working population. At the same time, the campaign over urban deprivation in the poorer suburbs of the town was gathering strength. The most recent grievances ranged from the rise in water-rates to a plague of rats that had infested one of the working-class estates. A third expression of dissent was the campaign for amnesty for political prisoners and exiles launched by the opposition, to which 34 legal organizations in the town had put their name, including the residents' associations, the boy scouts, cinema clubs, the local Bar Associations, and various Catholic institutions.

The discontent among many layers of Sabadell's population increasingly focused on the Town Council, whose Mayor was a particularly intransigent Falangist. The Council, appointed as a result of the indirect system of elections peculiar to Francoism known as organic democracy, could hardly be said to represent the local people. Of the 22 councillors the majority were members of the Falange, 14 were industrialists, and 4 were right-wing officials of the OSE.[52] The Mayor showed a degree of

---

[51] The following account is based on a number of sources: *Sabadell*, issues between 30 Jan. and 10 Mar. 1976; Guardia Civil reports, 16 and 29 Feb. 1976, CG archives nos. 27 and 47; *Cambio 16*, 19 Feb. and 8 Mar. 1976; D. Giménez Plaza, *Sabadell: el pueblo unido* (Hospitalet, 1976); *Unió Jove*, [1976]; X. Vinader Sánchez and J. M. Benaul i Berenguer, 'Sabadell, febrero 1976: una semana de huelga general política', unpublished manuscript.

[52] Vinader and Benaul, pp. 42–3; *Sabadell*, 21 Feb. 1976.

insensitivity towards the problems of working-class families that was in marked contrast to the earlier occupant of the office, Josep Marcet. In place of much-needed urban infrastructure in the suburbs, the Mayor had been lavish in the development of ambitious projects, such as the building of an arterial road through the town centre that had hardly benefited the vast majority of the population. His authoritarian response to any opposition to his plans drew the fire of numerous civic organizations. Matters came to a head at the last Council meeting of 1975, when he had refused to consider the petition for amnesty. Several of the Falangists present at the meeting had reacted to the protest of onlookers by assaulting three of them. Thereafter, the campaign for the resignation of the Mayor became one of the central issues of local agitation.

In mid February, the three different movements of protest converged. As was often the case, the spark of collective action was police brutality. The local schools had been closed down as a result of the teachers' strike and for several days groups of parents and schoolchildren had been demonstrating in the town centre. On the 13th their march was roughly broken up by riot police and several young children were hurt.[53] A widespread strike was held on the 19th in protest, during the course of which another demonstration was brutally set upon by the police and the convener of one of the largest factories in the town critically injured by a rubber bullet. The next day, flying pickets from the plant went round other engineering factories in the area pulling out their work-force. Unlike that of nearby Baix Llobregat, the labour movement of Sabadell had less control of the local OSE, and attempts to organize a general strike from within the State Union were frustrated initially when the strikers found the building locked and surrounded by police. It was Comisiones Obreras, therefore, in a clandestine meeting in a wood on the outskirts, that co-ordinated efforts to bring the town's industry to a halt. Its manifesto, addressed to workers and the population of Sabadell at large, called for a general strike, 'for all our demands, and against the economic policy of the Government; for a democratic and representative Town Council; for union and political freedom as a form of struggle against repression'.

---

[53] Reporting on an earlier police action, the local right-wing paper *Sabadell* (13 Feb.) stated, 'The police were obliged to intervene with several charges, using modern methods of dissuasion.'

The strike began on 23 February and spread rapidly to engineering factories, building-sites, and textile plants. The police began making arrests. On the day the strike began, the OSE, bowing to mass pressure, opened its doors. A thousand branch delegates from all the industries in the town met and elected a committee called the *Comisión Interramos*, or Joint Union Committee, to run the strike. That same evening, the unofficial strike committee was in the office of the Civil Governor in Barcelona, to which the Mayor of Sabadell had been summoned, laying down terms for a return to work. Two days later, some 45,000 workers from 800 firms downed tools and the majority of shops and bars in the working-class suburbs of the town closed down in support. On the 26th and 27th, the strikers met in local stadiums made available by the besieged authorities. The meeting demanded the release of all people recently arrested, a halt to police violence, and a guarantee that no one would be penalized or sacked as a result of the strike. In an unusual move to restore industrial peace, the local employers met and agreed to a policy of no penalties or dismissals. On the 27th, the 25,000 demonstrators in the stadium refused to leave until all the detainees were released. According to one account, the Minister of the Interior, Manuel Fraga Iribarne himself, intervened in the matter, while the Mayor of Sabadell was said to have paid for the bail of eight of the detainees out of a municipal fund destined for the victims of the recent earthquake in Guatemala.[54] That evening, in the midst of great emotion, the eight were let out of prison and received in triumph in the stadium and the strike was called off.

The February general strike in Sabadell was the result of an altogether more spontaneous process than that of Baix Llobregat in January or indeed in 1974. In the course of the month, the different grievances of groups of workers, residents' associations, and a civic movement for democracy flowed together into a common protest. Although the national situation—the almost tangible approach of political change, the rise in the cost of living, the new wage freeze—was the backcloth to the events, the general strike arose from local tensions. One of the most important of these was the turmoil caused by agitation over the renewal of collective agreements. In mid February, many of the trades in the town were involved in separate disputes. The local building workers were on strike as part of a province-wide action. The wool workers who joined the strike on the 19th did so mainly because their demands had just been thrown out by the employers. Conversely, the 200 branch delegates of the dyers and bleachers voted not to participate in the same strike 'because it lacked any labour motives'.[55] It was significant that industrial unrest continued for some weeks after the general strike. The dyers and bleachers themselves downed tools in March over their own provincial contract.

Another factor that contributed towards the atmosphere of disruption in the town was the closure of schools and the enforced idleness of 20,000 pupils as a result of the teachers' dispute. The general dissatisfaction with the poor funding of education led to the demonstrations in the town by parents and children in support of the teachers, and it was the police assault on one of these that sparked off the first widespread strike. The Mayor took the blame for the violence that ensued. Indeed, he became the target of the exasperation accumulated for years over the Council's neglect of the working-class suburbs. Nor had his arrogant handling of civic protest endeared him to middle-class sectors of the population. The isolation of the Town Council was made even more complete by the evident distaste for the Mayor among the more progressive employers of the town. The manager of a textile firm, in an interview after the strike, asserted, 'I believe it all started because of a lack of political sensitivity on the part of the Council. The mayors of other towns have been able to deal perfectly well with the same sort of problems we have here. They haven't dug themselves in their Town Hall . . .' In a similar vein, the President of the local Union of Engineering Employers stated, 'These days, the Town Council must be much more truly representative.'[56]

In many respects, therefore, the Sabadell general strike of February 1976 was a microcosm of the National Democratic Action that the Communists hoped would overthrow the regime. The local representatives of the Francoist State, the Town Council, found themselves overwhelmed by the breadth of

[55] *Sabadell*, 20 Feb. 1976.
[56] Quoted in Vinader and Benaul, op. cit.

popular opposition. The local branch of the State Union was overrun and for the duration of the strike replaced by a democratic structure based on the mass meeting of Sabadell workers. The authorities were forced to accept the unofficial committee, elected by an illegal meeting of union delegates, as representing the will of the local population.

Nor was this kind of action limited to Sabadell. A similar process had taken place in Baix Llobregat a month previously. During the course of the general strike in that area, most of the local Councils had felt obliged to allow mass meetings of strikers to take place in the municipal stadiums. The Civil Governor and the employers had been forced to recognize a committee of five workers elected by the unofficial *Intersindical* as the spokesmen for the labour movement of the whole area. Moreover, all five were known to the authorities as members of the Communist Party and leaders of Comisiones Obreras.[57] If the so-called democratic break with the regime, or *ruptura democrática*, envisaged by the opposition was a fast-diminishing prospect in early 1976, an apparent *ruptura sindical* and *municipal* had been carried out in Baix Llobregat and Sabadell.

Yet this local agitation was highly circumscribed. This was most vividly illustrated in the case of the general strike of Sabadell. The latter followed closely on the heels of the Baix Llobregat strike of January, and yet the call for a general stoppage in the province in support of the sacked Laforsa workers was not answered in Sabadell, despite the considerable unrest that had already broken out among its working population. Barely three weeks after the abortive call, the workers of Sabadell were on strike themselves.

Moreover, the political repercussions of a general strike confined to an industrial suburb were considerably less than those that paralysed the city centre. It was no coincidence that public order was more severely imposed during demonstrations in the city of Barcelona than elsewhere in the province. The authorities took great care to prevent marches that began in the suburbs from reaching the centre. On 22 January, for example, a huge procession of strikers from different towns of Baix

---

[57] For the January general strike in Baix Llobregat see Riera and Botella, ch. 7; Cuadernos Primero de Mayo, *Hacia la Huelga General—Baix Llobregat* (Barcelona, 1976).

Llobregat set out on the 12-kilometre march from Cornellá to the Civil Government in the city centre. The only direct road into the capital ran across a bridge spanning a deep ravine that divides Baix Llobregat from the municipality of Barcelona. On that day, the bridge at Esplugues was blocked by the massed ranks of riot police. A baton charge forced some of the demonstrators to turn back and they made their way to Barcelona via a long detour to the north. Others slid down into the ravine and clambered up on to the other side beyond the wall of police. The knots of marchers who finally arrived in the city centre hardly made any impact among the crowds that thronged the streets.[58] The divisions that prevented the spread of general strikes into a movement embracing the whole region were reinforced by the brute power of the police.

The parochial character of the labour movement, however, was also its strength. The success of the general strikes in Sabadell and Baix Llobregat rested on a sense of mutual identification that had developed among workers of different trades in the same area and among different layers of the local population. Yet in each case, the sequence of events depended on the convergence of industrial unrest and protest at the victimization of known people. If the functions of the local administration and the local Union had ground to a halt temporarily, they were not contested by a durable form of alternative power. The demands of the strike movement were surprisingly moderate in relation to the mobilization that had taken place. Without the extraneous factor of repression, moreover, the local general strike of workers tended to peter out, as in the case of the Terrasa strike in March 1976 and six months later in Sabadell again, because no common objective united the different trades.[59]

For all the solidarity that the labour movement displayed on a local level, the source of strike action was economic grievances. The foundations of the labour movement lay in the experience of over a decade of economic expansion during which well-

---

[58] Cano interview; Riera and Botella, p. 183.

[59] For the Terrassa action, see *Tarrassa Información*, issues from 11 to 23 Mar. 1976; *Mundo Diario*, 13 Feb. 1976; and *Tele-Exprés*, 24 Mar. 1976. For the September 1976 strike in Sabadell see *Correo Catalán*, 16 Sept. to 13 Oct. 1976; R. Cliville *et al.*, *Metal: 30 días de huelga* (Barcelona, 1976); D. Fábregas and D. Giménez, *La huelga y la reforma* (Madrid, 1977).

organized workers had been able to push up their living
standards through stopping production or threatening to go on
strike. Their main demands had been about pay, in terms of
wages, bonuses, and overtime rates, and to a lesser extent about
hours of work. In the agitation over these demands, however,
new values of mutuality and shop-floor democracy had taken root.
It is true that support for political demands had an important
ideological dimension. Aspirations for democratic rights had
been nourished by increasing contact with other countries
where they were taken for granted. Furthermore, the examples
of May 1968 in France, the overthrow of the Greek junta, and
above all the Portuguese Revolution of 1974, were not lost on
many Spanish workers. But political demands such as amnesty,
democracy, and free trade unions stemmed also from the
experience of bargaining and the day-to-day disputes, in which
the absence or loss of representative delegates eroded the
capacity of workers to defend living standards.

The labour movement, then, moved between two poles of
political and economic demands. Attention has also been drawn
to a parallel dichotomy between the programmatic unity that
existed among workers throughout the region and the diversity
of forms of agitation that separated different areas and trades.
Whilst there was no segregation between political disaffection
and industrial unrest, the link that brought the two kinds of
demands together in action was solidarity. However, this vital
connection was made only on a local level. On the other hand,
the 'middle ground' between pay and politics—union questions
of working conditions, and shop-floor control—was less well
developed. Although it is hazardous to generalize, for there were
undoubtedly many workplaces where conditions had been
vastly improved by militant pressure, it can be argued that
matters connected with health and safety, equal pay, factory and
office regulations or *ordenanzas*, and a host of other labour
issues had not received the same attention because they were less
likely to mobilize workers.[60]

---

[60] A survey of delegates to the first legal Congress of Comisiones Obreras in
1978 revealed that these matters were low in their priorities. It is true that their
overriding concern for action on unemployment and union rights reflected the
new problems created by economic crisis and the delay over union legislation.
Yet it can be argued also that the survey showed a lack of tradition of union
organization on the shop-floor. CONC report 1978, unpublished manuscript.

Some of the problems that would face the labour movement in the coming democracy stemmed in part from those characteristics that had been its strength under the dictatorship. Of these, the parochialism of collective protest and the tradition of spontaneous mobilization around issues of pay and local solidarity were two of the most important. In the different context of the post-regime period, dominated by economic crisis and political negotiation, the traditions built up during the struggle against Franco were to prove a mixed blessing.

THE EMERGENCE OF THE NEW UNION MOVEMENT

The multitudinous agitation that shook Spanish society in 1976 thus took no concrete political shape. The mass strikes that broke out in some areas such as Sabadell and Baix Llobregat may have posed a momentary challenge to the local representatives of the State, but they did not throw up new centres of political power such as Workers' Councils. The organizations that led them were alternative forms of democratic representation, substituting for free trade unions and representative local Councils. Indeed, the form that the self-organization of workers took (characterized, as we have seen, by shop-floor unity and the election of unofficial representatives in mass meetings that were the centres of decision-making) was more a reflection of the constraints of an authoritarian system in which free unionism was denied than evidence of the advanced union consciousness that some leaders of Comisiones Obreras claimed to identify.[61]

The eventful year of transition between Franco's death and the approval of the Suárez government's plans for democratic reform saw a proliferation of such alternative forms of representation throughout Spain. Committees elected by mass meetings of workers or local residents to negotiate with employers and authorities sprang up everywhere. It was a measure of the greater transcendence of the social movements over political forces that discussions to bring the mass strikes to an end were held, not with the united fronts of the local opposition, such as the *Assemblea Democrática de Sabadell*, but with delegates elected

---

[61] For example the essay of Nicolás Sartorius, written in Carabanchel jail in the winter of 1975, 'Introducción: prospectiva sobre CCOO', in *El sindicalismo de nuevo tipo* (Barcelona, 1977), 9–50.

by spontaneous workers' assemblies. Yet in the absence of a political alternative with roots in forms of popular power, and with the emergence of a reformist project within the State itself, the process of democratic change moved to a plane of political discussions between the government and the opposition. In these negotiations, the only bargaining weapon that opposition forces could wield was their claim to represent this effervescent and multiform grass-roots movement. How far they would use this power to push for the social and economic demands of the movement for which they were the self-appointed spokesmen or to carve out a political space for themselves in the coming democracy will be discussed in the next chapter.[62]

With the shift to political forces as arbiters of a limited process of democratic reform, the vision of a congress to set up a united union in the new democracy faded rapidly. The re-emergence of the Socialist Party, which in 1975 could claim only a few thousand members throughout Spain, owed not a little to this deflection of social struggles towards political bargaining. Yet the PSOE could not stake its claim in the coming democracy without a strong base among organized workers.[63] The Socialist leadership was therefore more intent on rebuilding the UGT, which had relegated itself to the sidelines of the new labour movement during the dictatorship, than on promoting a united union that the seasoned shop-floor leaders of the Communist Party would dominate.

The declining prospects for an establishment of a single union of Spanish workers left Comisiones Obreras in a cleft stick. As we have seen, its leaders had correctly perceived it not as the embryo of a free trade union but as an instrument of mobilization suited to the peculiar conditions of working-class struggle under the dictatorship. Moreover, they had attributed to it a dominant

[62] An editorial in *Treball* (30 Aug. 1976) commented: 'The reformist attempt to keep the Communists outside the bounds of the law is equivalent to reducing as far as possible the influence of the working class and the mass of workers in the city and countryside over the process of change and in the future democracy . . . The Communists are the guarantee of the basic defence of the political rights of workers.'

[63] In a press conference at the beginning of 1978, Felipe González said: 'The development and strengthening of the UGT is of vital importance for us. It is absolutely clear that the PSOE could not govern if, next to its parliamentary representation, it did not have strong roots in the trade-union movement.' *El País*, 19 Jan. 1978.

role in the political fight against Francoism; hence it had always been defined as a social and political movement rather than as a labour organization. The strategy of Comisiones Obreras had been part of the grand design of the *ruptura democrática*, that is, the overthrow of the regime and its replacement by a new democratic State based on a high level of mobilization on the part of the working-class and popular movement. Such a triumphal process of events would have strengthened the sense of unity among workers of different aspirations and levels of consciousness.

It must have been difficult, in the midst of the popular struggles which took place in the last years of the dictatorship, to have foreseen the divisions that were soon to break up the labour movement. Unity and solidarity were strong impulses among workers who had organized to improve their pay and conditions. Comisiones Obreras enjoyed an unrivalled support among masses of workers. In hundreds of workplaces and in whole areas, such as Baix Llobregat and Mataró, Comisiones Obreras was effectively the single united union of workers that it aspired to create on a national level. The pressure to move towards a congress to found a united union organization was strongest in those areas where Comisiones Obreras had achieved almost complete hegemony within the working class.[64]

Yet, however broad its base, Comisiones Obreras had been able to mobilize only a small minority of the working class across the country.[65] In the coming democracy, a multitude of workers with little or no experience of workplace organization would need to be unionized. Among the profusion of trades and occupations, from hotel staff to garment workers, from dustmen to clerks, there was no tradition of collective struggle of the sort shared by the militant sections of workers. Moreover, almost 40 years of dictatorship had destroyed any common political culture that workers might have once shared through institutions such as

[64] See for example the call by the workers of Pirelli in Cornellá for a *Congreso Sindical Constituyente*, reported in *Tele-Exprés*, 26 May 1976. For the polemic over the question of the congress, see also *Mundo*, 11 May and 3 July 1976, and Cuadernos Primero de Mayo, *Marcelino Camacho y el debate de Comisiones Obreras* (Barcelona, 1976).

[65] A joint statement by UGT and USO pointed out, '. . . the organized movement represents a minimal proportion of workers and cannot decide on unity in their name'; *Cambio 16*, 21 June 1976.

the anarcho-syndicalist unions and the republican clubs. The reliance on the fluid links that had bound the movement together during the dictatorship would no longer be appropriate in the new context of free trade-unionism.

The problem was given an added urgency in April 1976 when the UGT, still outside the law, held its 30th National Congress in Madrid with the tacit approval of the government, which was already anxious to encourage the growth of divisions within the trade-union movement.[66] By the spring, only a minority of militants in Comisiones Obreras were still convinced about the possibility of founding a united union of Spanish workers. The real problem that now faced its leaders was not whether but in what way to convert the movement into a union. However, it was not till October that the decision was taken to create the new Confederation of Comisiones Obreras. It was made, not in a mass meeting of delegates, but by no more than the 70 delegates of the National Co-ordinating Committee. The Catalan branch of Comisiones had argued that the new union should be built from the grass roots upwards on the basis of shop-floor assemblies and meetings of workers in each industry and area.[67] Such a process, of course, would have made it more difficult for the UGT, which lacked any organized base in Catalonia, to construct its own union. The reluctance of the national leadership of Comisiones to organize the new Confederation on this basis was not unconnected with the desire of the Communist Party, to which the overwhelming majority of Comisiones leaders belonged, to avoid any friction with the Socialists with whom they were united in the *Platajunta*.[68] It was not to be the last occasion that the interests of the new Union would be subordinated to those of the Communist Party.

The fledgeling union movement that emerged at the end of

---

[66] *Tele-Exprés*, 14 and 19 Apr. 1976; *Mundo Diario*, 16, 17, and 19 Apr. 1976; and *Hoja del Lunes*, 19 Apr. 1976.

[67] López Bulla interview.

[68] According to *Mundo* (27 Nov. 1976), '. . . the followers of Carrillo changed their mind' (about a united approach to building a single union) 'after the formation of the Junta Democrática. The need for *rapprochement* with the PSOE began to dominate its policy and this had to mean allowing the UGT a space in which to build its organization.' See also *Mundo*, 30 Oct. 1976. Of the 26 members of the General Secretariat of Comisiones Obreras in January 1978, that is before its first Congress in the new democracy, 24 were members of the Communist party, according to *Cambio 16*, 29 Jan. 1978.

1976 could not have faced more unpropitious circumstances in which to build its foundations. It was confronted with numerous obstacles, the most important of which was the economic crisis that was beginning to gather strength and that would play havoc among the most militant sections of industrial workers. Moreover, the new unions, without any funds except those they could raise from abroad, had to contend with an unsympathetic government and a largely hostile body of employers unused to democratic industrial relations. Nor were they helped by being left on the sidelines of the political negotiations leading to the new democratic State. Finally, as will be examined in the next chapter, the legacy of almost 40 years of Francoism would weigh heavily against the development of a strong union movement: more so, indeed, than the extraordinary popular mobilization that occurred in the last years of the dictatorship had suggested.

7

The Labour Movement in the Post-Franco Era

> The new Spain, prudent, conciliatory, was being born; it was being born as Franco was dying, at an . . . imperceptible pace. As if one had to be watchful not to wake someone up, someone not clearly defined but menacing, more than a group or a man, a sort of Thing which, if resuscitated, would turn everything to blood and catastrophe.
>
> (Rossana Rossanda, *Un viaje inútil*, p. 150)

THE UNIONS IN THE TRANSITION TO DEMOCRACY

The success of the Suárez government's project for political reform in the December 1976 Referendum marked the end of opposition hopes of controlling the process of democratic restoration. The strategy of the Left became one of forcing the pace and extent of reform by attempting to mobilize the relatively autonomous movements of social protest. That they were able to rally large sections of workers had been clear in the mass stoppage on 12 November 1976 called by the short-lived united front of the main unions, the *Coordinadora de Organizaciones Sindicales*, against the government's decree restricting wages and job security. The two-year consensus that followed between the opposition and the Suárez government was, in reality, a contest to determine the parameters of reform. The result was a series of measures—the elections in June, the Pact of Moncloa in October, and the drawing up and promulgation at the end of 1978 of a new Constitution—which, if they went beyond what the establishment had intended to concede, also neglected areas vital to the new labour movement. While the Socialist and Communist Parties were able to set themselves up in the new political arena, the union movement was left on the margin of reform. Crucial matters affecting the capacity of the new unions to recruit and negotiate were subordinated to establishing the political framework of the new parliamentary democracy.

In the Moncloa Pact, signed by eight representatives of the new configuration of political forces including Santiago Carillo for the Communists and Felipe González for the PSOE, it was agreed to keep wage rises below the level of inflation, a cut of over 7 per cent in the living standards of workers. In exchange, a number of social and economic reforms were promised. Several years later, they remained on paper. For example, the pledge to distribute to the union movement the *patrimonio sindical* (the enormous funds accumulated by the State Union during almost 40 years through the confiscation of the property of the old unions and through the obligatory dues of employers and workers alike) was still not properly fulfilled over a decade after the coming of democracy. Similarly, questions of trade-union rights, bargaining structures, and industrial relations in general, were left aside in the discussion between political forces. If indeed the strength of the opposition lay in its ability to mobilize the labour movement, those reforms that might have consolidated its only organized base were postponed. When finally these matters began to be addressed several years later, in the Workers' Statute of 1980 and the Organic Law of Union Freedom of 1985, it was in circumstances far less favourable to the unions.

In addition to the lack of funds and the absence of a new industrial relations framework, the unions, in particular Comisiones Obreras, were hampered by the many obstacles put in their way by the government and employers. Until their legalization in April 1977, Comisiones was harassed by the authorities whenever it tried to hold public meetings.[1] The greater tolerance of the government towards the Socialist UGT, whose 30th Congress was allowed to be held a year before legalization, gave way to hostility when it became clear that the Socialists were an electoral force to be reckoned with. In the spring of 1977, attempts were made to create scab unions or *sindicatos amarillos* using pro-management or OSE-sponsored groups of workers in an unsuccessful endeavour to create a right-

---

[1] Over lunch in a Madrid restaurant, four members of the Comisiones Secretariat complained to the Minister for Labour Relations, De la Mata, that over a four-month period meetings of Comisiones had been banned 51 times: *Tele-Exprés*, 8 Feb. 1977.

wing counterbalance in the new union movement.[2] The first democratic shop-floor elections in spring 1978 were hedged with numerous restrictions; in many workplaces, the employers did their best to obstruct the process of the ballot.[3] To the union movement at least, democracy would come drop by drop.

Despite all the obstacles, the legalization of the unions in April 1977 was greeted with euphoria by labour leaders. Recruitment soared after the general elections of June. Comisiones Obreras professed to have signed up almost half a million workers across the country in 20 days. By October it claimed a total of over one and a half million members, more than one-fifth of Spain's wage-earners.[4] In parts of the industrial belt around Barcelona, the proportion of recruits was even higher; in Baix Llogregat, claims were made that up to 65,000 workers (out of an active population of about 168,000) had joined Comisiones.[5] The UGT, in turn, made the extravagant contention in March 1978 that it had recruited over two million people, more than the old Union had had even at the height of its popularity in 1936.[6] So great were expectations among union organizers that the Madrid Comisiones leader, Marcelino Camacho, was led to assert that union membership in Spain would soon be the highest in Europe.[7]

The UGT was faced with an altogether bigger task than Comisiones Obreras in its attempt to rebuild the Union. It was true that in some parts of Spain, such as Asturias and the Basque Country, the Socialist Union had not entirely lost its roots among workers. It was no coincidence that the highest levels of abstention in the union elections had been registered in these two areas. The Catalan UGT, however, had been overshadowed by the anarcho-syndicalists in the years before the Civil War, and could not rely on historical memory or tradition upon which to build a new constituency. Moreover, the Socialist movement

[2] For details, see *Cambio 16*, 29 Jan. 1978.

[3] See, for example, J. Ariza Rico, 'Gobierno y elecciones sindicales', in *El País*, 1 Feb. 1978; and G. Cabarrocas, 'Trabas a las elecciones sindicales', *Lluita Obrera*, 15–30 Mar. 1978.

[4] Gaceta de Derecho Sindical, quoted in J. Setién, *El movimiento obrero y el sindicalismo de clase en España* (Madrid, 1982), 47.

[5] *Tele-Exprés*, 28 Apr. 1978.

[6] *El País*, 19 Mar. 1978. The same paper in its edition of 14 Dec. 1979, however, points out that only just over 70,000 UGT members' dues were received at headquarters.

[7] *Diario de Barcelona*, 19 July 1977.

there had broken into fragments in the sixties, one of which, as we saw in Chapter 3, had chosen to work within Comisiones Obreras. The roots of the new Catalan UGT lay in a group of Asturian workers, exiled to the region in 1947, who had continued to meet throughout the long purgatory of the dictatorship. They had been joined in the early seventies by some young workers who identified politically with the PSOE and rejected the Communist-dominated Comisiones Obreras. The nucleus of the new leadership was formed among a handful of workers of the typewriter factory Hispano Olivetti.[8] But it was only in 1976 that the Catalan branch of the UGT began to reach beyond the few dozen activists who had built up the organization in the first half of the decade.

The growth of the Socialist Union nationally was helped by the high profile of the Party and indeed of the political process in general in the new climate of reform. Many militants who identified politically with the PSOE but who had worked within Comisiones Obreras were now encouraged to join the UGT. A survey of shop-floor leaders of the UGT in Madrid and Barcelona in 1980 suggested that a sizeable proportion of them had participated in the Comisiones movement and that, while the clandestine UGT had boycotted the State Union, almost a fifth had been shop stewards or branch delegates in the OSE.[9] The reorganization of the Socialist Union was also helped by the very fact that it had not taken part on any scale in the struggle against the dictatorship. Its lack of experience enabled it to adapt more quickly than Comisiones to the changing situation of the post-Franco period. The UGT was more attuned to the mood of moderation among workers in the gathering economic crisis, and its adoption of a social-democratic model of unionism evidently had a growing appeal among many workers. But the pool of workplace leaders from which the Catalan UGT could draw was very small and the branches that it set up in the early stages were improvised and totally unrepresentative.[10] Moreover, the UGT nationally drew mainly on white-collar workers as its cadres, 11

---

[8] Interviews with Valentín Antón (19 Apr. 1983), José Luis Rodríguez, and Gil Pachón.

[9] R. Fishman, 'Working-class Organization and Political Change', Ph.D. thesis (Yale, 1985).

[10] According to the Organizational Secretary of the Catalan UGT at the time, 98% of the 197 local branches set up by 1978 were unrepresentative: Rodríguez interview.

per cent of whom were managerial or technical staff, while over 60 per cent of Comisiones shop-floor leaders were blue-collar. Ironically, among its new officials were ex-bureaucrats of the State Union, which the UGT had so determinedly shunned throughout the dictatorship.[11]

The 1978 union elections drew the profile of the new union movement in Spain. Comisiones Obreras was confirmed as the largest union in the country, followed at a short distance by the UGT. In Catalonia, the former won a majority of all the votes cast and over $2\frac{1}{2}$ times as many as the Socialist union. The results were paradoxical, for they suggested that large numbers of workers who voted for the PSOE in the general elections supported the Communist Union on labour issues. Together, the two confederations dominated the new union movement; neither USO nor least of all the Revolutionary Left unions were able to muster any significant support.

As for the anarcho-syndicalist union, the CNT, it was clear, although it took no part in the elections, that it had failed to recover its old hegemony among the working-class in Catalonia. The libertarian movement of which it was part had always been a heterogeneous body, and Francoist repression had only served to scatter and divide its components even further. Moreover, the transformation of Catalan society in the sixties had given rise to a new social structure and new values that accorded ill with the moral principles of the old movement. The small Anarchist movement that emerged in the post-Franco period was marked by a painful gap between the old guard of militants who had survived the dark years of the dictatorship in exile or in clandestinity and a generation of young Anarchists whose reference-point was the youthful rebellion of the sixties.[12] It was not long before the Anarchists split up once again. Nevertheless, anarcho-syndicalism exerted a subterranean influence on the modern labour movement. While it would be wrong to see any continuity between the CNT of the thirties and Comisiones Obreras of the seventies, it can be argued that the old culture of anarcho-syndicalism had effected a junction in the sixties with the localized and participatory style of the new movement.

[11] *Mundo Diario*, 21 Sept. and 11 Oct. 1977. Figures for the composition of union members are from Fishman (1985), 140–1.

[12] See, for example, I. Guardia Abella, *Conversaciones sobre el movimiento obrero* (Madrid, 1978).

The euphoria of the period of mass union recruitment in 1977–8 turned sour in a matter of a few years. By the early eighties, it had become clear that, far from being one of the strongest movements in Europe, the Spanish unions had one of the lowest levels of union membership. If the calculations about the number of workers signed up after the unions became legal had been over-optimistic, the drop in membership was nevertheless dramatic.[13] Although no reliable figures are available, it is likely that less than a fifth of Spain's wage-earners were union members at the end of 1981 and that the proportion had dropped even further in subsequent years, reaching a level as low as 12 per cent.[14] Indeed, the unions entered a profound crisis of identity. Having been the main actor in the struggle against the dictatorship between 1962 and 1976, the labour movement became the poor relation of the new democracy.

THE CRISIS OF UNIONISM IN THE EIGHTIES

Three major causes of the impasse that faced the union movement in the eighties can be singled out: the effects of the economic crisis, the consequences of the political form taken by the transition to democracy, and the legacy of Francoism.[15] Of the three, it was undoubtedly the economic crisis that most weakened the emerging unions. The recession that hit the Western economy in the aftermath of the rise in oil prices in 1973 affected Spain more deeply than other European countries. Not only was the Spanish economy more reliant on oil imports

[13] In a 1978 survey, Pérez Díaz found that 56.3% of industrial workers were unionized. By 1980, in a follow-up survey, this had dropped to 33.8%. Pérez Díaz, 'Los obreros españoles', op cit.

[14] J. A. Sagardoy and D. León, in *El poder sindical en España* (Barcelona, 1982), 130, put the figure at 20% in 1982. J. Estivill and J. M. De la Hoz, basing their calculations on figures declared in Union conferences in 1983, put total paid-up membership at 10.7%: 'L'evolució del sindicalisme a Europa', *Mon Laboral*, 2nd semester 1986, pp. 7–32.

[15] For a study of the economic crisis in Spain see Fundación Fondo para la Investigación Económica y Social, 'Los ajustes a la crisis de la economía española', *Papeles de Economía Española*, no. 21 (1984). For the effects of the recession on the Catalan economy see M. Casals Couturier and J. M. Vidal Villa, *L'economía de Sabadell* (Sabadell, 1983), vol. i. Some public discussion of the causes of the crisis has taken place in Union conferences and in the Union press: see for example the General Report to the Second Congress of Comisiones Obreras (Barcelona, 1981) and J. Aznar, 'Sindicalizar más las Comisiones Obreras', *Lluita Obrera*, July 1980.

but its main activities were located in industries most vulnerable to the fall in world prices: steel, shipyards, and textiles. The period of transition to democracy had seen a rise in the cost of labour (but not a rise in real wages per capita, because of growing unemployment), a low level of investment, and a fall in savings. The three pillars on which the 'economic miracle' had rested—foreign investment, tourism, and emigrant remittances —were severely eroded by the world crisis.

The economic recession had a devastating effect on the traditional industries of Catalonia. Because it was an overwhelmingly industrial region, dominated by three of the industries particularly hit by the crisis—textiles, engineering, and construction for the tourist sector—Catalonia suffered a severer recession than most other areas of Spain with the exception of the Basque Country. Between 1973 and 1979, the rate of growth of per capita income in Catalonia rose more slowly than the average for Spain, while its rate of unemployment soared above the national average.[16] The social effect of the recession was especially marked in towns such as Sabadell whose economic activity had centred on one industry. The textile sector in this old wool-spinning town went through a new and more radical process of reconversion in the seventies than that which it had experienced during the previous decade. The closure and rationalization of old firms broke up many work-forces that had played an important role in the labour movement under the dictatorship. Alongside the newly converted and trimmed-down firms, a black economy had grown whose workers it was impossible to unionize. It was calculated that some 30% of the industrial turnover of Sabadell in 1982 was generated by non-registered firms.[17] Textile machines could still be heard rattling behind the closed gates of many old factories dotted around the town, but the workers inside no longer worked for the firm whose name appeared, in crumbling signs, on the façade.

Another centre of militant shop-floor organization, Baix Llobregat, was also badly hit by the recession. The area of Almeda, for example, once a bustling industrial centre, seemed laid waste in the eighties. In one corner stood the tall gaunt ruins of the Laforsa steel-mill, its roof caved in and its gates thick with

---

[16] Casals and Vidal, vol. i.
[17] Ibid. See also *El País,* 29 May 1983.

weeds. Around the conurbation, dozens of small factories and workshops lay in various states of deterioration. Those firms still in business continued production with a considerably reduced work-force. The dirty tracks around the industrial estate were virtually empty of vehicles and on a weekday an eerie silence hung over the area as if it were a Sunday.

In Barcelona, the old industrial centres continued to wither. The once flourishing industry of Poble Nou was virtually derelict, ravaged by real-estate speculation and economic recession. Alongside the ruins of factories, dozens of transport depots had crept in to take advantage of the proximity of the motorway to the north. Blocks of old buildings and warehouses were being razed to the ground in preparation for the 1992 Olympics. The traditional industry of Poble Nou had virtually collapsed. By the early eighties, few of its old dyeing and bleaching firms were left. In the city and its suburbs, most such companies had folded between 1965 and 1975.

The engineering industry had also been badly hit. In the country as a whole between 1979 and 1982, over 44,000 jobs were lost in the 150 largest plants, a total of 16.5 per cent of their work-force. In Barcelona in 1976, an average of one firm each day was declaring itself in crisis.[18] The best-organized factories had suffered severe manpower cuts or closed entirely. The Poble Nou plant of Motor Ibérica had disappeared after a prolonged and determined struggle in 1976 had failed to keep it open. The nearby factory of Hispano Olivetti cut its staff from 3,000 to 900 despite a bitter fight by its workers to preserve their jobs. SEAT, La Maquinista, Macosa, and other large plants saw a drastic fall in the strength of their work-forces.

The rash of closures and the sudden rise in unemployment not only weakened or broke up the traditional centres of labour militancy, but also undermined the confidence of workers in their ability to defend their jobs and living standards. The mounting crisis, of course, affected the capacity of the new unions to offer benefits to workers. But they played a particularly defensive role, negotiating redundancy terms or restraining struggles over closures in the belief that further resistance was pointless. Leaders of fierce struggles against cuts in the last years

[18] *Mundo Diario*, 6 Aug. 1977. The first figure is according to calculations by Comisiones Obreras, *El País*, 26 Mar. 1983.

of the dictatorship could be found agreeing to closures and pocketing redundancy payments without further ado. After over a decade of rising living standards, the unions were now reaching agreements in some cases to cut real wages.

The economic downturn had begun precisely at a time when the new union movement was beginning to recruit members, with the result that its appeal was diminished for masses of workers with no experience of unionism. Moreover, the problem of how to deal with the effects of the recession created a bitter polemic in the union movement that further weakened its image among workers. The divisions were particularly acute within the Catalan Comisiones Obreras, in which a large minority were arguing for a policy of resistance to all closures against the majority line of negotiating redundancies where the cost of outright opposition was thought too high.[19]

The second cause of the union crisis was the subordinate and sometimes ambiguous role the two major unions played in the transition to democracy. The difficulties they faced were partly of their own making. It was not just that they and the specific interests they represented were deprived of funds, excluded from the political negotiations of 1977–8, and hamstrung by the government's filibustering over trade-union rights. Their problem lay also in the ambiguity of their relationship to the parties to which they were linked. This was highlighted in the divisions within Comisiones Obreras over the Moncloa Pact. The agreement was signed by the Communist leadership without any discussion, even among high-ranking Party members, and it was endorsed enthusiastically by Madrid Comisiones leaders as if the Union itself had been involved in the talks. Yet it became clear that large numbers of workers disapproved of the Pact and that within Comisiones there was widespread criticism, not just of the agreement itself but of any social pact with the government.[20] The vociferous defence of the Moncloa Pact by some leaders reinforced the impression not only that Comisiones played second fiddle to the Communist Party but also that, in its anxiety

---

[19] This was the main polemic in the Second Congress of the Barcelona Comisiones Obreras in June 1983. It also lay at the roots of the split within the PSUC that led to the formation of the pro-soviet Partit dels Comunistes Catalans. See *El País,* 13 Apr. 1982, and *Noticiero Universal,* 12 Apr. 1982.

[20] Péréz Díaz (1979), 51, and Fishman (1985), 395.

to be involved in the political negotiations, the leadership was neglecting the bread-and-butter issues affecting workers.[21]

Indeed, a wide gap seemed to have opened up within Comisiones Obreras between the concrete tasks of union organization—recruitment, bargaining, training, and so on—and the political concerns of the leadership. 'It was like Jekyll and Hyde,' the Secretary-General of the Catalan Comisiones remembers.

There was a divorce between the union work being done at the base and the concerns and general discussion of the Union. Union leaders did their shop-floor work but when they went to the Union, a curious sort of cultural, even psychological metamorphosis took place. When they went to the top levels of the Union, the talk was about 'grand' politics while in the factory it was about restructuring or redundancies.[22]

Referring to the Union's attempt to mobilize workers over broader issues, one of the leaders of the Catalan Comisiones most critical of the Moncloa Pact wrote, '. . . the explanation and defence of our position on these questions has not been linked sufficiently with concrete union work over the everyday problems facing workers . . . The result is that we seem to workers to be more concerned with global policies than with the problems that affect them directly every day.'[23] The old practice among may Communist leaders of seeing Comisiones as part of the wider policy of the Party died hard. It did little to strengthen the image of Comisiones Obreras as an independent labour union.

For their part, the Socialists were intent on building the UGT as an organized base for their party, and it is unlikely that they were ever serious about their professed desire for a united confederation of workers.[24] The UGT's zigzags between united action with Comisiones Obreras and unilateral action such as abandoning the united union front COS in April 1977 and, more importantly, signing an independent pact with the employers' organization in 1979 (the *Acuerdo Marco Interconfederal*) responded in part to the electoral ambitions of the PSOE. But the UGT's policies were also dictated by a different conception of

[21] See for example Marcelino Camacho's declarations to the press in *Mundo Diario*, 13 Oct. 1977.   [22] López Bulla interview.

[23] J. M. Rodríguez Rovira, '¿Qué ha pasado en Seat?' *Lluita Obrera*, June 1980.

[24] See for example P. Castellano, 'Problemática sindical', *Cambio 16*, 1 Mar. 1976.

the role of unions to that of Comisiones Obreras. By the late seventies it was clear that the UGT had espoused a social-democratic model of unionism as a provider of services within a system of free collective bargaining. In contrast, Comisiones Obreras' reference-point was the Italian model of global negotiations between unions, political parties, employers, and government, backed by mobilization.[25]

The divisions between the two Union Confederations and their lack of independence from political parties did much to erode the image of the union movement among many workers who did not identify strongly with their political orientation. These two related problems were taken seriously by shop stewards. A survey of workplace representatives in Madrid and Barcelona in 1981 revealed that while 83 per cent chose the economic crisis as one of the main causes of the crisis of unionism, over 62 per cent also put it down to the divisions among the unions and almost half attached importance to the subordination of the unions to the political parties.[26]

Moreover, the relationship between union leadership and rank and file had been transformed. The spontaneous forms of agitation that had characterized the grass-roots protest movements of the early seventies were gradually replaced from the middle of 1976 by politically controlled mobilizations. Self-organization gave way to delegation and later to the new structures of the democratic State and the unions. In the process, the level of rank-and-file participation began to fall, until, by the early eighties, the regular factory-floor assemblies were virtually no more than a memory of the past and the residents' associations a pale shadow of their former selves. The almost continuous climate of mobilization that had existed in areas such as Baix Llobregat and Sabadell had evaporated and with it the active bond between the labour movement and the local population, and between militants and rank and file. The impulse towards unity that had characterized the movement during the dictatorship had thereby been weakened.

Underlying the new mood of *desencanto*, or disenchantment, was the sense of failure that after so much struggle little had been

---

[25] For the UGT's policy see Nicolás Redondo's speech to the 32nd Congress of the UGT, published in *Mundo Obrero*, 27 June to 3 July 1980. For that of Comisiones Obreras, see its *Plan de Solidaridad Nacional* (Madrid, 1980).

[26] Fishman (1985), 377.

achieved beyond a formal system of parliamentary democracy. The terms of the new political order did not reflect the mass mobilizations that had taken place all over the country against the dictatorship. Instead, the opposition parties seemed to have been more concerned with placating the Right. A Baix Llobregat workers' leader expressed his disappointment thus, 'Since I had had no experience of democracy, I could afford to dream.'[27] An erstwhile clandestine organizer of Comisiones in Barcelona faced a different sort of paradox: 'I have the feeling that in those days [during the dictatorship] I was in a much better position to influence the life of the city on the following day than now when everything is legal and there are no problems about meeting-places and making telephone calls etc.'[28] For many militants the aphorism, 'Against Franco, we lived better' (an adaption of the much-repeated lament among some Spaniards that life was better under Franco), had a bitter ring of truth.

The third major cause of the crisis of unionism in the eighties was the shadow that 40 years of dictatorship cast over the new union movement. There were two sides to this legacy: firstly, the social effects of the prohibition of free unions and the imposition of an authoritarian system of industrial relations controlled by the State; and secondly, the repercussions of traditions of struggle developed over almost two decades by the labour movement.

However widespread the labour movement had been in the last years of the Franco regime, it had mobilized only a minority of workers. The vast mass of people in industry had had no experience of collective organization or solidarity. To some extent, therefore, the Francoist aim of disorganizing the working class had been successful. Many of the new recruits who flocked into Comisiones Obreras and UGT in 1977–8 had little notion of what a union was. Indeed, for all the hostility which workers felt towards the old regime, its system of industrial relations had laid deep roots in their response to labour problems. The paternal role that the State had claimed to play as defender of the lone worker against any arbitrary action of the employer has been stressed in previous chapters. It could almost be said that an unwritten contract existed whereby workers enjoyed a relatively high degree of job security in lieu of the loss of the right to

[27] Cano interview. [28] Boix interview.

organize collectively. This tacit exchange was dramatically reversed in the new democracy when the freedom to form unions was swapped for the right of the employers to fire virtually at will. From the 1980 Workers' Statute (the new law governing industrial relations) onwards, the employers were given increasing flexibility to hire and fire. It would not be surprising that many workers blamed the drastic rise of unemployment on the loss of the Francoist legislation protecting jobs. To possess the right to join a union might seem poor compensation for losing one's job.

The reliance on the State as arbiter of industrial relations and the law as dispenser of individual justice created habits that were poor soil for the growth of collective behaviour vital to the new union movement. The heritage of constitutionalism also held back the development of forms of arbitration and mediation. Its sway could be seen in the eighties in the array of legal advisers that the new unions were forced to provide and in the full waiting-rooms of private labour lawyers.[29] But the most important latent influence on the attitudes of masses of workers towards unionism was that exerted by the OSE. While it had evoked widespread cynicism for its corruption and subjection to the State, the OSE had provided the only mechanism through which most workers could improve their living and working conditions. In addition to collective bargaining and legal advice, the State Union had offered an astonishing range of services, from holiday camps to housing, through which it had built an extensive network of patronage. The funds it had wielded were enormous, flowing not only from the property confiscated in 1939 from the parties and unions of the Left, but also from State subsidies and the obligatory dues it collected from all employers and employees alike. The income of the OSE in 1972 alone was over 12,000 million pesetas (about £72 million), of which, according to its accounts, more than 5,000 million were spent promoting social and welfare activities such as housing and professional training.[30] In a speech at the 1968 Congress of the OSE, the national head of the organization, José Solís, boasted

[29] The Catalan Comisiones Obreras employed no fewer than 70 labour lawyers in 1983: López Bulla interview.

[30] Organización Sindical, *Síntesis de actividades sindicales en el período 1968–1972* (Madrid, 1973).

that it had set up over 23,000 co-operatives with more than $2\frac{1}{2}$ million members, established 125 technical schools for training youth, dispensed 700 million pesetas (over £4 million) in study grants in 1968 alone, and arbitrated almost $2\frac{1}{2}$ million individual labour disputes since 1943.[31] In Barcelona in the early seventies, the OSE had employed 130 lawyers to give legal advice to workers. During the previous decade, some 30,000 people in the province had been enrolled in its sports and leisure clubs.[32] Indeed, at one point or another, most workers and their families came into contact with the ubiquitous OSE.

While there was no mourning when it sank without trace in 1978, the OSE left a profound mark on industrial relations in Spain. The problem was not just that many shop-floor leaders had acquired their experience of bargaining and organization within its structures but that hundreds of thousands of workers had gained a distorted idea of unionism: as a form of social insurance and a source of benefits, on one hand; and on the other, as a quasi-State institution for which money was taken out of their pay-packet each week. It was significant that one of the hardest tasks facing the new unions was to ensure that subscriptions were being paid up.[33] Nor had the experience of industrial relations under the dictatorship encouraged the view that unionism involved mutual responsibilities between officials and rank and file. After the first flush of union recruitment in 1978, and in the steadily deteriorating economic situation, it must have seemed to many workers that they were not getting much for their union dues. Yet the drop in membership was not completely synonymous with a fall in support for union policies. One of the surveys already mentioned found considerable backing for the confederations among non-unionized workers.[34] The combination of a low level of union membership and a relatively high degree of mobilization was a contradictory feature of the labour movement of the eighties.

Indeed, the very success of this mobilization during the last

[31] The speech can be found in CG archives no. 1763 (11).

[32] OS, *Memoria del Delegado Provincial de la Organización Sindical* (Barcelona, 1973); Candel (1968), 158–9.

[33] See for example the problems of UGT over unpaid dues in *El País,* 19 Mar. 1978.

[34] Almost 20% of non-unionized workers in the sample supported one confederation or another: Pérez Díaz, 'Los obreras españoles', 42.

years of the dictatorship had concealed weaknesses that were to surface in the new democratic period. The traditions of struggle that had grown in the labour movement left militants ill prepared for the tasks that lay ahead. The first most obvious problem was that of adapting to the new and unexpected environment of the democratic transition. The scenario of the post-Franco period that activists of the opposition had been encouraged to rehearse in their minds for years bore no relation to the drab scene that confronted them after the first flush of democracy. The result of so much personal sacrifice, imprisonment, exile, or torture, was meagre indeed. The heroic struggles of the past were replaced by the mundane tasks of organizing, collecting dues, and bargaining in bitterly adverse conditions in which the labour movement found itself on the retreat. Charismatic leaders had to learn to become bureaucrats; victims of torture had to learn to live with their torturers; solidarity gave way to division; the mass meetings on the shop-floor rapidly dwindled; and the rank-and-file base began to evaporate. It was not surprising in these conditions that many militants became burnt-out cases.

In fact, there was a striking lack of continuity in shop-floor leadership between the last years of Francoism and the new period. In a 1981 survey, fewer than 60 per cent of Comisiones shop stewards from Madrid and Barcelona had been involved in the labour movement during the dictatorship. The same percentage held for those who participated in strike action under the former regime, while only around a third had held elective posts or had taken part in negotiations with employers. Conversely, a third of those who had had no contact with the clandestine Comisiones had experienced strike action, and just under 20% had been shop stewards or branch delegates in the OSE.[35] Two conclusions may be drawn from these figures. The first is that Comisiones Obreras (and the labour opposition as a whole) did not embrace all the activity of the labour movement under the regime; this was indeed the suggestion made in our analysis of the 1975 elections.[36] The second is that there was a significant drop-out rate between the 1975 and 1980 union elections among militants who had stood in the Comisiones-sponsored electoral platform of 1975, the *Candidaturas Unidas y Democráticas.*

[35] Fishman (1985), 184 and 195.
[36] It is also Fishman's conclusion, ibid. 196–7.

The workplace union leaders of the eighties were by no means those militants forged in the struggle against Franco.

Moreover, the relative ease with which militants were able to mobilize workers in the early seventies had discouraged the idea that on-going organization was important. Of course, it was not possible, in the conditions of the dictatorship, to build a union with a mass membership, as the CNT had found out in brutal terms in the late forties. But the main form of militant workplace organization that had developed since the late fifties, the strike committees or comisiones which had emerged and disappeared according to the rhythm of dispute, had nourished a tradition of spontaneity that retarded the growth of union structures on the shop-floor. It was significant that of the two forms of workplace organization which the union movement attempted to set up after 1977, it was the *comité de empresa* (the new works council, to which any worker could be elected regardless of whether he or she was a union member) that got off the ground rather than the union branch.[37]

Nor had the peculiar and highly effective organizational model that Comisiones militants had adopted—the reliance on the OSE structures as a framework of agitation, on the small clandestine networks of Comisiones for co-ordination, and on the mass shop-floor meetings for mobilization—prepared the new Union for the task of building nation-wide bodies to service all aspects of working life in each trade and profession. The disappearance of the OSE left a vacuum in which militants were forced to improvise organization. The reluctance to abandon the 'movement' of Comisiones Obreras in favour of its constitution as a union had been a strong impulse among many militants in Catalonia. Neither their traditions nor their aspirations inclined them towards the more bureaucratic models of unionism of neighbouring countries. Furthermore, a tradition of blue-collar workerism in Comisiones weighed against the spread of unionism to new layers of white-collar workers. The vacillations about how to organize the teachers, nurses, lawyers, and other professions within the Union did not help to draw them into its ranks.

[37] Though the UGT and Comisiones Obreras were divided over which to stress in their shop-floor organization. For the views of the different unions on shop-floor organization see *Cambio 16*, 17 July 1977.

The most damaging legacy of 40 years of Francoism, however, was that it had succeeded to some extent in atomizing labour protest. This was most obvious on a national scale, but it was also true on a regional level.[38] Variations in patterns of behaviour among workers of different regions and industries were magnified under the dictatorship by the effects of repression, atomized bargaining, and the divisive structures of the OSE. Even within the city, as we have argued in the case of Greater Barcelona, the labour movement in each district or locality developed its own culture of militancy distinct from that of a neighbouring area that may have lain only a few miles away. It has also been argued that in certain industries in Barcelona, in particular that of engineering, militant work-forces developed their own style of struggle that set them apart from each other, though they may have shared the same industrial estate. This parochialism had been a source of strength during the latter part of the old regime, but it had not prepared the ground for the broader tasks that lay before the union movement in the new democracy. Militant groups of workers were called on to dilute concessions they had won from their employers after many years of struggle in order to accommodate the needs of workers who had never been able to organize. The Baix Llobregat engineering workers, for example, had to forgo part of a bonus that they had negotiated with local employers as the price of strengthening the provincial agreement.[39] There was resistance to move towards more generalized bargaining that would embrace the weaker lower-paid sections of workers. The print-workers of Catalonia, for example, were reluctant to broaden the scope of their provincial agreement to encompass a national contract.

Indeed, the segregation of labour protest under Francoism had been such that shop-floor and local labour leaders emerged during the transition, from the intense, almost claustrophobic atmosphere of their workplace or area, with only a hazy notion of what had been happening elsewhere. A textile workers' leader from Sabadell confesses, 'As a worker, I know what I am doing in my factory. But when it comes to running a union you've got to

---

[38] Only in a few very special instances was some form of national co-ordination possible—among railway workers because of their mobility, and among bank employees, as we saw in Chapter 6. For the railway workers, see J. L. Martino de Jugo, *Los ferroviarios en Comisiones Obreras* (Madrid, 1980).

[39] Cerdán interview.

know the industry from another point of view and in this sense we were ignorant.'[40] In some cases, militants were reluctant to leave the close network of solidarity that had been built over years of struggle in their area to assume broader responsibilities in the new union movement. Local traditions still coloured the responses of militants to national problems, and yet decisions were being made centrally that affected their capacity to continue defending the interests of workers in their area.

This was graphically illustrated in the case of the Comisiones Obreras of Baix Llobregat. Overwhelmingly dominant in the labour movement of the area, the Union attempted to reach an agreement with local employers in the so-called Pact of Baix Llobregat to preserve jobs and raise productivity.[41] But the problems that faced local industry were part of a more general crisis which reached into all corners of the country. They could not be solved at a local level any more than the Baix Llobregat labour movement could extend the better conditions it had negotiated to other parts of Spain. Even the best-organized work-force in the area, that of Siemens, could do little to prevent the effects of economic recession from eroding its more favourable terms of contract. The 40 per cent drop in the national market for the small motors that Siemens produced led to negotiated redundancies, until over a third of the work-force had left the company.[42] The Baix Llobregat branch of Comisiones Obreras, one of the strongest local union branches in Spain, was hardly in a position to influence negotiations about technological reconversion involving multinational firms, employers' organizations, ministerial departments, regional government, and national unions. The new situation required broader forms of union organization embracing industrial sectors across the boundaries of towns and provinces. Local mobilization was no longer a sufficient condition of a successful defence of workers' interests.

[40] J. A. García interview.

[41] It was no coincidence that the Baix Llobregat employers were among the first in Spain to set up their own association in response to the organized strength of the local labour movement. But it did not survive the establishment in 1978 of centralized employers' organizations, the most important of which was the *Confederación Española de Organizaciones Empresariales.* For more details of the Pact, see *Mundo Diario,* 25 Jan., 1 Feb., 6, 8, 12, and 13 July 1978, and *Tele-Exprés,* 30 Jan. and 14 July 1978.

[42] Interview with Carlos Blasco, 10 Mar. 1983.

The transition to democracy itself was part of a broad offensive by government and employers to establish the most profitable terms for Spanish-based capital to compete in the cutthroat conditions of the recession. The Francoist State had been abandoned mainly because it had proved incapable of dealing with social conflict and had, moreover, aggravated it. Yet the terms of the new democratic system were less favourable to the new unions than the mobilized power of the labour movement under the old regime had merited.

During an earlier period of economic crisis in the early thirties, the alliance of the employers, the landowners, the Church, and the military had set out to destroy the organized working class and the parties associated with it in order to protect their own interests. The crisis that faced Spain in the seventies was not of the same magnitude. What was at stake was not the existing social and economic order but its political representation. Neither economic recession nor social conflict posed the sort of challenge that could not be dealt with by political reform. The fundamental reason for this greater social stability was the legacy of 20 years of economic growth during which living standards had risen dramatically. But another important cause lay in the effects of almost 40 years of dictatorship. The regime failed in its attempt to banish class conflict either in the period of austerity in the first two decades of its rule or during the economic boom of the sixties and the early seventies. But it did succeed to some extent in disorganizing the working class through the use of force, the imposition of an authoritarian and divisive industrial relations system, and the offer of some of the benefits of economic growth. For all the power of mobilization that the labour movement was able to wield, especially in Catalonia, it was the working class that paid the price of the economic crisis in the post-Franco period.

In conclusion, the history of the labour movement between 1939 and the present day is marked by discontinuity. The old institutions of the working class were destroyed after the victory of the Nationalists. Its traditions were then buried by the radical social, economic, and urban changes of the sixties. In turn, the forms of collective organization developed by the new labour movement in the latter half of the dictatorship were cut short by the economic crisis and the political upheaval of the post-Franco period.

The Spanish labour movement was indeed remade between

1960 and 1976, but not in ways determined by the opposition. Though it shared a common programme of demands, it was a fragmented movement, rooted in the particular conditions of each urban centre, industry, and workplace. The organized workers in that period were fundamentally concerned with raising their low living standards inherited from the repressive conditions of post-Civil-War Spain. It was only in the mid seventies that broader questions of union organization and shop-floor control began to be addressed. The source of these weaknesses can be attributed in large measure to the adverse circumstances in which the labour movement developed. One of the main obstacles to its growth was the multiple forms of social control exercised by the regime. Equally important was the lack of experience of collective organization of the Spanish working class as a result of the swift industrialization of Spain. Another cause of the weakness of the new union movement was the tendency of many sections of the opposition to ignore basic union matters in the belief that Spain was on the brink of revolution. When it became clear that political change would come through a process of negotiation with regime reformists, the opposition parties put the achievement of moderate parliamentary consensus before the building of independent union organization.

The history of the Spanish labour movement since 1939 illuminates some of the key problems of political change under authoritarian regimes, and parallels can be drawn with the experience of the labour movement in France and Italy in the immediate post-war years, Argentina and Portugal in the seventies, and more recently in Poland. In all these cases, in which the self-defence of workers' interests has been prohibited or curtailed, it is impossible to separate economic from political struggle. But the level of workers' mobilization is not the same as the degree of their politicization. The political strength of the labour movement in Spain, as in Portugal, and in Poland with Solidarność, derived from a shared conviction in the right to possess basic freedoms accepted without question elsewhere, of which the most important was the right to form free trade unions. The extent of militancy—the street clashes with the police, the occupations, the general strikes—was more an expression of resistance against State repression than a token of radical consciousness.

The shape of the new post-authoritarian society has depended on the relationship between the strength of the labour movement and its allies and the ability of the prevailing order to reform itself. Even the most radical example of political change in an autocratic society, the 1917 Russian Revolution, suggests that the politicization of workers flowed largely from the failure of Tsarism to solve their social and economic problems because of the continued war campaign. The vacillations of Kerensky's provisional government led the small Russian labour movement to go beyond its initial demands and support the Bolsheviks' call for the seizure of state power. During more recent moments of political upheaval when the working-class movement seemed to challenge the State itself, as in France in May 1968 and Portugal in the spring of 1974, the margin for political reform and economic concession was considerably greater. In Spain, the ruling order was able to abandon the Francoist State 'as one abandons an old coat in spring'.[43]

The strength of the labour movement as it emerges from an authoritarian system into a parliamentary democracy has depended, of course, on the circumstances of the political transition. Where it is the result of the collapse of an old regime under the weight of social and political dissent or war, as in the case of Italy in 1945, the labour movement has wrung economic and social concessions from the new political order. The Italian working-class movement emerged victorious out of 20 years of dictatorship; it was the FIAT workers of Turin in March 1943 who struck the first major challenge to the Axis powers, and the workers' insurrection in Milan and Turin in April 1945 that marked the end of Fascism in Italy. In Spain, on the other hand, the new labour movement had grown in the sixties in circumstances of ferocious repression. Moreover, the conditions of the transition to democracy were negotiated with the real or imagined threat of authoritarian restoration hanging above, and the terms were vague or modest over economic and social reform while expansive over constitutional reform. Unless the transition to democracy marks a moment of expansion of the potential for working-class organization, the negative consequences of authoritarian rule—the fragmentation of struggle,

---

[43] Rossana Rossanda, p. 145.

the lack of experience of unionism, the legacy of State intervention in industrial relations—are likely to undermine its ability to organize and defend workers' interests.

However, even where the labour movement has been on the ascendancy, as in France and Italy in the immediate post-war years, Chile between 1969 and 1973, Portugal in 1974, and Spain in the post-Franco era, its immediate needs have been subordinated by the principal parties of the Left to maintaining a consensus with the political and economic establishment, misleadingly termed as the 'national interest'. The consequence has been, to a greater or lesser extent, the weakening of the labour movement and the erosion of the influence of the parties of the Left whose main power base it is. The splits that occurred in the union movement in France, Italy, Portugal, and Spain were not the result simply of ideological differences among workers, economic crisis, or foreign interference, but also of the parliamentary preoccupations of the established Left.[44]

The paradox posed in the Preface to this book—the power of the Spanish labour movement under Franco and its organizational weakness in the new democracy—is perhaps not so great after all. The fledgeling unions were faced with formidable handicaps—the deepest world recession since the thirties, the pervasive legacy of Francoism, the subordination of labour to political compromise. In these circumstances, it is perhaps wrong to talk of the crisis of unionism. On the contrary, what is striking about the Spanish labour movement is how, in the adverse conditions of the dictatorship, it developed at all, and how, confronted with so many obstacles in the post-Franco period, it faced up to the challenge of a new era.

The task confronting the union movement at the end of the eighties is to reconstruct the defence of workers' interests, including those of the unemployed. It can no longer continue to fight struggles that draw their energy from circumstances of the past. The new context in which it has to operate is extremely

[44] For the policy of 'moderation' imposed by the Italian Communist leader, Togliatti, see his 1944 speech, 'The Communist Policy of National Unity', in P. Togliatti, *On Gramsci and Other Writings* (London 1979), 29–64; also D. Sassoon, *The Strategy of the Italian Communist Party* (London, 1981), 41–4; for that of the French Communists see ·Maurice Thorez's 1946 interview in *The Times,* quoted in R. Tiersky, *French Communism 1920–1972* (New York, 1974), 149; also I. H. Birchall, *Workers against the Monolith* (London, 1974), 28–9.

complex. Economic recession and technological change are making deep inroads into the traditionally organized sections of workers. The working class itself is changing shape as new areas of exploitation open up. Indeed, the depth of the crisis makes this task no less formidable than that which faced the labour movement in the very different conditions of the Franco dictatorship.

APPENDIX

LIST OF PROTAGONISTS INTERVIEWED BETWEEN 1982 AND 1987

(including notes on their role during Francoism relating to the interviews, as well as party and union affiliation)

Albéndiz, Nicolás—Vice-President of Provincial Transport Union. PSUC. CCOO (Comisiones Obreras).

Alcaina Caballero, José—President of Provincial Engineering Union. Ex-CNT.

Alibés, José María—Architect.

Almendros, Fernando—Labour lawyer.

Antón, Valentín—Secretary-General of UGT Catalonia (post-Franco). PSOE. UGT.

Arán Trullas, Josep—AEG worker. CCOO. Liga Comunista.

Avilés, Montserrat—Labour lawyer. PSUC.

Aznar, Jaime—Editor of *Lluita Obrera*. PSUC. CCOO.

Baños, Bartolomé—Metal worker. PSUC organizer. CCOO.

Blasco, Carlos—Siemens shop steward (post-Franco). CCOO.

Boix, Isidor—PSUC and CCOO industrial organizer.

Bosch, Ana—Metal worker. Mayor of Mollet (post-Franco). CCOO.

Botella, José—Journalist. CCOO. PSUC.

Cano, José—President of San Feliu Engineering Union. Convener of Matacás. PSUC. CCOO.

Cases, José—Delegate to National Union of Entertainment. National Committee of CNT.

Castañé i Colomer, Josep—JOC leader.

Castañé, García, Josep—AEG worker. PSUC. CCOO.

Cerdán, Esteban—Convener of Laforsa. Vice-President of Cornellá Engineering Union. PSUC. CCOO.

Chicharro, Tomás—La Maquinista worker. HOAC. FOC. PSUC. CCOO.

Claudín, Fernando—Writer. Executive Committee PCE (to 1965).

Clemente, Alfredo—Bank worker. PSUC. CCOO. PCC (post-Franco).

De la Hoz, José María—Ex-priest. Metal worker. USO.

Escudé, Ramón—Secretary of Institut de Industria de Terrassa.

Fanlo, Carlos—Director of OS Provincial Employment Exchange. Director of OS Provincial Information and Publications Service.

Fernández, Ginés—Engineering worker. PSUC organizer. CCOO.

Frutos, Paco—Textile and engineering worker. PSUC and CCOO organizer.

Fuentes, Roc—Labour lawyer. PSUC.

García, Cipriano—Building worker. PSUC organizer. National co-ordinator of CCOO.

García, Emilio—Engineering worker. Sectores. PSUC. CCOO.

García, Juan Antonio—Textile worker. PSUC. CCOO.

García-Nieto, Juan—Priest. CCOO.

Gilaberte, Silvestre—SEAT worker. PSUC. CCOO.

Giménez, Paco—Bank worker. USO organizer. Secretary-General of USO (post-Franco).

Gispert, Rafael—Engineering worker. Movimiento Comunista.

Gordillo, Francisco—Textile worker. PSUC organizer. Secretary-General of Terrassa CCOO (post-Franco).

Gutiérrez, Antoni—Michelin worker. Delegate to National Co-ordinating Committee of CCOO. Secretary-General of CCOO (1988).

Huertas Clavería, Josep María—Journalist. Poble Nou Residents' Association.

Iglesias, Rodrigo—Secretary-General of Foment de Treball (post-Franco).

Lleonart, Francesc—Bank worker. President of Junta Coordinadora of Mataró Unions. PSUC. CCOO.

López, Ramón—SEAT worker. CCOO.

López Bulla, José Luis—Print-worker. Organizer of Catalan Comisiones Obreras. Secretary-General (post-Franco).

Molas, Juan—Engineering worker. JOC. PSUC. CCOO.

Morales, Pablo—Textile worker. PCC (post-Franco).

Navales, Carlos—Glass-worker. President of Glass and Ceramics Union of Cornellá. Secretary-General of Baix Llobregat CCOO (post-Franco). Sectores. PSUC. CCOO.

Ossets, Agustí—Bank worker. CNT.

Pachón, Gil—Hispano Olivetti worker. Secretary-General of Barcelona UGT (post-Franco).

Pagés, Manel—Technician. Vice-President of Engineering Union of Sabadell. PSUC. CCOO.

Pla, Ramón—Engineering worker. PSUC. CCOO.

Prats, Agustí—Textile worker. Delegate to Provincial Committee of Dyers and Bleachers Union. Secretary-General of CCOO Textile Federation (post-Franco). PSUC. CCOO.

Puiggrós, Ramón—Textile worker. President of Terrassa Wool Union. National Delegate of Wool Union. Secretary-General of Catalan CCOO Textile Federation (post-Franco). HOAC. USO. CCOO.

Pujol, Josep—Engineering worker. MSC. UGT. CCOO.

Ramírez, Remei—Co-ordinator of Solidarity Committee of Barcelona Bishopric.

Rivas, María-Angeles—President of Nueve Barrios Residents' Association. PSUC.

Rodríguez, José Luis—Chemical worker. Secretary-General of Catalan UGT Chemical Federation and Organization Secretary UGT (post-Franco).

Rojas, María Dolores—Textile worker.

Rozas, Angel—Building worker. Delegate to National Commmittee of Construction Union. Delegación Exterior de CCOO. PSUC.

Sartorius, Nicolás—Journalist. PSUC. CCOO.

Trives, Antonio—Engineering worker. Delegate on Sabadell Engineering Union. PSUC. CCOO.

Valdivieso, Juan Ignacio—Building worker. Secretary of Sabadell Construction Federation of CCOO (post-Franco). PSUC. CCOO.

Villanueva, José Miguel—SEAT worker. SEAT convener (post-Franco). UGT.

BIBLIOGRAPHY

PRIMARY SOURCES

1. *Interviews with protagonists*

For list of people interviewed see Appendix.

2. *Unpublished documents*

2.1 Archives of the Civil Government of Barcelona Province:

2.1.1 Jefatura Superior de Policía de Barcelona, VI Brigada Regional de Investigación Social: *Notas informativas* and untitled secret and confidential reports on industries, workplaces, collective bargaining, collective disputes, and union elections; on anti-regime activities in general; and on the political, social, economic, and labour situation; from 1961 to 1977.

2.1.2 Dirección General de la Guardia Civil, Servicio de Información de la 231 Comandancia: as above.

2.1.3 Organización Sindical, Delegación Provincial de Sindicatos: confidential reports to the Civil Governor and unpublished documents on collective bargaining, disputes, and union elections; correspondence between the Civil Governor and the head of the Provincial OS (Delegado Provincial); 1962–77.

2.1.4 Town Councils of Barcelona, Sabadell, Terrassa, Mataró, Hospitalet, Santa Coloma, Cornellá, Esplugues, and Prat: confidential reports to and correspondence with Civil Governor from Mayors.

2.1.5 Delegación Provincial de Trabajo: confidential reports to Civil Governor, 1966–9.

2.1.6 Confiscated clandestine anti-regime leaflets, bulletins, and newspapers; transcripts of illegal speeches and radio broadcasts, 1962–76.

2.2 Archives of the Organización Sindical, Barcelona Province (*Archivos de la Corona de Aragón, Depósito Regional*, Cervera): reports on union elections, collective bargaining, and collective disputes, 1963–75.

2.3 Clandestine shop-floor, union, and party leaflets and bulletins of the labour movement and confidential official documents passed on to labour opposition: in the following archives:

Archivo Agustí Serra (AAS archives)

Archivo de Documentación de la Unión Comarcal de CCOO de Baix Llobregat

Archivo Municipal de Historia de Barcelona (Centro de Documentación Política)

Archivo Municipal de Terrassa

Archivo Nacional de Catalunya (ANC)

Archivo del PCC de Mataró

Archivos del PSUC de Barcelona

Arxiu Historic de Sabadell

Arxiu Tobella

Centre d'Estudis Historics Internacionals (CEHI-FIES)

Centro de Documentación Histórica

Centro de Estudios Sociales

Private archives

3. *Clandestine press:* main periodicals consulted and period covered by research:

Agencia Popular Informativa (API), 1972–5
Asamblea Obrera, 1970–7
Avui, 1972–6
Bandera Roja, 1968–76
Boletín de la UGT de España, 1972–6
Catalunya Obrera, 1969–76
Cuadernos Rojos, 1971–4
Estrella Roja, 1970–6
Informaciones Obreras, 1970–3
Lluita Obrera, 1972–6
Luchas Obreras, 1973–5
Nous Horitzons, 1960–6
Nuestra Bandera, 1966–76
Oficina de Prensa de Euskadi (Eusko Deya) (OPE), 1950–7
Poder Obrero, 1967–9
Prensa Obrera, 1971–4
El Pulso, 1965–9
¿Qué Hacer?, 1969
Realitat, 1969–74
Servir al Pueblo, 1972–6
Solidaridad Obrera, 1940–76
Treball, 1943–76
Unidad, 1967–73

4. *Commercial and official press:* main periodicals consulted:

Acción Sindicalista
Arreu
L'Avenç
Cambio 16
Correo Catalán
Cuadernos para el Diálogo
Diario de Barcelona
Hoja del Lunes
Mundo
Mundo Diario
El País
Sabadell
Tarrassa (Información)
Tele-Exprés
La Vanguardia (Española)

5. *Published documents*

Ariza, Julián, *Comisiones Obreras* (Madrid, 1976).
Cámara Oficial de Comercio e Industria de Sabadell (COCIS), *Memoria comercial e industrial,* annual publication, 1939–74.
Castells, Andreu, *Sabadell: informe de l'oposició,* vols. i–vi (Sabadell, 1983–7).
Comisión Diocesana JOC, *Manifiesto de la juventud trabajadora de Cataluña y Baleares* (Barcelona, 1968).
Comisiones Obreras, *Plan de Solidaridad Nacional* (Madrid, 1980).
Commissions Obreres de Catalunya, *Acción sindical y libertades nacionales: primer congreso de Commissions Obreres de Catalunya 12–15 mayo 1978* (Barcelona, 1978).
Consejo Económico Sindical del Vallés Occidental, *Informe* (Barcelona, 1970).
Consejo Económico Social del Bajo Llobregat, *Ponencia de zonas y polígonos industriales: plan de estructuras generales del AMB* (1970).
_____ *Informe sobre las necesidades más urgentes de la comarca de Cornellá* (1972).
_____ *Plan de necesidades urgentes de la comarca de Cornellá* (1972).
_____ *Comisión de industria* (Barcelona, 1974).
_____ *Comisión de vivienda, urbanismo, y ordenación del territorio* (n.d.).
Delegación Exterior de Comisiones Obreras (ed.), *Documentos básicos de Comisiones Obreras* (n.p., n.d.).

Díaz, José Antonio, *Luchas internas en CCOO Barcelona 1964–70* (Barcelona, 1977).

Federación del Textil de CCOO, *2 Congreso: ponencias, conclusiones y resoluciones* (May, 1981).

García-Nieto, María Carmen, and Donezar, Javier María, *Bases documentales de la España contemporánea*, vol. xi of *La España de Franco 1939–1973* (Madrid, 1975).

González Alonso, Arcadio, *La construcción* (Madrid, 1977).

Gremi de Fabricants de Sabadell, *Memoria*, annual, 1940–76.

HOAC, *CCOO en sus documentos 1958–76* (Madrid, 1977).

Instituto de Estudios Sindicales, Sociales y Cooperativas (Delegación de Barcelona), *Estudio sociológico sobre el trabajador y su medio en la ciudad de Barcelona* (Madrid, 1969).

Ministerio de Trabajo, *Informes sobre conflictos colectivos,* annual, 1963–76.

Organización Sindical (OS) *Información de convenios colectivos sindicales,* monthly 1965–7, and quarterly 1968–73.

——— *Estadísticas de convenios colectivos de trabajo 1958–1967* (Madrid, 1968).

——— *Memoria de actividad sindical* (Barcelona, 1969).

——— *Convenios colectivos sindicales vigentes,* 1973.

——— *Memoria del Delegado Provincial de la Organización Sindical* (Barcelona, 1973).

——— *Síntesis de actividades sindicales en el período 1968–1972* (Madrid, 1973).

Plan nacional de higiene y seguridad del trabajo (Madrid, 1972).

Servicio Sindical de Estadística, *Bienestar social in España* (Madrid, 1976).

Sobre la unidad del movimiento obrero de masas, API, Feb. 1973.

Ucelay Da Cal, Enric, 'Documents (1936): els nacionalistes catalans al PSUC', *Arreu*, 25–31 Oct. 1976.

6. *Memoirs, contemporary accounts, and theoretical works by protagonists*

Alcaraz, Joan, 'Agustí Daura, preparant la revolució', *Al Vent*, Nov. 1982.

L'Avenç, 'Les condicions de treball d'ença de la guerra civil', *L'Avenç*, Jan. 1981.

Balcells, Ignasi (Isidor Boix), *Lucha solidaria—lucha política: una experiencia del movimiento obrero* (Barcelona, 1969).

Barba Hernández, Bartolomé, *Dos años al frente del Gobierno Civil de Barcelona* (Madrid, 1948).

Bellavista, Oleguer, *Evolució d'un barri obrer: Almeda-Cornellá* (Barcelona, 1977).

Boix, Isidor, and Pujades, Manuel, *Conversaciones sindicales con dirigentes obreros* (Barcelona, 1975).

Bruguera, Ignasi (Isidor Boix), *En el camino de la huelga general política* (Barcelona, 1971).

Camacho, Marcelino, *Charlas en la prisión* (Barcelona, 1976).

Carrillo, Santiago, *Después de Franco, ¿qué?* (Paris, 1965).

—— *Nuevos enfoques a los problemas de hoy* (Paris, 1967).

—— *Demain l'Espagne* (Paris, 1974).

—— *Hacia el post-franquismo* (Paris, 1974).

—— *Memoria de la transición* (Barcelona, 1983).

Castaño i Colomer, Josep, *Memories de la JOC a Catalunya 1932–1970* (Barcelona, 1974).

Centre de Treball i Documentació, 'Debat: Comissions Obreres, 1968–69; repressió i crisi', *Quaderns*, 1981.

Claudín, Fernando, *Documentos de una divergencia comunista* (Barcelona, 1978).

Cortes, Angel, 'Quan la memoria encara roman fidel', *L'Avenç*, Mar. 1983, pp. 8–12.

Cuadernos Primero de Mayo, *Marcelino Camacho y el debate de Comisiones Obreras* (Barcelona, 1976).

Damiano, Cipriano, *La resistencia libertaria: la lucha anarco-sindicalista bajo el franquismo* (Barcelona, 1978).

Edo, Luis Andrés, 'Trampa a la CNT', *Mundo*, 18 Dec. 1976.

Fabre, Jaume, and Huertas, Josep M., 'La fundació de CCOO a Barcelona', *L'Avenç*, Sept. 1982.

Fina, Albert, *Des del nostre despatx* (Barcelona, 1978).

García, Miguel, *Franco's Prisoner* (London, 1972).

Gilaberte, Silvestre, 'La lucha obrera en SEAT' (unpublished manuscript, 1976).

Guardia Abella, Isidro, *Conversaciones sobre el movimiento obrero* (Madrid, 1978).

Instituto de Estudios Laborales, 'Conversaciones sindicales' (unpublished manuscript, 1974).

Llonch, Jordi, and Comorera, Ramón, 'Cipriano García: un diputado Terrassense', *Al Vent*, Dec. 1977.

Marcet Coll, José María, *Mi ciudad y yo: veinte años en una alcaldía 1940–1960* (Barcelona, 1963).

Marco Nadal, E., *Condenado a muerte* (Mexico, 1966).

Martín Villa, Rodolfo, *Al servicio del estado* (Barcelona, 1984).

Martino de Jugo, J. L., *Los ferroviarios en Comisiones Obreras* (Madrid, 1980).

Molina, J. M., *El movimiento clandestino en España 1939–1949* (Mexico, 1976).

Orwell, George, *Homage to Catalonia* (London, 1938).

Pallach, Josep, 'Nosaltres i els Comunistes', *Endavant*, July 1959.

Pujol, Josep, 'El naixement de CCOO a Barcelona', *Debat*, no. 5 (July 1978).

Ricart Oller, Josep, *Egara: una parroquia obrera bajo el franquismo (1963-1977)* (Terrassa, 1979).

Sanz Oller, Julio (José Antonio Díaz), *Entre el fraude y la esperanza: las Comisiones Obreras de Barcelona* (Paris, 1972).

Sartorius, Nicolás, *El resurgir del movimiento obrero* (Barcelona, 1975).

_____ *El sindicalismo de nuevo tipo* (Barcelona, 1977).

Vinader, Xavier, 'Angel Abad, o l'enyorança del FLP', *Arreu*, 21-7 Mar. 1977.

SECONDARY SOURCES

Monographs and general works

Abella, Rafael, *La vida cotidiana en España bajo el régimen de Franco* (Barcelona, 1985).

Alabart Vilà, Ana, 'Els barris de Barcelona i el moviment associatiu veïnal', Ph.D. thesis (Universidad de Barcelona, 1981), 2 vols.

Alabart i Vilà, Ana, and Sapes de Lema, Jordi, *La població i l'habitatge a Sabadell* (Sabadell, 1983).

Alba, Victor, *La oposición de los supervivientes (1939-1955)* and *Historia de la resistencia antifranquista (1939-1955)* (Barcelona, 1978).

Almendros Morcillo, F., *et al.*, *El sindicalismo de clase en España (1939-1977)* Barcelona, 1978).

Amsden, Jon, *Collective Bargaining and Class Conflict in Spain* (London, 1972).

Anuario económico y social de España 1975 (Barcelona, 1975).

Anuario de las relaciones laborales en España 1975 (Madrid, 1976).

Anuario de las relaciones laborales en España 1976 (Madrid, 1977).

Aparicio, Miguel A., *El sindicalismo vertical y la formación del estado franquista* (Barcelona, 1980).

Artal, F., *et al.*, *Economía crítica: una perspectiva catalana* (Barcelona, 1973).

Balcells, Albert, *Trabajo industrial y organización obrera en la Cataluña contemporánea (1900-1936)* (Barcelona, 1974).

_____ *Historia contemporánea de Cataluña* (Barcelona, 1983).

Banca Catalana, Servei d'Estudis, *Catalunya: industria i demografia* (Barcelona, 1968).

Barbé i Durán, Lluis (ed.), *Dinámica y perspectiva del Vallés,* 14 vols. (Sabadell, 1970).

Benet, Josep, *Catalunya sota el regim franquista* (Barcelona, 1973, 2nd edn. 1979).

Berriatúa San Sebastián, Javier María, *Las Asociaciones de Vecinos* (Madrid, 1977).

Biescas, José Antonio, and Tuñon de Lara, Manuel, *España bajo la dictadura franquista (1939–1975)*, vol. x of *Historia de España* (Barcelona, 1980).

Birchall, Ian H., *Workers against the Monolith: the Communist Parties since 1943* (London, 1974).

Blanc, Jordi, 'Las huelgas en el movimiento obrero español', in Ruedo Ibérico, *Horizonte Español*, vol. ii (Paris, 1966).

Borja, Jordi, 'Urban Movements in Spain', in Michael Harloe (ed.), *Captive Cities* (Chichester, 1977).

Brademas, J., *Anarcosindicalismo y revolución en España 1930–1937* (Barcelona, 1974).

Bulnes, Ramón, 'Del sindicalismo de represión al sindicalismo de integración', in Ruedo Ibérico, *Horizonte Español*, vol. iii (Paris, 1966).

Cabana, Francesc, *Les multinacionals a Catalunya* (Barcelona, 1984).

Caja de Ahorros de Sabadell, *Dinámica y perspectiva del Vallés 1969* (Sabadell, 1970).

Calamai, Marco, *Storia del movimiento operaio spagnolo dal 1960 al 1975* (Bari, 1975).

Calvet i Puig, Jordi, 'Aproximació al creixement econòmic de Sabadell i Terrassa durant la postguerra (1939–1959)' (unpublished manuscript, 1982).

Caminal, Miquel, *Joan Comorera,* 3 vols. (Barcelona, 1984).

Candel, Francesc, *Els altres catalans* (Barcelona, 1963).

——— *Ser obrero no es ninguna ganga* (Barcelona, 1968).

——— *Apuntes para una sociología del barrio* (Barcelona, 1972).

——— *Emigrantes y trabajadores* (Barcelona, 1972).

Carr, Raymond, and Fusi, Juan Pablo, *Spain: Dictatorship to Democracy* (London, 1979).

Casals Couturier, Muriel, and Vidal Villa, Josep María, *L'economía de Sabadell: estructura, diagnòstic i perspectives*, 2 vols. (Sabadell, 1982).

Cassassas Simó, Lluis, 'La Gran Barcelona en la regionalización de Cataluña', in Asociación de geógrafos españoles, *La región y la geografía española* (Valladolid, 1980).

Castaño Colomer, José, *La JOC en España (1946–1970)* (Salamanca, 1978).

Centre d'Estudis de Planificació, *Reconocimiento territorial de Cataluña* (Barcelona, 1978).

——— *Industrialització a Catalunya 1960–1977* (Barcelona, 1982).

Chao, José, *La iglesia en el franquismo* (Madrid, 1976).

Círculo de Economía, *Gestión o caos: el área metropolitana de Barcelona* (Barcelona, 1973).

Claudín, Fernando, *Santiago Carrillo: crónica de un secretario general* (Barcelona, 1983).

Clavera, Joan, *et al.*, *El capitalismo español (1939–1959)* (Madrid, 1978).

Cliville, R., *et al.*, *Metal: 30 días de huelga* (Barcelona, 1976).

Clusa i Oriach, Joaquim, *Estudio-informe de los barrios de Can Oriach, Plana de Pintor, Torrent de Capellà* (Sabadell, 1967).

Clusa Oriach, Joaquín, *La localizacíon industrial en la comarca de Barcelona* (Barcelona, 1973).

Colectivo de Estudios por la Autonomía Obrera, *Luchas autónomas en la transición democrática* (Madrid, 1977).

Colomer, Josep M., *Assemblea de Catalunya* (Barcelona, 1976).

_____ *Nosaltres els catalans: una visió crítica de la Catalunya actual* (Barcelona, 1983).

_____ *Espanyolisme i catalanisme: la idea de nació en el pensament polític català (1939–1979)* (Barcelona, 1984).

_____ *La ideologia de l'antifranquisme* (Barcelona, 1985).

Comín, Alfonso C., *Per una estrategia sindical* (Barcelona, 1970).

_____ and García-Nieto, Juan M., *Juventud obrera y conciencia de clase* (Madrid, 1974).

CONC, 'Informe sobre afiliación' (unpublished document, 1978).

_____ 'Informe sobre el sector del metal' (unpublished document, 1978).

Costajussa Oliver, José, *Sabadell 1967* (Sabadell, 1968).

_____ *Sabadell 1972* (Sabadell, 1973).

Creixell, Joan, *Premsa clandestina 1970–1977* (Barcelona, 1977).

Crompton, Rosemary, and Jones, Gareth, *White-Collar Proletariat: Deskilling and Gender in Clerical Work* (London 1984).

Cuadernos Primero de Mayo, *Hacia la Huelga General—Baix Llobregat* (Barcelona, 1976).

Cunningham, Valentine (ed.), *Spanish Front: Writers on the Civil War* (Oxford, 1986).

Dalmau, Josep, *Crónica d'un combat obrer* (Barcelona, 1977).

_____ *La crisi del P.S.O.E. vista des del conflicte Pallach-Reventós* (Barcelona, 1979).

De la Villa, Luis Enrique, and Palomeque, Carlos, *Introducción a la economía del trabajo*, 2 vols. (Madrid, 1977–8).

Departamento de Derecho del Trabajo, Universidad Autónoma de Madrid, *La transición política y los trabajadores: anuario de las relaciones laborales en España 1977* (Madrid, 1977).

De Vicente, Ciriaco, *Trabajo y sindicatos 1974–1977* (Madrid, 1977).

Duocastella, R., *Estudio socioeconómico y de planificación de servicios sociales: Terrassa* (Barcelona, 1967).

Ederle, *Los conflictos laborales en 1976* (Madrid, 1977).

Ellwood, Sheelagh, *Prietas las filas: historia de Falange española 1933–1983* (Barcelona, 1984).

Equipo Confederal de la CNT, *Confederación Nacional del Trabajo* (Barcelona, 1976).

Equipo de Análisis Laborales, *Los trabajadores de la construcción frente a la crisis* (Barcelona, 1977).

Equipo de Estudios de Caritas Diocesana, *Visión sociográfica de Barcelona* (Barcelona, 1965).

Equipos de Estudio, *La lucha de barrios en Barcelona* (Barcelona, 1976).

Escudé i Pladelloreus, Raimon, *L'economía terrassença 1877–1977* (Terrassa, 1977).

Estivill, Jordi, *et al.*, *Apuntes sobre el trabajo en España* (Barcelona, 1973).

Fabre, Jaume, and Huertas Clavería, Josep M., *Tots els barris de Barcelona*, 7 vols. (Barcelona, 1976–7).

_____ Huertas, Josep M. and Ribas, Antoni, *Vint anys de resistència catalana (1939–1959)* (Barcelona, 1978).

Fabregas, Diego, and Giménez, Dionisio, *La huelga y la reforma: Sabadell, metal otoño 1976* (Madrid, 1977).

Fanés, Fèlix, *La vaga de tramvies del 51* (Barcelona, 1977).

Fernández de Castro, Ignacio, *La fuerza de trabajo en España* (Madrid, 1973).

_____ and Martínez, José, *España hoy* (Paris, 1963).

Ferras, Robert, *Barcelone: croissance d'une métropole* (Paris, 1977).

Ferrer, Joaquim, *La lluita pels ajuntaments democràtics* (Barcelona, 1977).

Ferrer Aixala, Amador, *Presentación y estadística de los planes parciales de la Provincia de Barcelona* (Barcelona, 1974).

Ferri, Llibert, Muixí, Jordi, and Sanjuán, Eduardo, *Las huelgas contra Franco 1939–1956* (Barcelona, 1978).

Figueruelo, Antonio, *Cataluña: crónica de una frustración* (Madrid, 1970).

Fina, Lluis, 'Convenios y salarios en el sector metalúrgico español 1960–1975', Ph.D. thesis (Universidad Autónoma de Barcelona, 1979).

Fishman, Robert Michael, 'Working-class Organization and Political Change: the Labor Movement and the Transition to Democracy in Spain' Ph.D. thesis (Yale University, 1985).

FOESSA, *Informe sobre la situación social de España* (Madrid, 1970).

Fondo de Documentación para la Información Anarcosindicalista, *Apuntes para una historia del movimiento obrero español de la post-guerra, años 1939–1970* (Barcelona, 1976).

Font, Joan, *La vaga de la Harry Walker a Barcelona (desembre 1970–febrer 1971)* (Paris, 1973).

Fontana, Josep (ed.), *España bajo el franquismo* (Barcelona, 1986).

Fraser, Ronald, *Blood of Spain: the Experience of Civil War 1936–1939* (London, 1979).

Fundación Friedrich Ebert, *La realidad sindical en 5.500 centros de trabajo españoles—estudio previo a las elecciones de 1980* (Madrid, 1981).

—— *Documentos y legislación laboral de la transición* (Madrid, 1982).

García, Cipriano, 'El modelo Terrassa', in Nous Horitzons, *Nuestra utopía* (Barcelona, 1986).

—— *et al.*, *Sindicalismo en Cataluña* (Madrid, 1977).

García, Soledad, 'Urbanisation, Working-class Organisation, and Political Movements in Barcelona', Ph.D. thesis (Hull University, 1983).

—— 'El movimiento obrero, de nuevo', in Nous Horitzons, *Nuestra utopía* (Barcelona, 1986).

García de las Heras, Gloria, 'La huelga general del 12 de marzo de 1951 en Barcelona', Tesis de Licenciatura (Universidad de Barcelona, 1980).

García-Nieto, J. N., *et al.*, *La nueva ley sindical (análisis de una protesta* (Barcelona, 1970).

Gilaberte, Silvestre, 'Los convenios colectivos en SEAT' (unpublished study).

Gilaberte Herranz, Silvestre, and Zamora Terrés, Juan, *Le lotte operaie alla SEAT: Barcellona 1952–1975* (Turin, 1977).

Gilmour, David, *The Transformation of Spain: from Franco to the Constitutional Monarchy* (London, 1985).

Giménez Plaza, Dionisio, *Sabadell: el pueblo unido . . .* (Hospitalet, 1976).

—— *Roca: organización obrera y desinformación* (Madrid, 1977).

Giner, Salvador, *Continuity and Change: the Social Stratification of Spain* (University of Reading, Graduate School of Contemporary European Studies, 1968).

—— 'La estructura social de España', in Ruedo Ibérico, *Horizonte español 1972*, vol. ii (Paris, 1972).

Giralt, Emili, *et al.*, *El franquisme i l'oposició: una bibliografia crítica 1939–1975* (Barcelona, 1981).

Goitia, Iñaki, 'El orden laboral y las magistraturas de trabajo', in Ruedo Ibérico, *Horizonte español 1966*, vol. ii (Paris, 1966).

Goldthorpe, John J., *et al.*, *The Affluent Worker* (Cambridge, 1968, 1969).

Grimaldos, Alfredo, and García, Andrés, *Contra el pacto de la Moncloa: algunas respuestas de la clase obrera* (Madrid, 1978).

Guinea, José Luis, *Los movimientos obreros y sindicales en España* (Madrid, 1978).

Harloe, Michael (ed.), *Captive Cities: Studies in the Political Economy of Cities and Regions* (Chichester, 1977).

Heine, Harmut, *La oposición política al franquismo de 1939 a 1952* (Barcelona, 1983).

Hermet, Guy, *Los comunistas en España* (Paris, 1972).

Hobsbaum, Eric, *Labouring Men: Studies in the History of Labour* (London, 1964).

—— *Worlds of Labour* (London, 1984).

Huertas Clavería, Josep M., *Obrers a Catalunya: manual d'historia del moviment obrer (1840–1975)* (Barcelona, 1982).

Ibarra Güell, Pedro, *El movimiento obrero en Vizcaya: 1967–1977; ideología, organización y conflictividad* (Bilbao, 1987).

Iglesias Selgas, Carlos, *Los sindicatos en España: origen, estructura y evolución* (Madrid, 1966).

Instituto de Estudios Laborales (IEL), 'Boletín Informativo', 1–10 (unpublished, Barcelona, 1971).

—— 'El conflicto obrero en España 1960–1970', 2 vols. (unpublished, Barcelona, 1972).

—— 'Documentos informativos' (unpublished, Barcelona, 1974).

Instituto Social de Pastorales Aplicados, *Estudio socio-económico y de planificación de servicios sociales*, 2 vols. (Mataró, 1967).

Izquierdo, Manuel P., *De la huelga general a las elecciones generales* (Madrid, 1977).

Jackson, Gabriel, and Centelles, Agustí, *Catalunya republicana i revolucionaria 1931–1939* (Barcelona, 1982).

Jáuregui, Fernando, and Vega, Pedro, *Crónica del antifranquismo*, 3 vols. (Barcelona, 1983–5).

Juliá Díaz, Santos, *Madrid, 1931–1934: de la fiesta popular a la lucha de clases* (Madrid, 1984).

Jutglar, A., *et al.*, *La immigració a Catalunya* (Barcelona, 1968).

Linz, J., *España: un presente para el futuro*, 2 vols. (Madrid, 1984).

Lleonart, Pere, Macías, Pere, and Ardèvol, Remei, *El Maresme: les claus de la seva contínua transformació* (Barcelona, 1981).

Llobet, Salvador, 'La industria moderna', in *Geografía de Catalunya* (Barcelona, 1968).

Lorenzo, César M., *Les Anarchistes espagnols et le pouvoir (1868–1969)* (Paris, 1969).

Lorés, Jaume, *Catalunya, política i socialisme* (Barcelona, 1984).

Ludevid, Manuel, *Cuarenta años de sindicato vertical* (Barcelona, 1976).

_____ *El movimiento obrero en Cataluña* (Barcelona, 1977).

Malerbe, Pierre C., *La oposición al franquismo 1939–1975* (Madrid, 1977).

Mallet, Serge, *The New Working Class* (Nottingham, 1975).

Maravall, José María, *El desarrollo económico y la clase obrera* (Barcelona, 1970).

_____ *Dictatorship and Political Dissent: Workers and Students in Franco's Spain* (London, 1978).

_____ *La política de la transición 1975–1980* (Madrid, 1981).

Marsal, Juan F., *Pensar bajo el franquismo* (Barcelona, 1979).

Martí, Francisco, and Moreno, Eduardo, *Barcelona ¿a dónde vas?* (Barcelona, 1974).

Martín, Eduardo, and Salvador, Jesús, *Las elecciones sindicales* (Barcelona, 1975).

Martín Moreno, Jaime, and De Miguel, Amando, *La estructura social de las ciudades españolas* (Madrid, 1978).

Miguélez Lobo, Faustino, *SEAT: la empresa modelo del régimen.* (Barcelona, 1977).

_____ *El sindicato obrero ante la organización capitalista del trabajo* (Barcelona, 1978).

Miró i Ardevol, Josep, *et al.*, *La Catalunya pobra* (Barcelona, 1974).

Molinero, Carme, and Ysàs, Pere, *L'oposició antifeixista a Catalunya (1939–1950)* (Barcelona, 1981).

_____ *'Patria, Justicia Y Pan': nivell de vida i condicions de treball a Catalunya 1939–1951* (Barcelona, 1985).

Monjo, Anna, and Vega, Carme, *Els treballadors i la Guerra Civil: historia d'una industria catalana collectivitzada* (Barcelona, 1986).

Montesinos, Jesus, *et al.*, *Anuario de relaciones laborales* (Madrid, 1975).

Morán, Gregorio, *Miseria y grandeza del Partido Comunista de España 1939–1985* (Barcelona, 1986).

Mujal-León, Eusebio, *Communism and Political Change in Spain* (Bloomington, 1983).

Muñoz, Xavier, *L'economia com a experiència diària a Catalunya* (Barcelona, 1984).

Navales, Carlos, and Ludevid, Manuel (eds.) *Hacia la huelga general: Baix Llobregat* (Barcelona, 1976).

Negre Rigol, Pedro, *El obrero y la ciudad* (Barcelona, 1968).

Nous Horitzons (ed.), *Nuestra utopía: PSUC; cincuenta años de historia de Cataluña* (Barcelona, 1986).

Paz, Abel, *CNT 1939–1951* (Barcelona, 1982).

Pérez Díaz, Victor, *Clase obrera, partidos y sindicatos* (Madrid, 1979).

Pérez Díaz, Victor, *Clase obrera, order social y conciencia de clase* (Madrid, 1979).

Picó, Josep, *El moviment obrer al País Valencià sota el franquisme* (Valencia, 1977).

Pinilla de las Heras, Esteban, *Estudios sobre cambio social y estructuras sociales en Cataluña* (Madrid, 1979).

Pla, José, *Cataluña* (Barcelona, 1961).

Preston, Paul, *The Triumph of Democracy in Spain* (London, 1986).

PSUC, *40 anys de lluita per la democràcia i el socialisme a Sabadell: Partit Socialista Unificat de Catalunya* (Sabadell, 1976).

—— *PSUC per Catalunya, la democracia i el socialisme* (Barcelona, 1976).

Recolons, Luis, *La població de Catalunya: distribució territorial i evolució demogràfica, 1900–1970* (Barcelona, 1976).

Reguant, Francesc, and Castillejo, Germán, *Juventud y democracia: crónicas del movimiento juvenil* (Barcelona, 1976).

Reyes Mate, *Una interpretación histórica de la USO* (Madrid, 1977).

Riera, Ignasi, *Pàries, sindicalistes, demagogs: notes sobre sindicalisme i cultura obrera* (Barcelona, 1986).

—— and Botella, José, *El Baix Llobregat: 15 años de luchas obreras* (Barcelona, 1976).

Rodríguez, Angel, and D'Alòs-Moner, Raimon, *Economía y territorio en Catalunya: los centros de gravedad de población, industria y renta* (Barcelona, 1978).

Roig, Joan (Francesc Vivens), 'Veinticinco años de movimiento nacional en Cataluña', in Ruedo Ibérico, *Horizonte español 1966*, vol. ii (Paris, 1966).

Romero Maura, Joaquín, *La Rosa de Fuego: el obrerismo barcelonés de 1899 a 1909* (Barcelona, 1974).

Rosenhaft, Eve, *Beating the Fascists? German Communists and Political Violence 1929–33* (Cambridge, 1983).

Rossanda, Rossana, *Un viaje inútil o de la política como educación sentimental* (Barcelona, 1984).

Ruedo Ibérico, *Horizonte español 1966*, 2 vols. (Paris, 1966).

—— *Horizonte español 1972* 3 vols. (Paris, 1972).

Sabat, Francisco, *Los anarcosindicalistas tarrasenses en el exilio* (Barcelona, 1979).

Sagardoy, Juan Antonio, *La realidad laboral española* (Madrid, 1976).

Sagardoy Bengoechea, J. A., and León Blanco, David, *El poder sindical en España* (Barcelona, 1982).

Sala, A., and Durán, E. (José Antonio Díaz), *Crítica de la izquierda autoritaria en Cataluña 1967–74* (Paris, 1975).

Sanz, Jesús, *El movimiento obrero en el País Valenciano* (Valencia, 1976).

Sartorius, Nicolás, and Díaz Cardiel, Victor, *Clase obrera y multinacionales: una denuncia de los metalúrgicos de Madrid* (Madrid, 1975).

Sassoon, D., *The Strategy of the Italian Communist Party* (London, 1981).

Serrano, Angel, and Malo de Molina, J. L., *Salarios y mercado de trabajo en España* (Barcelona, 1972).

Setién, Julio, *El movimiento obrero y el sindicalismo de clase en España (1939–1981)* (Madrid, 1982).

Solá-Morales, M. de, et al., *Barcelona: remodelación capitalista o desarrollo urbano en el sector de la Ribera Oriental* (Barcelona, 1974).

Solé, Carlota, *La integración sociocultural de los inmigrantes en Cataluñya* (Madrid, 1981).

_____ *Los inmigrantes en la sociedad y en la cultura catalanas* (Barcelona, 1982).

Solé Barberá, Josep, *La fundació del PSUC* (Barcelona, 1977).

Solé i Sabaté, Josep M., *La repressió franquista a Catalunya 1939–1953* (Barcelona, 1985).

_____ and Villarroya i Font, Joan, *Catalunya sota les bombes (1936–1939)* (Barcelona, 1986).

Solé-Turà, Jordi, *Catalanismo y revolución burguesa* (Madrid, 1974).

Termes, Josep, *La immigració a Catalunya* (Barcelona, 1984).

Tezanos, José Félix, *¿Crisis de la conciencia obrera?* (Madrid, 1982).

_____ et al., *Las nuevas clases medias: conflicto y conciencia de clase entre los empleados do banca* (Madrid, 1973).

Tiersky, Ronald, *French Communism 1920–1972* (New York, 1974).

Togliatti, Palmiro, *On Gramsci and Other Writings* (London, 1979).

Trías Fargas, Ramón, *Introducción a la economía de Cataluña* (Madrid, 1972).

Tuñón de Lara, Manuel, *Variaciones del nivel de vida en España* (Madrid, 1965).

_____ *El movimiento obrero en la historia de España*, 3 vols. (Madrid, 1972).

Ucelay Da Cal, Enric, *La Catalunya populista: imatge, cultura i política en l'etapa republicana (1931–1939)* (Barcelona, 1982).

Ullman, Joan Connelly, *The Tragic Week: a Study of Anticlericalism in Spain 1875–1912* (Cambridge, Mass. 1968).

Unión Sindical Obrera de Catalunya (ed.), *Dossier: otoño–invierno caliente; análisis sobre las luchas obreras y represión peninsular 73–74* (Catalonia, 1974).

Unzueta Y Yuste, Abelardo de, *Estructura económica de España* (Barcelona, 1980).

USO, *Spagna: sindacato e democrazia; la presenza dell'Union Sindacal Obrera USO sindacato 'illegale' nella Spagna Franchista* (Rome, 1976).

Vazquez Montalbán, Manuel, *Los demonios familiares de Franco* (Barcelona, 1987).

Vega, Eulalia, *El Trentisme a Catalunya: divergències ideologiques en la CNT (1930–33)* (Barcelona, 1980).

Vilar, Sergio, *La oposición a la dictadura* (Barcelona, 1976).

Vilasero, Manuel, and Huertas Clavería, J. M., 'Los barrios de Barcelona en conflicto', in *Las asociaciones de vecinos en la encrucijada: el movimiento ciudadano en 1976–77* (Madrid, 1977).

Villatoro i Lamolla, Vicenç, *et al.*, *Terrassa 1967–1977: anys de transició* (Terrassa, 1981).

Vinader, Xavier, Martí Gómez, José, and Ramoneda, Josep, *López Raimundo, lluita d'avui per u demà més lliure* (Barcelona, 1976).

Vinader Sánchez, Xavier, and Benaul i Berenguer, Josep M., 'Sabadell, febrero 1976: una semana de huelga general política' (unpublished manuscript, n.d.).

Wynn, Martin, 'Spain', in Martin Wynn (ed.), *Housing in Europe* (Kent, 1984).

Zaguirre, Manuel, and De la Hoz, José M., *Presente y futuro del sindicalismo* (Barcelona, 1976).

Articles

Acarín, Nolasc, and Sans, Carme, 'Equipamiento, organizacíon, y gasto sanitario en Barcelona', *CAU*, May–June 1976.

Alibés, Josep M., *et al.*, 'La lucha de los barrios de Barcelona 1969–1975', *CAU*, Nov.–Dec. 1975.

―――― *et al.*, 'La Barcelona de Porcioles', *CAU*, Sept.–Oct. 1973.

Alió, María Angels, 'La evolución de un núcleo suburbano barcelonés: San Boi de Llobregat', *Revista de Geografía*, Jan.–Dec. 1977.

Andes, Fernando, 'El paro y las horas extras', *Gaceta de Derecho Social*, Oct. 1975.

Arcadio, Alonso, *et al.*, 'El trabajo en la construcción: mesa redonda'. *Cuadernos para el Diálogo*, Feb. 1973 (extra).

Ariza Rico, Julián, 'Gobierno y elecciones sindicales', *El País*, 1 Feb. 1978.

Aznar, Jaime, 'Sindicalizar más las Comisiones Obreras', *Lluita Obrera*, July 1980.

Balfour, Sebastian, 'The Role of the Working-Class Movement in the Transition: the Case of Catalonia', in Bell, Tony (ed.), *Proceedings of the Fifth Conference of Hispanists in Polytechnics and Other Colleges* (London, 1983).

_____ 'The Origins of Comisiones Obreras', *Spanish Studies*, Summer 1984.

Baron, Enrique, 'Los obreros ante la magistratura', *Cuadernos para el Diálogo*, Feb. 1973 (extra).

Bonet, Teresa, 'El moviment de les Comissions Obreres a Catalunya', *Nous Horitzons,* 1–2 quarter 1965.

Borja, Jordi, 'Planeamiento y crecimiento urbanos de Barcelona (1939–1958)', *CAU*, Nov.–Dec. 1973.

_____ Tarragó, Marsal, *et al.*, 'La Gran Barcelona', *CAU*, 1972.

Borja de Riquer *et al.*, 'Dossier: el franquisme i la burguesía catalana (1939–1951)', *L'Avenç*, Jan. 1979.

Botey Vallés, Jaume, 'Cinquanta-quatre relats d'immigració', *Perspectiva Social*, Jan.–June 1980.

Bulnes, Ramón, Vidal, Andrés, *et al.*, 'Presente y futuro de las Comisiones Obreras', *Cuadernos de Ruedo Ibérico*, Aug.–Nov. 1968.

Cabarrocas, Gisela, 'Trabas a las elecciones sindicales', *Lluita Obrera*, 15–30 Mar. 1978.

Calvet i Puig, Jordi, 'El creixement industrial de Sabadell durant 1940–1960', *Arrahona*, Autumn 1981.

Carreño Piera, Luis, 'Proceso de suburbialización de la comarca de Barcelona', *Ciudad y Territorio*, Jan.–Mar. 1976.

Carreras, Francesc, and Vilagut, Josep R., 'La Obra Sindical del Hogar y el Patronato Municipal de la Vivienda en Barcelona: dos ejemplos de ineficacia', *CAU*, Nov.–Dec. 1978.

Carreras, Josep María, and Margalef, Joaquim, 'La evolución de las ciudades catalanas entre 1857 and 1975', *Ciudad y Territorio*, Apr.–June 1977.

Carrillo, Santiago, 'Características del trabajo de los comunistas en el período actual, *Nuestra Bandera*, Apr. 1943 (Mexico).

_____ 'En torno a la encuesta sindical de *Nuestra Bandera*', *Nuestra Bandera*, 4th quarter 1962.

Castellano, Pablo, 'Problemática sindical', *Cambio 16*, 1 Mar. 1976.

Castells, Andreu, 'El FOC i la vaga d'autobusos de Sabadell', *Debat* no. 4 July 1978.

Catalá, Jordi, 'Com es va fundar el PSU de Catalunya', *Nous Horitzons*, 3rd and 4th quarter 1971.

Claudín, Fernando, 'Analisis político del postfranquismo', *Avance/ Intervención*, no. 1 (Apr. 1976).

Clavera, Joan, 'Industrialització i canvi de conjuntura en la Catalunya de la postguerra', *Recerques*, no. 6 (1976).

Colomer, Josep M., Fabre, Jaume, and Huertas, Josep M. 'Els alcaldes de la Barcelona franquista', *L'Avenç* nos. 15, 17, and 21 (Apr., June, and Nov. 1979).

Construcción de la Ciudad (ed.), 'Barcelona como modelo de ciudad capitalista', *Construcción de la Ciudad,* 2 C (1972).

Cuadernos Rojos, 'Informe sobre el textil', *Cuadernos Rojos,* Feb. and June 1973.

Documentación Social, 'Sindicalismo, hoy en España', *Documentación Social,* Apr.–June 1976.

Elordi, Alberto, 'Bailar con la más fea', *Mayo,* Feb. 1983.

Esteban, Carlos, 'Paco Giménez: lluitar a banca', *Arreu,* 24–30 Jan. 1977.

Estivill, Jordi, and De la Hoz, Josep María, 'L'evolució del sindicalisme a Europa', *Mon Laboral,* 2nd semester 1986.

Fabre, Jaume, and Ribas, Antoni, 'La reorganització del PSUC després de la guerra', *Avui,* 25 Mar. 1977.

Fava i Compta, M., and Huertas Clavería, J. M. 'Conflictos laborales que dejaron huella: 1939–1972', *Cuadernos para el Diálogo,* Feb. 1973.

Ferri, Llibert, 'Traidores a la CNT', *Mundo,* 11 Dec, 1976.

Fina, Lluis, 'Política salarial i lluita de classes sota el franquisme', *Materiales,* no. 7 (1978).

—— and Toharia, Luis, 'Los mil y un salarios', *Mayo,* Feb. 1983.

Fishman, Robert, 'El movimiento obrero en la transición: objetivos políticos y organizativos', *Revista Española de Investigaciones Sociológicos,* Apr.–June 1984.

Frutos, Paco, 'El nuevo movimiento obrero: apuntes para un debate', *Materiales,* Jan.–Feb. 1978.

Fundación Fondo para la Investigación Económica y Social, 'Los ajustes a la crisis de la economía española', *Papeles de Economía Española,* no. 21 (1984).

García, Cipriano, 'Moviment obrer i qüestió nacional', *Nous Horitzons,* 2nd and 3rd quarter 1976.

García Birlán, Paco (Andreu Castells), 'Operación mandos rojos para la CNS', *Can Oriach,* Apr.–May 1974.

Gómez, Juan, 'Apuntes para una historia de los últimos años sabadellenses', *Can Oriach,* Mar. 1970.

Gómez Parra, Rafael, '¿Qué pasó con los enlaces sindicales?', *Gaceta de Derecho Sindical,* Feb.–Mar. 1975.

González Alonso, Arcadio, 'Situación del sector de la construcción', *Cuadernos para el Diálogo,* Sept, 1974.

Hernández, Jerónimo, 'Aproximación a la historia de las Comisiones Obreras y de las tendencias forjadas en su seno', *Cuadernos de Ruedo Ibérico,* Oct. 1972–Jan, 1973.

Herrero, José Luis, 'La superación de cauces', *Cuadernos para el Diálogo,* Feb. 1973 (extra).

Huertas Clavería, Josep M., 'Un muestreo de agravios para Barcelona', *CAU,* Nov.–Dec. 1978.

Jané Solá, José, 'Los salarios en la industria catalana', *Información Comercial Española,* May–June 1968.

Lawlor, Teresa, and Rigby, Michael, 'Contemporary Spanish Trade Unions', *Industrial Relations Journal*, Autumn 1986.

Logan, John R., 'Affluence, Class Structure and Working-Class Consciousness in Modern Spain', *American Journal of Sociology*, Sept. 1977.

―――― 'Rural–Urban Migration and Working-Class Consciousness', *Social Forces*, June 1978.

―――― 'Bases socials de la consciència de clase a Barcelona', *Papers*, no. 12 (1979).

Lowder, Stella, 'The Evolution and Identity of Urban Social Areas: the Case of Barcelona', *Occasional Papers*, no. 4, (Geography Department, Glasgow University, 1980).

Ludevid Anglada, Manel, 'Vint-i-cinc anys de moviment obrer a Catalunya', *Taula de Canvi*, Mar.–Apr. 1977.

Maragall, Pasqual, 'Un instant de reconstrucció de la historia del FOC', *Debat*, July 1978.

Marcet i Gisbert, Xavier, 'La Guerra Civil a Terrassa', *Terme*, Nov. 1986.

Martí, Ernest (Joaquim Sempere), 'Ciudad y lucha de clases', *CAU*, May–June 1977.

Martínez Alier, Juan, 'Pacto de la Moncloa: la lucha sindical y el nuevo corporativismo', *Cuadernos de Ruedo Ibérico*, July–Dec. 1977.

Màximi, M. 'Amb motiu de l'onze de setembre', *Nous Horitzons*, 3rd quarter 1968.

Miguélez, F., Alvarer, G., and Santolaria, J. J., 'Planificación y conflictos urbanos: el caso de L'Hospitalet de Llobregat', *CAU*, July–Aug. 1975.

Miguélez Lobo, Fausto, 'La negociación colectiva 1969–1975: el caso de Barcelona', *Revista de Estudios Sociales*, nos. 17–18 (1976).

―――― 'Inmigración e integración', *Papers*, no. 18 (1982).

―――― 'Sindicalismo y conflicto social en la España de la transición', *Mientras Tanto*, Sept. 1985.

Morera, Julio, 'La fundación de USO: circunstancias políticas y objetivos', *Debat*, no. 5 (July 1978).

Mujal-León, Eusebio, 'Cataluña, Carrillo, and Eurocommunism', *Problems of Communism*, Mar.–Apr, 1981.

Mundo (ed.), 'The Spanish Workers' Commissions', *International Socialism*, Summer 1968.

Naylon, John, 'Politics and Urban Growth in Franco's Spain: the Case of Barcelona', in Lalaguna, Juan A., *Proceedings of the Fourth Conference of Hispanists in Polytechnics and Other Colleges* (London, 1982).

Olivé, María José, 'Crecimiento urbano y conflictividad en la aglomeración barcelonesa: el caso de Santa Coloma de Gramenet', *Revista de Geografía*, Jan.–Dec. 1974.

Papers, 'Estructura social de Catalunya', *Papers*, no. 12 (1979).

Pérez Díaz, Victor, 'Los obreros ante el sindicato y la acción colectiva en 1980', *Papeles de Economía Española*, no. 6 (1980).

Pinilla de las Heras, Esteban, 'Inmigración y movilidad en Cataluña', *Papers*, no. 4 (1974).

Pujades, Manuel, 'La classe obrera davant la transició política: dues qüestions actuals del sindicalisme de masses', *Taula de Canvi*, Mar.–Apr. 1977.

Pujol Marigot, Rafael, 'Localización de la industria en Cataluña', *Información Comercial Española*, May–June 1968.

Rebert, Lluis (Pere Ardiaca), 'La burguesía nacional catalana i la unitat antifranquista', *Nous Horitzons*, 4th quarter 1964.

Riera, Ignasi, 'Moviment obrer i qüestió nacional sota el franquisme', *Taula de Canvi*, Mar.–Apr. 1977.

—— 'Comunistes i catalans', *Nous Horitzons*, Dec. 1977.

Rodríguez Rovira, '¿Qué ha pasado en SEAT?', *Lluita Obrera*, June 1980.

Roig, Salvador, 'El paper de les Commissiones Obreres en el moment actual', *Nous Horitzons*, 1st quarter 1976.

Ruedo Ibérico, 'El año X de las Comisiones Obreras: historia y análisis de un proceso de degradación política', *Cuadernos de Ruedo Ibérico*, June–Sept. 1971.

Seidman, M., 'Work and Revolution. Workers' Control in Barcelona in the Spanish Civil War', *Journal of Contemporary History*, July 1982.

Servei d'Estudis de la Banca Mas Sardà, 'Les industries metal·liques a Catalunya', *Mon Laboral*, 2nd semester 1986.

Siguan, Miquel, 'L'assimilació dels immigrants en la societat catalana: el punt de vista de psicòleg', in Jutglar, A., et al., *La immigració a Catalunya* (Barcelona, 1968).

Solé, Carlota, 'Integración versus catalanización de los inmigrantes', *Sistema*, Sept. 1981.

—— et al., 'Sobre el problema de la integración sociocultural de los inmigrantes en Cataluña', *Materiales*, May–June 1978.

Soler, Ricard, 'The New Spain', *New Left Review*, Nov.–Dec. 1969, pp. 3–27.

Taberner, Josep Lluis, and Oset, Agustí, 'La Huelga General de 1951', *Destino*, 29 Dec. 1976.

Tarragó, Marçal, Brau, Lluis, and Teixidor, Carlos, 'Planificación y crecimiento de Barcelona (1958–1971)', *CAU*, Nov.–Dec. 1973.

Tezanos, José Félix 'Identificación de clase y conciencia obrera entre los trabajadores industriales', *Sistema*, Sept. 1981.

—— (ed.), 'La transición democrática en España', *Sistema*, Nov. 1985.

T. P., 'Associacions de veïns; perspectives', *Nous Horitzons*, 3rd and 4th quarter 1974.

Ucelay Da Cal, Enric, 'Els nacionalistes catalans al PSUC', *Arreu*, 25–31 Oct. 1976.

Verrié F. P., *et al.*, 'Història del socialisme a Catalunya 1939–1972', *Debat*, nos. 4–5 (1978).

Vidal, Andrés, 'Peligros y posibilidades de las Comisiones Obreras', *Cuadernos de Ruedo Ibérico*, Aug.–Nov. 1968.

Vidal Villa, J. M., 'La industria en Cataluña', *Ciudad y Territorio*, Apr.–June 1977.

Vidiella, Rafael, 'Com va neixer el PSU de Catalunya', *Nous Horitzons* 2nd and 3rd quarter 1976.

_____ 'El veritable problema no son els immigrats', *Nous Horitzons*, 1st quarter 1967.

Vinader, Xavier, and Esteban, Carlos, 'Ram de l'aigua . . . una llarga agonia', *Arreu*, 25–31 Oct. 1976.

Wynn, Martin, 'Barcelona: Planning and Change 1854–1977', *Town Planning Review*, Apr. 1979.

_____ 'Peripheral Growth in Barcelona in the Franco Era', *Iberian Studies*, Spring 1979.

_____ 'San Cosme, Spain: Planning and Renewal of a State Housing Area', *Journal of the American Planning Association*, Jan. 1980.

_____ 'The Residential Development Process in Spain—a Case Study', *Planning Outlook*, xxiv 1 (1981).

INDEX